Dutch Societ

1588–1713

Dutch Society

1588–1713

J. L. PRICE

An imprint of **Pearson Education**

Harlow, England · London · New York · Reading, Massachusetts · San Francisco
Toronto · Don Mills, Ontario · Sydney · Tokyo · Singapore · Hong Kong · Seoul
Taipei · Cape Town · Madrid · Mexico City · Amsterdam · Munich · Paris · Milan

Pearson Education Limited
Edinburgh Gate
Harlow
Essex CM20 2JE
England

and Associated Companies around the world

Visit us on the World Wide Web at
www.pearsoneduc.com

First published 2000

ISBN 0 582 26425 1 CSD
ISBN 0 582 26426 X PPR

British Library Cataloguing-in-Publication Data
A CIP catalogue record for this book can be obtained from the British Library

Library of Congress Cataloging-in-Publication Data
Price, J. L.
Dutch society, 1588–1713 / J.L. Price.
p. cm.
Includes bibliographical references and index.
ISBN 0-582-26425-1 (csd) -- ISBN 0-582-26426-X (paper)
1. Netherlands--Social conditions. I. Title.
HN513 .P75 2000
306'.09492--dc21   00-061375

Typeset by 7 in 11.5/13pt Van Dijck
Produced by Pearson Education Asia Pte Ltd.
Printed in Singapore

Contents

Part Two Apogee and the Portents of Decline, 1648–1713

Preface

T HE NEW Dutch state rose to the position of a major power with
surprising rapidity in the years after about 1588, and it continued
to play a major role in European politics for the rest of the seventeenth
century. Not coincidentally, and also with a speed which astonished
contemporaries, it became the dominant economy in Europe in the
course of the last decade of the sixteenth and the early years of the
seventeenth century. Impressive as these successes were, in retrospect it
is clear that the cultural achievements of the Dutch in the seventeenth
century, particularly but not only in art, were if anything even more
remarkable, even if they made less impression at the time. The society
which underpinned these extraordinary achievements has, however,
attracted rather less attention, then or since. Yet the economic
developments of the sixteenth and the early seventeenth century
produced a new phenomenon in the social history of Europe, possibly
the first capitalist society, and certainly a form of society which
provides an instructive contrast to that of the rest of Europe at this
time. However, as well as representing an important stage in the
development of European society, the social history of the Dutch in the
seventeenth century has characteristics which make it fascinating in its
own right.

   In recent years there has been a heartening increase in the numbers
of works in English on the history of the Dutch Republic, particularly
in the seventeenth century, both by means of translations of the work
of Dutch historians and through original contributions from British
and, increasingly, American scholars. This development has been a great
help for those trying to persuade their students of the interest and
importance of Dutch history both on its own terms and as an
indispensable aspect of the history of the early modern period in
Europe. There are still gaps, however, and the lack of an overview of
Dutch society in the Golden Century is one of the most glaring of

them. It is not too difficult for students to find general accounts of Dutch political, economic and even cultural history, but similar coverage of social history is lacking. There are monographs, some admirable and others at least useful, available on various aspects of the social history of the period, and works on economic history necessarily provide at least oblique light on society as a whole, but there is no single work which attempts to cover the social history of all the Republic for the whole of the seventeenth century. It is this gap that this book is intended to fill.

Although the interpretation of Dutch social history to be found here is, for better or worse, my own, this account could not have been written without the work of other historians, and I trust that my debts are made clear through the notes and bibliography. More immediately, I should also like to acknowledge the helpful and encouraging comments made by the publisher's anonymous reviewer. At this point, however, I feel that I should acknowledge a much longer standing debt – that to my first mentors in Dutch history. Ernst Kossmann's teaching first aroused my interest in the Dutch seventeenth century when I was a student at University College London, and he also guided my initial and distinctly hesitant steps into research. The late Koen Swart took over the perhaps rather difficult task of supervising a somewhat wayward research student. Without the encouragement of the first I would almost certainly never have embarked on historical research in the first place, and without the encouragement of the latter I might never have completed my doctorate. Whether either would consider the long term result to be altogether a good thing is not for me to say.

For reminding me, often forcibly, that there are other things in life, and encouraging a just sense of proportion, my thanks again go to Michael and Jonathan. Sue and Dick too have played their part, not to mention Cassie.

Hull
February 2000

The Northern Netherlands in the late Sixteenth Century

T HE LATER sixteenth century was a dramatic period in the Netherlands: the Revolt against Spanish rule, the assault on established beliefs and practices in religion, and the beginnings of the Eighty Years War between the new Dutch state and the apparently invincible Spanish *monarchía*. Underneath this surface turmoil, more fundamental and, perhaps, more significant changes were taking place in the economic and social structure of the region. Without descending to crude materialism and interpreting political and religious developments as simply the consequences of changes in the economic and social infrastructure, it does not seem unreasonable to suggest that – at the very least – neither the Revolt nor the rise of protestantism in the Netherlands can be properly understood without taking into account the far-reaching economic and social changes that were taking place at this time – that, indeed, had to some extent already taken place. Similarly, the strength and character of Holland's economy and the peculiar social profile of this province must be seen as an important part of the explanation why the North and not the South was able to break away from Spanish rule and eventually achieve its independence.

The Netherlands had already been an important centre of trade and manufacturing for centuries before the beginning of the sixteenth century. The number and size of its towns together with their political as well as economic importance already made the region distinctive in a Europe where the vast majority of the population still lived and worked in the countryside. The leading towns were in the South: by the early sixteenth century, Antwerp had overtaken the now rather faded glories of Ghent and Bruges and become the main centre for trade and finance not only of the Netherlands but of Europe north of the Alps as well. The production of the highly successful 'new draperies' was also based in the main in the southern Netherlands, though chiefly outside the old manufacturing towns of Flanders and Brabant. In contrast, the northern provinces seemed on the surface relatively backward, and for most of them this appearance was not deceptive. However, almost imperceptibly the province of Holland was undergoing a quiet but profound transformation – outlined in the final section of this chapter – which was eventually to make it the economic powerhouse of the Dutch Republic. It is not just the Revolt and the simple emergence of the new Dutch state that cannot be properly understood without taking into account the economic and social background. The ability of the Dutch Republic to become a major power in Europe within a few decades of its effective foundation also cannot be satisfactorily explained without taking into account the economic and social developments which were already well-advanced before the troubles of the late sixteenth century even began.

Revolt in the Netherlands

The Dutch Revolt was one of the most dramatic events of the early modern period – and in some ways one of the most surprising. Revolts in this period, whatever their temporary success, almost invariably failed in the long term; even the English Civil War resulted, after nearly twenty years of armed struggle and political experiments, in a return to something very like the pre-war situation, at least on the surface. The rising in the Netherlands, however, succeeded: Spanish rule was rejected and a new independent state eventually emerged. This is only part of the story, however, as the revolt can also be said to have failed: the southern Netherlands, which had been at the heart of much of the early opposition to the Spanish, returned to obedience or was reconquered – depending on one's perspective – and an exclusive catholicism was re-imposed in these provinces along with Habsburg rule. Perhaps it is better, then, not to think in terms of a single revolt in the Netherlands, but of a number of movements only one of which, in the end, succeeded – and even in this case the outcome was quite different from anything that had been envisaged or intended by any of the participants. The Revolt can be regarded as consisting of at least three different revolts which, although in some ways similar and to an extent overlapping, did not necessarily have quite the same causes and certainly had very different outcomes. In consequence, no single line of analysis is likely to be adequate for them all.

The first opposition movement failed after promising beginnings. In the early 1560s, both the nature of Spanish rule in the Netherlands and some of the policies that were being pursued by the government in Brussels came under attack. The Spanish were seen as trying to introduce absolutist rule by undermining the right of states (i.e. representative assemblies), nobles and towns. Specifically they were accused of using such methods to force onto the Netherlands an intransigent policy of persecution of protestants. The opposition was led initially by the high nobles, prominent among them Willem of Orange, and then spread to the distinctly more militant lesser nobility. After some apparent successes, the movement was caught between Philip II's determination to make no concessions on the religious issue and the iconoclastic riots of 1566 which frightened most of the nobility back to obedience. This first movement of opposition was intended neither to throw off Spanish rule nor to bring about the triumph of protestantism, but to check what were seen as absolutist tendencies and to moderate in a rather unspecific way the policy towards religious dissenters. After the shock of the inconoclastic movement, the revolt collapsed or was crushed by military force, and the duke of Alva arrived in the Netherlands intent on strengthening the central government and imposing a hard-line policy of ruthless prosecution of rebels and persecution of protestants. Not only had the first opposition movement failed, the outcome seemed to be a decisive strengthening of Spanish authority in the Netherlands.

Whereas this first movement had been focused in the south and led by the high nobility, the risings in Holland and Zeeland in the summer of 1572 were based on the towns and were quickly restricted to these provinces alone by decisive Spanish military action. Although obviously related to the general causes for discontent in the Netherlands, both the causes of the revolt and the reasons for its survival have to be understood in the specific circumstances of these provinces. This resistance of a handful of towns in the north of the Netherlands was regarded by the Spanish authorities at first rather as a temporary embarrassment than a significant threat to their control of the Netherlands; it hardly seemed likely that the rebels would be able to resist the might of the Spanish *monarchía* for long. Yet it was this initially unprepossessing movement which in the end succeeded: the Dutch Republic had its roots in the risings of 1572 in the towns of Holland and Zeeland, not in the broader opposition movements of the first half of the 1560s or the late 1570s.

The towns in rebellion were able to hold out, if precariously, until their position was eased by the third phase of opposition which broke out in 1576. A combination of the death of the Spanish governor-general, Requesens, increasing discontent in the 'obedient' provinces after four years of indecisive civil war, and mutinies by unpaid Spanish troops, allowed opposition to surface again in the south and take control of the government. An agreement with the rebels in Holland and Zeeland was reached in the Pacification of Ghent in November of that year, and the Netherlands were briefly united in support of their political privileges and of some moderation in the policies towards protestants. Within three years this unity had collapsed as a result of Spanish military pressure combined with fundamental disagreements among the rebels over political aims and religious attitudes. The leading nobles of the south had never aimed at a complete break with Spain, but rather a compromise to secure their own rights and privileges. Moreover, they had mostly remained loyal to the old church and felt threatened when religious radicals began to take over the towns of Flanders and Brabant forcing out catholics from the governments of these towns. Such conservative elements led the southernmost provinces to a peace with Philip II in 1579 by the treaty of Arras which, on paper at least, conceded most of their political demands and certainly secured the future of catholicism in the South. The Pacification failed because of the disparate aims of the various parties involved. In particular, Holland and Zeeland were committed to protestantism and this meant that their goal was effectively independence, as Philip was never going to make significant compromises on this issue. The southern notables were committed neither to protestantism nor to independence but were looking for a compromise settlement with Spain. In the end, it was the religious issue which made a negotiated settlement for the whole of the Netherlands unattainable.

The collapse of the hollow unity created by the Pacification marked the defeat of the third phase of the Revolt, but it left the rebellion which had started in Holland and Zeeland in 1572 in a much stronger position than it had been before the agreement at Ghent. The causes of the movement in these provinces were not so different in general terms to those operating more widely in the Netherlands – resentment at encroachment by central government on local rights and privileges and concern at the damaging consequences of the persecution of protestants – but its social location was very different. In marked contrast to the South, here the role of the nobles was distinctly limited and that of the towns vital; the rebellion in Holland and Zeeland started in the towns, and produced a political system that gave the towns almost complete domination. Perhaps even more important than their initial take-over by the Sea-Beggars was the ability of the towns to hold out for four years against Spanish military pressure until the situation eased decisively in 1576. The reasons why this handful of towns was able to resist the most powerful military force of the period – outside the Ottoman empire – can be found in the peculiar circumstances, as much social as political and military, of these provinces.

Holland in particular was able to provide effective leadership to the revolt because it already enjoyed a considerable degree of administrative and fiscal autonomy before the Revolt. In the course of the first half of the sixteenth century, the States of Holland had become used to floating loans on its own credit, and to collecting and spending a large part of the taxes levied in the province.[1] This considerable degree of control over fiscal matters enabled the province to gain a reputation for reliability and so borrow money at relatively low rates of interest. So when the Sea Beggars took the town of Den Briel in the south Holland islands on 1 April 1572, an administrative system was already in existence which could both run and finance a government for the province. The Beggars, helped by supporters on the inside, gained control of most of the towns in a matter of months, and were able to summon a rebel States of Holland on 19 July. Representatives from towns other than those normally represented in the States answered the summons, and this was the first step in a process which eventually led to its membership expanding from six towns to eighteen.[2] The take-over of power did not always go smoothly, and in general lack of resistance to the rebels was more conspicuous than enthusiastic support for them. One important exception to this passivity was Amsterdam, already one of the most important towns of Holland, which remained firmly in the grip of a loyalist government, and was to remain the centre of Spanish activity in the province until 1578.

Control of the administrative machinery and of a fiscal system that worked would not have been enough to sustain the revolt, had it not been for the economic strength of Holland. The province was already highly urbanised – which was what made control of the towns so crucial – and trade, manufactures and fishing produced the wealth that could be tapped to support the rebel cause. Moreover, much of Holland's trade was sea-borne and the Spanish were never able to mount a successful blockade of the coast of the rebel provinces. In the crucial early years of the Revolt, the Spanish lacked an effective naval force and so could neither starve the rebel provinces out nor seriously disrupt their commerce; these were hard times for the rebel towns, and for the countryside of Holland and Zeeland they were worse because of the movements of troops and widespread defensive inundations, but the economy survived.

The rebel cause might nevertheless have failed right at the beginning had it not been for a combination of the strategic decisions taken by the Spanish leadership and the tactical advantages the rebels enjoyed. In the summer of 1572, Alva withdrew the bulk of his forces from the north in order to concentrate them against the invasions in the south led by Willem of Orange and his brother, Lodewijk, which he saw as the main threat. This move left the Sea Beggars as the major armed force in the north and enabled them to make considerable gains in the short term; by the end of September, when the threat in the south had been cleared and Alva was ready to deal with what he regarded as a minor problem, not only Holland and Zeeland but much of the north of the Netherlands was in rebel hands. Nevertheless the campaign of reconquest progressed smoothly for the Spanish until they reached the heart of the revolt at the borders of its core provinces. Here they found that, given the military techniques of the time, conditions in Holland and Zeeland gave the defensive great, and perhaps decisive, advantages. Zeeland was a collection of islands, the southernmost part of Holland also, and North Holland was so divided by lakes and inlets as to be effectively an archipelago. In addition, a considerable part of the area in revolt was below or barely above sea-level. Low-lying land, damp earth and, above all, an abundance of water allowed the rebels to produce effective defence-works for their towns very quickly; low and thick earth walls combined with moats and ditches proved to be formidable obstacles. Towns defended in this way could be taken, but only after long and debilitating sieges: Haarlem was invested in December 1572 but fell to the Spanish only in July 1573, Alkmaar resisted successfully, while the relief of Leiden on 3 October 1574 after a siege of over a year was a crucial setback for the Spanish. Nevertheless, with Amsterdam remaining loyal and Haarlem in Spanish hands, the rebel position in Holland at this stage was split in two, and although the insurgents were hanging on with grim determination the future looked bleak.

The Pacification of Ghent of November 1576 transformed this situation: although this agreement only survived three years, the political and military situation of the rebels was immeasurably stronger after its collapse than it had been at the beginning of 1576. Although the disintegration of the Spanish position was sparked off by the sudden death of the governor, Requesens, the underlying cause was the fiscal crisis which hit the *monarchía* at this time. The expense of protracted warfare in the Netherlands combined with the major efforts against the Ottomans in the Mediterranean proved too much for Spanish finances and the crown had eventually to repudiate its debts.* The Spanish effort in the Netherlands had never been adequately financed and their troops, besides having to fight in unfamiliar and unpleasant circumstances, went unpaid for months. By the beginning of 1576, with bankruptcy looming, mutinies on a very large scale over arrears of pay broke out in the Spanish army.[3] The mutineers levied contributions from the civilian population to maintain themselves and to back their demands. They could also act with terrifying violence, and it was their attack on Antwerp at the beginning of November which helped to push through the signing of the Pacification a few days later.

The failure of Philip to fill Requesens's position as governor-general of the Netherlands quickly left the direction of affairs temporarily in the hands of the Council of State. This body proved unable to resist pressure to enter negotiations with the rebels in the hope, not only of ending hostilities, but also of getting help in dealing with the disobedient Spanish troops. The need to deal with the mutineers added urgency to a more general desire among the towns, nobles and provincial states of the South to bring an end to four years of inconclusive and destructive civil war. The effect of the Pacification was to unite the Netherlands, for a time at least, in opposition to Spanish policies as well as mutinous Spanish troops. The treaty proved ephemeral, of course, with the religious issue as the crucial sticking point. The risings of 1572 had brought protestants into key positions in the North and four hard years of war had only increased their influence in the rebel provinces; they could not, and would not, accept any settlement which

---

* or, rather, convert short-term high-interest loans into long-term low-interest ones.

did not offer convincing safeguards for their religion. Philip II, however, was determined to make no concessions at all on this issue as the protection of the true faith, which for him was unquestionably the Catholic Church, was central to his idea of his duty as a ruler. The southern leaders were caught between the two, committed to a compromise settlement where none was available. The Pacification was undermined by the different interpretations of the signatories concerning what had been agreed about the religious issue. Some sort of fudge on this question had, perhaps, been necessary before any agreement could be reached, but it rapidly became apparent that the southern leaders saw the Pacification as protecting the position of the Catholic Church, while the North claimed that it guaranteed toleration for protestants in the South.

In these circumstances the combination of renewed Spanish military pressure and the take-over by religious and political radicals of a number of towns in Flanders and Brabant broke the back of the Pacification. Don Juan of Austria, the new Spanish governor, after a brief flirtation with the new power holders in the Netherlands, seized the fortress of Namur and began an attempt to re-establish Spanish control by military force. After Don Juan's death, the duke of Parma took over and began to reveal his skills not only as a soldier but as a politician as well. The task facing him was considerably eased by the hostile reaction of southern nobles and patricians – not to mention clergy – to the protestant seizure of power in first Ghent in October 1577 and then other towns in Flanders and Brabant. This radical movement combined religion with a restoration of the political power of the artisan guilds, a move of considerable historical resonance in these provinces and a direct challenge to the position of the patricians in the towns and more generally to noble power and influence. This double attack on their position in society and on their religion pushed the southern notables into the arms of Parma: first the conservative forces came together in the Union of Arras in 1579 and then made peace with Spain in the same year. However, this left all of the northern Netherlands and most of the major towns in the South still in rebel hands. At the beginning of 1576 Spanish forces had been firmly lodged in the heart of Holland, dividing the province in two, and were poised to take Zierikzee in Zeeland; in 1579 the Spanish army under Parma was faced with the task of reconquering the greater part of the Netherlands. Moreover, by 1578 Amsterdam had been brought over to the new regime and Haarlem recovered, finally uniting Holland in opposition to Spanish rule.

The Union of Utrecht in 1579 became in effect the founding document of a new state, and the nearest thing to a constitution the Dutch Republic was ever to have, although it was never designed as such. As the Pacification began to fall apart those most committed to the rebel cause were brought together in this alliance, while the more conservative elements moved inexorably towards an agreement with Parma. The Union was intended to bring together those members of the States General of the Netherlands who were most determined to continue the struggle against Spain and, besides the northern provinces,[4] most of the towns of Flanders and Brabant also joined the Union eventually. It is perhaps at this point that the Revolt transmuted into the Eighty Years War: that is, the rebellion against Spanish rule began to turn into a war between a new Dutch state and Spain,[5] although Philip II's rule was not formally repudiated until two years later in 1581.

The first years after the signing of the Union of Utrecht were difficult in the extreme, and it is only in retrospect that they can be seen as even the uncertain beginnings of the new Dutch state. The town of Groningen in the north east was betrayed to Spain in 1580, and Parma pursued his systematic and seemingly irresistible reconquest of the South, culminating in the taking of Antwerp in the summer of 1585. Dutch resistance was ill-organised and ineffective, and the attempt to draw in French aid by giving the sovereignty to the duke of Anjou ended in failure when, frustrated by restrictions on his authority, he launched an abortive but nevertheless destructive coup. The assassination of Willem of Orange a year later, in 1584, threatened to deprive the Dutch of any effective leadership. In desperation the sovereignty was first offered to Henri III of France and then to Elizabeth of England, who both in turn refused. However, after the fall of Antwerp England agreed by the treaty of Nonsuch to send military aid under a general who it was intended would provide much needed purpose and leadership to the direction of Dutch affairs. The effect of the arrival of the English troops was disappointing at first, and the earl of Leicester, sent by Elizabeth with a fatally ill-defined political role, proved predictably inadequate both as a general and a statesman. After Leicester left in despair, the Dutch seem to have accepted that they had to stop trying to find a foreign sovereign and attempt to survive on their own, however hopeless the task might seem. In the event, the departure of Leicester turned out to be the low point in Dutch fortunes, and within ten years their situation had been transformed. The embryonic Dutch state was saved by the diversion of Spanish forces, first to the Armada in 1588, and then to intervention in France to try to prevent the protestant Henri IV from establishing himself on the French throne. This respite gave the Dutch the opportunity to create a political system which worked and an army capable of defending it. These tasks were achieved before the end of the century.

Warfare

The origins of the Dutch Republic lay in the revolt of 1572 and the continuous warfare of the following decades, but one of the most important reasons why the Revolt was able to survive was that, after the first four years, the war was neither as socially disruptive nor as economically damaging as might have been expected, at least as far as the core provinces of the new state were concerned. The risings of 1572 brought warfare to the heart of Holland and Zeeland but after the Pacification in 1576 actual military operations in the main took place in the south and east of the Netherlands, allowing these provinces to recover socially and economically from the devastation of the first few years of the Revolt. Thus, despite the war, Holland in particular was able to resume the economic and social transformation that had got under way in the first half of the century after only a relatively short interruption.

The immediate disruption caused by the Revolt was nevertheless very great, and it says much for the resilience of both the towns and the countryside of Holland that recovery was so rapid and vigorous. After the rebel successes of the summer of 1572, the Spanish forces first cleared the rest of the north and then moved in on Holland and Zeeland. Naarden, on the border of Holland, was sacked, Alkmaar besieged and Haarlem taken; Amsterdam remained loyal and, in Zeeland, Middleburg also was held by the Spanish. Holland was divided in two by the Spanish forces, and the long siege of Leiden threatened to crush the Revolt in South Holland. Fighting, the movement of troops, and defensive inundations devastated the countryside of the two provinces. The relief of Leiden was achieved mainly by boat and involved the flooding of a good part of the south of Holland between the Maas and the threatened town – the Revolt was saved, but the cost to the farmers of the area was incalculable, literally. On the other hand, the commerce of loyalist Amsterdam was crippled by the Sea Beggar fleet until 1578, and the Spanish failure to establish an effective naval presence in the North Sea and Zuyder Zee allowed the hard-pressed towns under rebel control to maintain enough of their trade to survive economically during these hard years.

This first phase was a war of skirmishes and sieges, fought amid water and mud on land that was below or only a little above sea level. The essential difference between warfare in Holland and Zeeland and in the rest of the Netherlands was that these conditions very much favoured the defensive, given the military technology of the time. Defence was taking the upper hand in warfare generally in the later sixteenth century, and in the Netherlands throughout the Eighty Years War there were few battles, none of them decisive, and war became essentially a series of sieges of forts, fortresses and fortified cities. At best this was a slow process, all too often it was simply inconclusive. Holland and Zeeland were thickly studded with towns which could be brought into a state of defence with relative ease by throwing up low, thick earth walls. These were effective artillery defences in themselves and could be further strengthened by the use of existing rivers and lakes or by opening the drainage sluices to flood the areas before the walls. In these circumstances the task facing the Spanish army was a formidable one, especially as carrying out long sieges in such damp and often cold conditions was a particularly unhealthy business. Disease and desertion often took a more important toll of a besieging army in this period than death or injury through direct military action, and the conditions they had to face in Holland and Zeeland sapped the morale as well as the manpower of the Spanish. They were still capable of considerable military feats: Spanish soldiers waded almost shoulder-deep through the sea to take Zierikzee in 1576 – but then mutinied over lack of pay. As this suggests, despite the fall of Middelburg to the rebels and the relief of Leiden, the rebel provinces were only just clinging on through desperate defence, when the events of 1576 transformed the situation.

The Pacification of Ghent – together with the mutinies in the Spanish army – brought Holland and Zeeland an immediate relief from military pressure. The decision of most provincial and urban authorities throughout the Netherlands to support the States General and the Pacification meant that when military operation eventually started up again, they were far removed from the territory of these devastated provinces. The Spanish campaign to regain control of the Netherlands had to begin in the extreme south and, later, the north east. While in the years immediately after the rising of 1572 the war had mostly been fought on the territory of Holland and Zeeland, after 1576 these provinces were never again the scene of significant military action. The Pacification had provided them with a protective screen of territory which not even Parma's long and successful campaign could quite pierce. The rural economy could begin to make good the damage done by military action and the more general disruption of the war years, and the towns too could begin the work of recovery. It was of crucial importance for Holland that the temporary unification of the Netherlands against Spain undermined Amsterdam's resistance. In 1578 the loyalist government of the town was first persuaded to come to an agreement with the States of Holland, then replaced by an internal coup which turned the town into a bulwark of the Revolt. Now it could be reintegrated into the province's economy: its trade was released from the shackles of the blockade, and it could resume its role as one of the main motors of economic development in the region.

After the defeat of the army of the States General at Gembloux (January 1578) and the loss of the Walloon provinces through the treaty of Arras, the conflict in the Netherlands became increasingly like a conventional war – and one that Spain was winning. In the South Parma embarked on an unavoidably slow but seemingly inexorable campaign of sieges, and one by one the towns in revolt fell, culminating in the capture of Antwerp in the summer of 1585. After the fall of Groningen in 1580, Friesland, Overijssel and Gelderland were brought into the front line. The warfare here was perhaps on a smaller scale than that in the South, but no less devastating for that. Under Parma the Spanish effort was purposeful and well-organised; given sufficient time the return of the whole of the Netherlands to obedience to the Spanish crown seemed not only likely but inevitable. The rebel side, in contrast lacked effective political leadership, was militarily inept, and seemed permanently on the verge of financial collapse. Willem of Orange could do little to overcome the deep-rooted particularism which caused people to put their province, or even their town, before the common interest. His attempt to provide both effective leadership and French help by co-opting the duke of Anjou for the cause in the end only made matters worse as, chafing at the restrictions imposed by the States General on his powers, he left after an abortive coup in 1583. Willem's policy had failed and his assassination in the following year appeared to leave the Revolt in its worst situation since 1576.

It was the constant pressure from the Spanish which pushed the embryonic state towards collapse. The ability of Parma as a general together with his astute political tactics was important, but so was the steady supply of money that Spain was able to provide now it was temporarily free from major commitments elsewhere.[6] The number of troops under his command rose to over 60,000,[7] many of them the cream of an army that was beginning to earn the reputation of being the most formidable in Europe. It seemed unlikely that the progress of this force could be halted let alone reversed by a handful of dis-organised provinces with a negligible martial tradition, so Willem's policy of looking for substantial outside help was continued by his successors. The English troops sent as a consequence of the treaty of Nonsuch in 1585 proved useful in the longer term but were hardly enough – even on paper they only amounted to just over 7,000 men – to transform the military situation, and Leicester failed to provide greater unity and purpose either to the political or the military leadership. Indeed, in many ways he made matters worse, in particular by failing to establish a working relationship with the States of Holland, a body which became increasingly important as the territory under the States General's control shrank. His governorship was the last of the Dutch attempts to buy support by hawking the sovereignty around and, after he left in disgust at the end of 1587, they accepted the burdens but also the opportunities of full independence and this decision may well be the one positive legacy of Leicester's period as governor.

In 1588, however, the Dutch situation was still extremely fragile with only Holland, Zeeland and Utrecht free of enemy troops, and Parma's army pressing forward in an arc from Friesland in the north, through Overijssel and Gelderland to the remnant of Flanders and Brabant which still remained in Dutch hands. At this point the likeli-hood that these disunited and war-weary territories would become a viable new state seemed remote, yet within ten years that is exactly what had happened.

Social causes, social consequences

The Revolt succeeded in the North but failed in the South or, to put it another way, the revolts which centred on the South in the 1560s and in 1576 were defeated while the rising in Holland and Zeeland in 1572 eventually led to the foundation of an independent state. Of course the reasons for this disparity can be sought in military factors: the second revolt in the South was eventually crushed by the Spanish army, while the North was able to hold out. Pieter Geyl, in his attempt to explain why a permanent division between North and South in the Netherlands arose out of the Revolt, never tired of arguing that geographical conditions in the North made the region easier to defend. In particular, he claimed that the great rivers running through the centre of the Low Countries provided the North with a defensible barrier which in the end proved militarily decisive.[8] This particular explanation has not received much favour of late, but it would be foolish to ignore the *histoire événementielle* of political and military factors in trying to understand the outcome of the Revolt. If Parma's efforts had not been diverted into France after 1589, for example, the North might have been defeated in the end, whatever its defensive advantages, and historians would be trying to explain why this particular outcome was inevitable. Nevertheless, there are long term factors which, while they do not make the success of the Revolt in the North inevitable, at least helped to make it possible.

Looking at long term social and economic factors, it might have been expected that the South would be a more likely centre of successful revolt. Flanders and Brabant had been the economic powerhouse of the Netherlands in the late Middle Ages, and it was the great towns of this region – Ghent, Bruges and finally Antwerp – which were at the heart of this development, not to mention Lille and Tournai further south. The southern towns also had a tradition of political turbulence which was largely lacking in the North. For much of the fourteenth century the three leading towns of Flanders had dominated the county in despite of its count, and both here and in Brabant the artisan guilds had a far stronger history of participation in urban government than could be shown by most of the towns further north. Economic strength and the notorious turbulence of the towns suggested that when it came to the success or failure of a revolt, the South would be the key area – indeed, just such thinking may have lain behind what turned out to be Alva's crucial strategic mistake in 1572. The invasions by Orange and his brother Lodewijk were aimed at the South, and Alva gave priority to defeating them there. Both sides saw the South as crucial and the risings in the North as of secondary importance, and for many years afterwards it seemed evident to contemporaries that the Revolt could only survive in the long term with the support of the great towns of the southern Netherlands.

However, while the social and economic developments in Holland may have been less spectacular than those in Flanders and Brabant, they possibly went deeper and were arguably more disruptive of traditional social structures. While in the South as a whole the nobility still played a crucial role in political life, in Holland and Zeeland the social and economic foundations of noble influence had already been decisively weakened by the early sixteenth century. The extent of this process may have been exaggerated and its nature oversimplified in the past – nobles were still present and still influential before, during and after the Revolt[9] – but the essential truth remains that the position of the nobility here was fragile, and probably more so than anywhere else in the Netherlands. In this respect the maritime provinces of the North were at the cutting edge of social change. The extent of the transformation of society in Holland is perhaps shown even more clearly by its high degree of urbanisation. The towns of the county were not large, certainly in comparison with the chief towns of the South, but they were numerous and by the middle of the sixteenth century something approaching 50 per cent of the population of Holland lived in them – a considerably higher proportion than in Flanders or Brabant, which in turn were very highly urbanised by contemporary standards. Thus in two very important respects – the erosion of the social and economic importance of the nobility and a high and rising degree of urbanisation – the core province of the future Republic was already demonstrating its distinctiveness before the Revolt.

Much of the rest of the North was much more traditional in its social and economic structure: Zeeland and parts of Friesland also experienced the changes which were taking place in Holland, at least to some extent, but even by the general standards of the Netherlands the eastern regions were somewhat backward. (On the other hand, in comparison with Europe as a whole even these areas were relatively highly urbanised.) However, in trying to explain the causes and outcome of the Revolt it is Holland and Zeeland that matter: if the Revolt had been defeated in these provinces there would have been no Dutch Republic. The success and then survival of the movement here determined its outcome for the North as a whole. So in seeking to understand the role of social and economic change in the Revolt, it is the maritime region of the North, and Holland in particular, which is of crucial importance.

Although overshadowed by the more spectacular successes of the leading cities of the southern Netherlands, the towns of Holland taken as a whole were a considerable trading force, and artisan production and fishing were already important sectors of the province's economy by the early sixteenth century. Perhaps more fundamental to the transformation of Holland's society, however, were the challenges facing the rural sector and the ways in which these challenges were met. At this time the county as a whole was facing serious problems of water control with profound effects on the rural economy.[10] Holland had more and larger lakes and inlets from the sea than after the great drainages of the later sixteenth and early seventeenth century: North Holland at this time has been described as more an archipelago than a solid land mass,[11] and the landscape of South Holland was deeply marked by the effects of the great floods of the late Middle Ages. The difficulties arose in part from what appear to have been significant changes in sea-level: there seems to have been a regression in the late medieval period, and serious incursions by the sea became more frequent and led to permanent loss of land as well as to damaging floods. The maintenance of defences against the sea became more difficult and more expensive, as did the drainage of low lying land. This latter problem was made more acute by the settling of land in the older polders which meant that natural drainage became increasingly ineffective. In some areas water control was made more difficult by the effects of peat-digging. Peat was the chief fuel naturally available in the province, but its extraction on a large scale could create areas vulnerable to flooding. The threat from the sea and the growing problem of drainage in general demanded in the short term greater local efforts and in particular better cooperation between neighbouring *waterschappen* (local water-control boards). In the longer term these problems were to be tackled by the great drainage projects of the late sixteenth and early seventeenth century which turned major stretches of water into agricultural land and North Holland into a solid land-mass, but in the meantime increasingly damp conditions stimulated fundamental changes in the way people in the Holland countryside lived and worked.

The changes which took place in agriculture and the rural economy in general may have been less spectacular than the boom in trade and the growth of manufactures, but they nevertheless played a fundamental part in the economic and social transformation of Holland in the sixteenth and early seventeenth century. The developments in the countryside were facilitated in part, of course, by the changes which were taking place in the urban economy of the province at the same time but, equally, they were an essential stimulus to overall economic growth.[12] The transformation of the rural economy was not just a dependent variable of what went on in the towns but was an equal partner in the rapid growth of the province's economy. Indeed, it might be argued that, while the distinction between the urban and rural economies may be a useful analytical tool, it should not be allowed to obscure the extent to which the whole of Holland was already well on the way to becoming an integrated economic system even before the Revolt.

The nature of the response to the increasing wetness of the land is an example of this complex relationship. As it became more difficult to grow bread grains, a large-scale shift from arable to pasture took place. Dairy farming and the fattening of beef calves became increasingly important, and the consequent shortage of locally produced grain was made up for by imports, particularly of rye from the Baltic ports. Thus this move in agriculture away from arable to a greater emphasis on pasture was facilitated by the availability of cheap grain through the increasing dominance in the Baltic grain trade of Holland merchants, but this change in the rural sector in turn increased the demand for grain imports which helped to stimulate this trade with the Baltic. Holland farmers had long moved away from anything which can be described as subsistence farming, but the shift to pasture was an important move towards greater specialisation and thus a greater dependence on the market, both to find buyers for butter, cheese and meat and to provide farmers with bread and the other necessities of life which they were no longer providing for themselves. Another important aspect of the response to the difficulties facing agriculture at this time was a greater diversification of the rural economy. The growth in the amount of goods moving both ways between town and countryside brought an increasing demand for transport facilities, especially by boat and barge. The ease of access to water and the sea also encouraged country people to take part in fishing, at sea as well as in rivers and lakes, and to find employment in the merchant fleet. In this harsh world, surplus population could also move out of the countryside to fuel the growth of the towns, which is another way in which the two sectors of the economy displayed a positive relationship.

More conventionally, the growth of trade has been seen as the motor of the economic development of the maritime region of the northern Netherlands in the sixteenth century, but in the first half of the century the commerce of the north was still overshadowed by the more spectacular achievements of the southern towns. Antwerp in particular was the great success of the early sixteenth century, becoming the commercial hub of the economy of Europe north of the Alps.[13] On the other hand it is not hard to find in the pattern of Holland's trade in the years before the Revolt clear foreshadowings of the successes which were to come in the seventeenth century. Most obviously there was the trade with the Baltic region: thanks to the Sound Toll records[14] there are fairly reliable, though not undisputed, statistics for this important branch of European commerce, and from these it is clear that ships and traders from the maritime region of the northern Netherlands were already playing an important role in the region by the first years of the sixteenth century. At this point their share seems to have approached 50 per cent of the total number of ships passing through the Sound, and they consolidated and even increased their percentage of Baltic trade over the next half century even though the volume of the trade increased markedly in this period. To give an idea of the numbers involved, in 1558 over 1,000 ships from the northern Netherlands passed through the Sound and in 1562 the total was well over 2,000 with around 1,700 coming from Holland alone.[15] The greater part of the cargoes carried west by these Dutch ships consisted of bread grains, particularly rye. The grain trade served in the first place to make up the short-fall in production resulting from the switch to pasture in the maritime region, but met a growing demand elsewhere in Europe as well and so was a significant early example of the staple function that was to become so important an element of later Dutch economic success.

The large number of ships employed in the Baltic trade is also a forceful reminder of a major difference between the commercial patterns of the towns of Holland and of Antwerp: the former carried the goods they traded in their own large and growing merchant fleet while the latter largely used the carrying services of others. The ships used by northern merchants were mostly quite small – in 1562, for example, the great majority of Dutch ships involved in the Baltic trade were under 100 tons – but, as has been seen, there were already a lot of them before the Revolt, and in terms of employment alone the size of this merchant fleet must have had a significant impact on the economy of the whole northern maritime region. With so many ships operating it becomes less surprising that going to sea at least for part of the year became a common feature of the employment pattern not just in the towns but also in the countryside, notably of North Holland. The growth of the trading fleet was also an important stimulus to ship-building and ancillary industries such as sawmills and rope- and sail-making. Holland not only built its own ships – and its herring-boats, barges and a host of small ships for inland transport – but began to develop new types of specialised trading vessels, culminating towards the end of the century in the appearance of the classic *fluit* (flute-ship) in Hoorn. This large merchant fleet, together with the manufactures associated with it, was one of the fundamental strengths of the economy of Holland in particular. The economic successes of Antwerp might have been more obvious, especially to foreign observers, but the maritime region of the North was quietly laying down very sound foundations for later growth.

Another unglamorous area of economic activity which was an important component of later Dutch economic success was the herring fishery. Fishing in lakes, rivers and inshore was an important element in the economy of many parts of the maritime region, and fish were a significant source of protein in the popular diet. The herring fishery, however, was a major industry: it offered opportunities for small-scale entrepreneurs, was an important source of employment, made a significant contribution to the food supply of the region, and – not the least important – provided a valuable export article. High quality Dutch herring found a ready market in the Baltic area and helped to finance the grain trade, as well as being much in demand in the Rhineland and northern France. On the eve of the Revolt there may have been as many as 400 or 500 specialised boats (*buizen* or 'busses' in English), employing perhaps 10–15,000 men – fishing boats needed more hands to work them than merchant ships – regularly engaged on the North Sea fishing grounds. Add to this the stimulus to ship-building and -repairing, the demand for barrels to pack the herring into, and the transport needed to take them to their ultimate markets, and the overall importance of the fisheries for the economy of the region begins to emerge. Although the chief bases of the herring fleet were the towns on the Maas in South Holland and the Zuyder Zee, in this earlier phase the role of smaller towns and even some of the larger villages was also significant. The countryside not only produced hands for the *buizen*, many of them had their owners and home bases in the economically diversified villages of Holland.

Just as the growth of the merchant and fishing fleets encouraged the development of shipbuilding and ancillary manufactures, so the general growth of Holland's economy helped to boost its manufactures. Here, however, the picture is rather less fundamentally healthy than the other sectors that have been dealt with so far. In particular, some of the manufactures which had once been important in the towns of Holland, and the maritime region as a whole, were going through a difficult time in the earlier part of the sixteenth century. Some, indeed, would never regain their former importance. The brewing industry, for example, had provided Holland with an important export article in the late Middle Ages, but for reasons which remain unclear it was beginning to lose ground in this period and was increasingly reduced to serving only local needs. Cloth manufacturing in the province, too, was suffering serious problems for much of the century, as it was in some of the southern towns, but in sharp contrast to the boom in textile production in the newer centres such as Hondeschoote. The new techniques used and types of cloth produced – the 'new draperies' of the period – in places free of the guild restrictions of the old towns were only to come to the rescue of the industry in the North after, and partly as a result of, the Revolt. The service sector was, however, stimulated by urban growth, the rising proportion of the population living in the towns, and the increased specialisation of the farming sector.

This rapid economic development brought with it fundamental changes in the society of the maritime region of the North, a transformation that was already well advanced by the eve of the Revolt, and which goes some way towards explaining its outcome if not its outbreak. As with economic developments, of course, these changes were most marked in the maritime region of the North, with Holland as the epicentre of the social upheaval. The most obvious aspect of these shifts was the urbanisation of Holland which has already been touched upon: already by c.1525 around 44 per cent of the population of this county could be found in towns with more than 2,500 inhabitants, while the proportion in the northern Netherlands as a whole was 27 per cent and the latter figure rises to 31 to 32 per cent if smaller towns are included in the calculation.[16] These figures mean that the North as a whole was more urbanised than the South and, which is even more surprising, Holland was more urbanised than Flanders or Brabant, traditionally the great centres of urban growth and power in the Netherlands. Apart from this high degree of urbanisation, the distinctive characteristic of the population distribution was that there were no towns which could match the great cities of the South, but a large number of small and medium sized towns. Even the rapidly growing Amsterdam had a population which was probably less than 30,000 on the eve of the Revolt, and Haarlem, Leiden, Delft and Dordrecht were all under 15,000. Outside Holland, the town of Utrecht almost matched Amsterdam in size, and Groningen, Deventer, Zwolle and Nijmegen were all over 10,000.[17] These figures are a reminder that, though the most obvious and far-reaching changes took place in Holland, there is a case for arguing that the North as a whole had already embarked on the course which was to produce a society which was quite distinctive in early modern Europe.

One of the motors behind this process of urbanisation was the rapid demographic growth which marked the North as a whole but, again, Holland in particular. Between 1525 and 1622 the population of Holland rose from around 275,000 to about 672,000. This rate of growth may have been followed, though at some distance, by the rest of the maritime region, and the eastern provinces also expanded steadily, though here growth was severely interrupted from the 1580s onwards by the effects of war. It is worth noting that population growth in Holland up to the Revolt was at least as fast in the countryside as in the towns, reflecting the extent to which the rural economy was at the forefront of change. Not only were more people being born in the countryside, more were able to find a living there as well. However, the extent to which the population rise in the towns was fuelled by the demographic *élan* of the rural areas must remain speculative. While towns in the early modern period generally had a negative demographic profile – put simply, more people died than were born there – this is neither a simple matter[18] nor did it necessarily apply to the towns of Holland in this period. Epidemic disease, especially recurrent outbreaks of bubonic plague which may well have become endemic in the Netherlands in these years,[19] was a major killer, but it is not clear that its impact was more severe in towns than in a countryside which was not only densely settled but was also in regular and frequent contact with the towns for economic reasons. It is also worth noting that it seems probable that the population in the county grew at least as fast in the early sixteenth century as it was to do in the half century or so up to 1622.

The economic changes that were taking place in the countryside were bringing about fundamental changes in employment patterns throughout the maritime region of the North. The sheer size of the merchant and fishing fleets indicates that a considerable proportion – perhaps as much as a third – of the working population must have been involved in these sectors for at least part of the year. If ancillary manufactures and transport are added, then the proportion of the population not directly involved – at least full-time – in agriculture rises yet further. Indirect evidence for a significant manufacturing presence in the rural areas comes from the concern of the towns of Holland to suppress or limit such activities which they saw as a threat to their interests and prosperity. In some areas it would seem that agriculture was becoming almost a secondary economic activity: this is certainly true of some of the larger villages in North Holland – De Rijp or the nearby Graft come to mind – and the pattern for the maritime region as a whole is of a specialised agricultural sector supporting a growing transport and service sector. These circumstances also encouraged a combination of different activities at different times of the year or at different periods of life: some involvement in farming, river and lake fishing, together with service as a sailor or in the herring fleet.

Along with the increasing urbanisation and far-reaching modifications of employment patterns went changes in religious life and perceptions. While it would be going too far to see the transformation in where people lived and how they earned their living as being the cause of the rise of protestantism in any simple sense, it would be flying in the face of both evidence and plausibility to deny the importance of these circumstances in both undermining traditional attitudes to the Church and facilitating the progress of the Reformation. Of course, there are many reasons for caution, not least being that the various protestant movements, despite the attention their activities have received both from contemporaries and from later historians, attracted rather few committed supporters. Up to the outbreak of the Revolt – and, indeed, for many years after – protestants remained a small minority in the northern Netherlands as a whole, and the various strands of the Reformation appeared to be markedly stronger in the towns of the South. An observer in the early 1560s might well have predicted that a protestant rising was much more likely to occur in Flanders or Brabant than in Holland or Zeeland. However, it can be misleading to count only fully committed adherents to one or other of the protestant movements and assume that all the rest remained in some significant sense loyally catholic. There was a wide range of discontent with the state of the Church throughout the North, from a corrosive popular anticlericalism[20] to a fastidious disdain among Erasmian intellectuals for its failure to live up to its own ideals.

The Church in the Netherlands remained unreformed until the 1560s, and the moves towards catholic reform which were then attempted became entangled with that distrust of the motives of the Spanish government which was so characteristic of the time. Until counter-reformation preaching and teaching made it clear, most of the population must have been uncertain quite where the line between protestant and catholic lay, and many will have preferred not to make a definitive choice between the two until compelled to do so. Intense trading contacts with the Holy Roman Empire, where protestantism made its first impact, and France, where calvinism began to take root in the 1550s, brought successive waves of protestant ideas into the Netherlands. The concentration of the population into numerous towns, and the relatively high levels of literacy of this urban public, facilitated the spread of the Reformers' message. The vulnerability of many artisans in this rapidly changing economy with its marked cyclical patterns[21] seems to have been at least in part the cause of the religious volatility of some towns. In the North, the textile workers of Leiden and Haarlem produced the *élan* behind the more fiery wing of the early anabaptist movement and produced both the leaders and many of the rank and file of the movement which instituted the Kingdom of God at Münster (1534–35) in the nearby Rhineland, with ultimately tragic consequences. In reaction, the anabaptist movement in the Netherlands took on a much more pacifist stance, especially under the influence of Menno Simons, but continued to attract support particularly among artisans in the towns and, notably, the countryside of the maritime region of the North.

With a few notable exceptions, the anabaptists' support came from the lower reaches – though not the lowest – of society. In contrast, the educational and social level of the followers of the early reformed movement was considerably higher, and their influence appears to have been much greater than their absolute numbers might seem to have warranted. Again, in the years up to the Revolt calvinism seems to have been stronger and better organised in the southern towns – including those in the Walloon (i.e. French-speaking) region which came under the influence of the Huguenot movement in France – than the northern. There was modest support for the embryo reformed churches in the numerous small towns of the North, but what was perhaps stronger here was the resistance to persecution. A number of motives were involved – including particularist reluctance to obey orders from Brussels – but local authorities throughout the North seem to have been unwilling to prosecute those whose only crime was adherence to protestant beliefs – anabaptists who seemed a threat to social order as much as to the Church were a different matter. If commitment to one or other of the new movements was rare, so was unconditional loyalty to the old church. The disruption of traditional society brought by the economic changes of the period was paralleled by the crumbling of old ideological certainties.

In the short term the upheavals of the Revolt and the first decade of the Eighty Years War damaged the economy of the northern Netherlands, but for the core territories of Holland and Zeeland at least this interruption to the rapid growth of the earlier part of the century was only temporary. After 1576 the war itself moved away from these provinces for good and Spanish naval weakness meant that there could be no serious disruption of Holland's sea-borne commerce. For the eastern provinces of the North the situation was very different and for many years they were where the war was largely fought and the disruption this brought with it had profound effects on their economies. The modest but steady growth of the earlier sixteenth century was halted and it was only in the following century that it could be resumed.

For Holland and Zeeland the take-off to economic success was being prepared in the 1580s. Paradoxically, this process was materially helped by the consequences of one of the greatest military setbacks which the North had to face in these years. The loss of Antwerp, together with much of the South, led to a wave of refugees with capital, expertise and skills moving to the towns of the North. The resuscitation of the textile manufactures of Leiden and Haarlem, the expansion of Amsterdam's position in international trade and finance, and even the development of Dutch art, have all been attributed to the influx of these southern refugees. There may be some exaggeration in all this, but that this population movement had an important and positive impact on the economy of the North can hardly be questioned. To this extent the loss of the South, together with the blockade of the Schelde to strangle the trade of Spanish-controlled Antwerp, was a stimulus to the economic growth of Holland in particular. If, in general, it is hard to say that the Dutch economy benefited from the Revolt, nevertheless the recovery was remarkably swift. It may well be that growth would have been faster and smoother without these upheavals – and certainly the land provinces would have fared better – but on the other hand the continuation of a Spanish regime with little interest in or sympathy for the needs of trade and manufacture in the Netherlands, and with a determination to enforce religious uniformity, might well have been a serious drag on the development of the economy.

By 1588, however uncertain the political situation, the economic and social foundations of the new society which was to emerge in the Dutch Republic in the next century were firmly laid down. The take-off of the 1590s and the economic supremacy of the early seventeenth century were already implicit in the developments within the society of the northern Netherlands, and in particular within the county of Holland, up to that point – the rest was, to a significant extent, a tautology.

Notes

1   James D. Tracy, *Holland under Habsburg Rule 1506–1566* (Berkeley, 1990); James D. Tracy, *A Financial Revolution in the Habsburg Netherlands: 'Renten' and 'Renteniers' in the County of Holland, 1515–1566* (Berkeley, 1985).

2   The *ridderschap* representing the nobility now had only one vote against the eighteen for the towns, on the face of it a considerable diminution of its influence.

3   For the nature of these mutinies, see G. Parker, 'Mutiny and Discontent in the Spanish Army of Flanders, 1572–1607', in *Spain and the Netherlands 1559–1659* (London, 1979), 106–21.

4   Overijssel, however, did not sign the Union of Utrecht although it did become part of the new state.

5   To give the right count, the Eighty Years War has to start in 1568 but it would seem unnecessarily pedantic to try to rename it the Seventy Years War (or the Sixty Nine Years War) at this late date.

6   G. Parker, *The Army of Flanders and the Spanish Road 1567–1659* (Cambridge, 1972), 241–3.

7   Parker, *Army of Flanders*, Appendix A.

8   E.g. Pieter Geyl, *The Revolt of the Netherlands, 1555–1609* (London, 1958), 179.

9   See H.F.K. van Nierop, *The Nobility of Holland. From knights to regents* (Cambridge, 1993), chap.7.

10 J.L. van Zanden, *The Rise and Decline of Holland's Economy. Merchant Capitalism and the Labour Market* (Manchester, 1993), 30–1.

11 A.M. van der Woude, *Het Noorderkwartier*, 3 vols (Wageningen, 1972), I, 32–3.

12 This point was first argued forcibly by Jan de Vries, *The Dutch Rural Economy in the Golden Age 1500–1700* (New Haven, 1974).

13 H. van der Wee, *The Growth of the Antwerp Market and the European Economy (fourteenth-sixteenth centuries)*, 3 vols (The Hague, 1963).

14 The Sound Toll was levied by the Danish crown on ships and cargoes entering and leaving the Baltic.

15 N.E. Bang and K. Korst, *Tabeller over skibsfart og varetransport gennen Oresund, 1497–1660, 1661–1783*, 7 vols (Copenhagen/Leipzig, 1906–53).

16 Jan de Vries and A.M. van der Woude, *The First Modern Economy. Success, failure and perseverance of the Dutch economy, 1500–1815* (Cambridge, 1997), 60–1.

17 Jonathan I. Israel, *The Dutch Republic. Its Rise, Greatness, and Fall 1477–1806* (Oxford, 1995), 114.

18 A.M. van der Woude, 'Population developments in the Northern Netherlands (1500–1800) and the validity of the "urban graveyard" effect', *Annales de démographie historique, 1982*, 55–75.

19 Leo Noordegraaf and Gerrit Valk, *De gave gods. De pest in Holland vanaf de late middeleeuwen* (Bergen, NH, 1988), 46–7.

20 A.C. Duke, 'The face of popular religious dissent in the Low Countries, 1520–1530', in *Reformation and Revolt in the Low Countries* (London, 1990).

21 Herman van der Wee, 'The economy as a factor in the start of the Revolt in the Southern Netherlands', *Acta Historiae Neerlandica*, v (1970).

PART ONE

The Dutch Republic,
1588–1648

I

The Emergence of a New State

WHEN THE earl of Leicester left the Netherlands, his ambitions thwarted and his hopes disappointed, in the autumn of 1587 never to return, the situation of the rebels seemed if not hopeless then certainly extremely precarious. Since the peace with the Ottomans, effectively from 1578, and the absorption of Portugal at the beginning of the following decade, the Spanish *monarchía* had been able to concentrate its resources on the campaign in the Netherlands, and the advance of Parma's army had come to seem virtually unstoppable. The inexperienced and poorly supplied English troops who had arrived in the Netherlands as a result of the treaty of Nonsuch (August 1585) had proved an ineffective foil to the veterans – regularly paid for once – of the Spanish Army of Flanders. The chances of survival for the rebel provinces were further weakened by internal divisions and political uncertainty. Although Willem of Orange's grip had perhaps been slipping in his final years, his assassination nevertheless deprived the provinces of what little leadership they had. The sovereignty had been offered to Henri III of France and then to Elizabeth of England in vain, and Leicester's period as governor-general seemed only to have further undermined the fragile political structure of the embryo state. The earl's authority in the Netherlands had been fatally weakened from the start by Elizabeth's angry disavowal of the quasi-sovereign powers he had accepted from the States General on his arrival, and his later attempts to strengthen his position, culminating in a failed coup in September 1587, only led to more confusion. Yet in little over a decade, the situation of the provinces had been transformed both internally and externally, and within another ten years the truce of 1609 was negotiated on the basis of almost complete equality between the Dutch and the Spanish. Just over twenty years after Leicester's departure, the Dutch Republic had effectively achieved its independence.

1589–1609: Foundation

One of the initial reasons for Dutch survival, if not for the degree of its success, was the diversion of the Spanish military effort. Financial support for the army of Flanders had perhaps not been over-generous in the 1580s but it had been regular,[1] and this had been the prime basis of Parma's success. From 1588 onwards, however, Philip II felt compelled to adopt other priorities. Firstly, the Armada campaign against England not only swallowed up an enormous amount of resources, but also the need to keep a force ready for transport to England hamstrung Parma's military actions in 1588. Spanish impetus was regained somewhat in the following year, notably with the taking of Geertruidenberg, but in 1590 the army was diverted to intervention in France and this remained its main task until the peace of Vervins in 1598. By the time the Spanish were again able to concentrate on the situation in the Netherlands they found that they had to face an altogether more formidable opponent.

The slackening of Spanish pressure from 1588 onwards gave the Dutch a breathing space in which to turn a collection of squabbling rebel provinces into a viable new state. In these ten years, first highlighted by the eminent Dutch historian Fruin in the last century,[2] a way was found of making the political system work and, which was in the circumstances equally necessary, the army of the States was turned into one of the most effective military organisations of the time. The chief architect of the Dutch state was Johan van Oldenbarnevelt, who had been appointed *Advocaat van den Lande* of Holland in 1585 and used this basis to become the effective leader of the Dutch Republic until his fall in 1618.[3] The key to his success was that he went with the grain of provincial particularism rather than trying to override it. As *Advocaat* he was formally only an appointed official of the States of Holland, its legal adviser, but in fact he became the political leader of the province, and the system he created established the predominance of this province in the Republic as a whole.

The States General, where Holland could make its economic strength felt, became effectively the centre of government, taking the place of the Council of State (*Raad van State*) through which Leicester had tried to govern the country. Seven provinces – Gelderland, Holland, Zeeland, Friesland, Utrecht, Overijssel and Groningen – were represented in the States General and each had only one vote in the assembly. However, unanimity was necessary on important matters and so a majority vote in the States General could not force Holland to accept any policy it did not want to support, while the financial strength of this province ensured that nothing could be done without its backing. Holland's nominal share in the budget of the state was nearly 60 per cent, but in these early years – with Gelderland, Groningen and Overijssel in the front line of the war and able to contribute little to the central treasury – its real contribution was even greater. Working through the States General enabled Holland to use its fiscal superiority to establish its political leadership and prevented it from being out-voted by the lesser provinces. As one of Holland's representatives in the States General and especially on the various committees which effectively took most of the decisions, Oldenbarnevelt was able to gain invaluable experience and expertise, which helped him in time to achieve unrivalled political authority in the new state. This system of government seems to have been acceptable to the other provinces as they knew they needed Holland to survive and, while the insistence on provincial autonomy ensured that the politics of the Republic were dominated by Holland, the same principle provided the other provinces with some protection against their powerful ally. They too had their vetos, though in practice these were not as effective as Holland's, and they could run their own internal affairs very largely without inter-ference, and this effective provincial autonomy was quite possibly a more important point for most of their regents.

As far as the war effort, and thus the survival of the new state, was concerned the construction of a fiscal system which could provide enough money to pay for the armed forces was an indispensable part of the creation of a workable state. Although money remained short, and squaring the fiscal circle required extreme ingenuity at times, Oldenbarnevelt and his collaborators managed to bring order and a degree of efficiency to the Republic's finances despite the insatiable demands of the war. That this was possible was only in part the result of skilful administration, more fundamental was the resurgence of the Dutch economy in these years: it has been argued that it was just in this period that the take-off to economic dominance in Europe occurred.[4] While it might be doubted that such a precise timing of Dutch economic development is possible, it is nevertheless reasonably clear that the economic growth of the pre-Revolt years was renewed with increasing vigour from the 1580s onwards, particularly in Holland. The consequent increase in prosperity provided not only a sound tax-base, but helped to ensure the success of the loans floated by the States of Holland to finance the war. A combination of a plentiful supply of capital and confidence in the soundness of Holland's finances meant that these loans could be floated at relatively modest rates of interest. At this stage, even more than later, the capacity of the Dutch Republic to continue to fight the war against Spain depended on Holland: on its tax payers, its ability to borrow relatively cheaply, and thus fundamentally on the health of its economy. The political dominance of the leading province in these years was a more or less just reflection of its economic and hence fiscal importance.

The political and fiscal consolidation of the new state was the necessary precondition for the vital task of reorganisation and modernisation of the Army of the Republic which was carried out by Willem of Orange's son, count Maurits, and his cousin, the stadhouder of Friesland, Willem Lodewijk. By the beginning of the new century, the Dutch army had become one of the most efficient military organisations in Europe, and was able to match in quality even the veterans of the Army of Flanders.[5] Besides the introduction of smaller units of manoeuvre, the improved training in tactics and weapon-handling, and deployment of the infantry in line to maximise fire-power, perhaps the most important development was the improvement in military discipline. In the main, the Dutch army did not fight battles – Nieuwpoort (1600) and perhaps Turnhout (1597) are the only notable ones in the whole period up to 1609 – but skirmishes and above all sieges, and here detailed and methodical planning by the leadership and disciplined conduct by the troops were of central importance. Underlying all this, however, was pay; what distinguished the Dutch army from all others of the period, and particularly from its Spanish opponent, was the regularity of its pay. Whereas mutinies over lack of pay were frequent in the Army of Flanders,[6] the Dutch, although sorely tried at times, were in the main able to pay their troops more or less in full and on time. Without this financial support, the strategic and tactical innovations would have been able to achieve little. The number of troops in the pay of the States General increased rapidly in the decade after 1588, and continued to grow in the first years of the new century from over 30,000 in 1595 to a peak of around 51,000 at the time of the cease-fire in 1607.[7] If local defence forces and the continuing naval effort are also taken into account, it is clear that by this time the Republic was able to sustain formidable armed forces.

With the Spanish army diverted into France, the Dutch began to consolidate the territorial base of their new state. The first important success came in 1590 with the taking of Breda, and in the following year Deventer, Zutphen and Nijmegen followed. In 1593 Geertruidenberg in the far south of Holland was retaken — it had been betrayed to the Spanish in 1589 — and in 1594 the fall of Groningen secured the north-east of the country. The eastern border was strengthened in 1597 by the taking of Ootmarsum, Enschedé and Groenlo, and by the end of the decade not only Holland and Zeeland but also Friesland, Groningen, Utrecht and substantial parts of Overijssel and Gelderland were firmly under Dutch control. The *Hollandse tuin* (the garden of Holland) was indeed firmly fenced in, but more importantly the territory of the new state as a whole had been very largely cleared of Spanish troops and the geographical shape of the Republic was at last becoming evident. After the peace of Vervins in 1598 which brought the war in France to an end, the Spanish were able to mount a new effort in the Netherlands but, despite some spectacular successes, such as the taking of Ostend in 1604 and the surprise of Groenlo in 1606, all the skill of the new Spanish general Spinola could do little more than dent the position which the Dutch had built up in the 1590s, and the cease-fire of 1607 marked a recognition on both sides that something like a stalemate had developed.

In these years the conflict between Spain and the new Dutch state also began to spread outside Europe. Up to this point merchants in the Netherlands had been happy to buy their spices and other Asian goods on the Lisbon market, but the Spanish embargoes of 1585–90 and 1598–1608 on trade with the rebel provinces also closed Portuguese ports to the Dutch. Consequently Dutch merchants had an incentive to open up direct trade with Asia, and the later Dutch colonial empire had its origins in the first expeditions of Dutch traders to the East Indies in the 1590s. Within a few years the Dutch presence in the East was so considerable — and the competition between rival Dutch companies so fierce — that it became expedient to found a chartered monopoly company to control trade with the region. The aim of the VOC (*Vereenigde Oost-indische Compagnie*, i.e. United East India Company), which was given its charter by the States General in 1602, was to give direction to the overall Dutch effort in the Indies, and to ensure that internecine rivalry did not force prices up in the East or down in Europe. The company needed a monopoly because of the expense of building up an infrastructure in the Indies and also because of the costs involved in undermining the established position of the Portuguese. The latter were a particular target, not only because of their dominance of the sea-borne spice trade to Europe, but also because they had become a part of the Spanish *monarchía* when Philip II enforced his claim to the Portuguese crown in 1580. The struggle for trade in the Indies thus came to have considerable strategic significance as part of the war against Spain: the VOC's campaign in Indonesia especially began to divert the profits of the spice trade away from Iberia and towards the Republic, and ensured that the already over-stretched Spanish military and naval resources would be further drained by attempting to protect the Portuguese position in the East. These developments also began to build up a powerful vested interest in the continued progress of the VOC, and thus made an overall settlement with Spain even more difficult to achieve. Dutch traders and privateers were also beginning to make an impact on the Caribbean and the Americas in general, which necessarily brought them into conflict with Spanish interests. These activities, too, created problems in the negotiations with Spain.

The inconclusive warfare of the first years of the new century strengthened the case of those on both sides who favoured a negotiated settlement. For the Spanish, confidence in an ultimate victory was waning, and the strains of the long years of warfare on this and other fronts was beginning to tell. The *monarchía* was in what seemed at times to be a permanent fiscal crisis, and the military organisation was beginning to collapse under the weight of the demands made upon it, leading to what might be called a devolution of responsibility or a privatisation of various aspects of the military effort by the end of the sixteenth century.[8] After the death of Philip II in 1598, the Spanish-controlled Netherlands had been granted a considerable degree of autonomy under the archduke Albert and here the desire to end what was seen as a futile and yet damaging war was particularly strong. On the Dutch side, the arguments of those who stressed the inordinate cost of the war and claimed that it was blocking the full development of the Dutch economy became more persuasive. This was particularly true for Holland: this province was the economic power-house of the Republic, had to pay for most of the costs of the war, and yet the conflict seemed to be getting nowhere at very great expense. Many leading politicians, and merchants as well, began to ask themselves what was the purpose of the war. For some, undoubtedly, the urge to free the South from Spanish occupation was still strong, but probably most inhabitants of the new state had lost interest in further conquests once their own province had been secured – or, at most, when the North as a whole had been freed of Spanish troops. In the end, Oldenbarnevelt took the lead in the movement working for peace and pushed through first the cease-fire of 1607 and then the Twelve Years Truce of 1609.

There was opposition to this peace policy from various quarters, however, most importantly from the ranks of orthodox calvinists and from count Maurits, both of them crucial foreshadowings of the future pattern of Dutch politics under the Republic. The motives of Maurits are difficult to assess. He clearly had a strong personal interest both in the continuation of the war and in opposing Oldenbarnevelt: as leader of the Republic's army, his importance would undoubtedly be diminished in peace-time; and as stadhouder of most of the provinces he may have come to resent the enormous authority which the *Advocaat* had acquired by this time. What had been tolerable to the younger and inexperienced Maurits was no longer, perhaps, acceptable now he had a long series of military successes behind him, and was beginning to be aware of the political potential of the combination of offices and positions which he held in the army and the various provinces. On the other hand, he may well have been perfectly sincere in his distrust of the peace and of the Spanish; he would not have been the only one to fear that a truce would only give Spain the opportunity to recuperate, with the intention of attacking the Republic at a later and more opportune moment. The Spanish were still regarded as the greatest power in Europe and thus an ever present and formidable threat; the Republic, it was argued, could not afford any let up in the pressure it was putting on them – after all, if they were ready to enter serious negotiations for peace, they must be weakening and thus vulnerable to a final Dutch effort.

Such attitudes had their emotional side, but were essentially based on practical considerations; the other main element in the campaign against the truce was ideological in nature and considerably more emotion-driven. For many of the calvinists in the country – still in all probability a minority of the population as a whole, but a highly influential one – the war against Spain was part of the apocalyptic struggle between the forces of Christ and of Antichrist which was felt to be the hallmark of the age in which they lived. Spain was the champion of catholicism, and it was still the orthodoxy in protestant circles to regard the Roman Church as the creation and tool of Antichrist designed to undermine the true church. It was the duty of all christians, thus, to oppose this power in the world and, as far as the Dutch were concerned, it was their god-given purpose to continue the war against the Spanish servants of antichristian forces in the world. In addition, in the eyes of many members of the Reformed Church, the Revolt had essentially been a religious movement, and the Republic in consequence had a providential purpose, a vital part of which was continuing to fight for the reform of the Church throughout Europe and the world. From this perspective, the peace with Spain was a betrayal of the meaning of the Revolt. On a more practical level, it was also argued that it was only the war which held together the very disparate provinces which made up the Republic; take away the war and the state would fall apart – as indeed at one stage during the Truce crisis it seemed about to happen.

Of all the opponents of the truce the most surprising in many ways was Amsterdam. In later years the great trading town was to become the archetypical supporter of peace in the interests of trade, but on this occasion its government worked against the negotiations for peace, and the signing of the Truce seems to have been instrumental in turning the town definitively against Oldenbarnevelt. One of the reasons for this attitude was economic: not all merchants believed that peace offered the best opportunities, in particular those involved with trade and privateering in American waters saw great possibilities for themselves if the war against Spain continued. However, the plans for the establishment of a chartered monopoly company, on the lines of the VOC, to organise and direct Dutch penetration of the 'West Indies' were blocked by Oldenbarnevelt in order to smooth the way to an agreement with Spain. Some of the leading Amsterdam regents appear never to have forgiven him for this.

A full peace proved impossible to achieve, partly because in the end the Spanish were not prepared to recognise the Republic as a fully-independent state, but a Truce of twelve years duration was signed at Antwerp (1609). However imperfect, this treaty marked the emergence of the Dutch Republic as a new state in Europe. Over the preceding two decades it had been able to deal on increasingly independent terms with England and France, and now Spain had recognised it as an equal, *de facto* if not *de jure*, in the talks leading up to the Truce. Unambiguous, formal recognition of the Republic's complete independence might have to wait until 1648, but the treaty of Antwerp was nevertheless a proud moment in the brief history of the young state.

1609–21: Crisis

Far from being an unalloyed triumph, the signing of the truce with Spain ushered in the most dangerous period of internal instability that the Republic was ever to experience. A dispute over doctrine within the Reformed Church, which had been gathering strength and bitterness for some years, now escalated into a political crisis which at one stage threatened to lead to civil war and perhaps even to the break up of the Dutch state. In the event the worst was avoided and the Republic stayed together, but only at the cost of a significant modification to the way in which its political system worked. Count Maurits carried out a successful coup in 1618, arresting Oldenbarnevelt and his chief collaborators and carrying out a series of *wetsverzettingen* – changes in the personnel of local government – to place his supporters in control of the voting towns of Holland. The *Advocaat* was tried, condemned and executed, and Maurits took his place as the *de facto* head of the Dutch state. A new way of running the Republic was established which was to last until the death of Willem II in 1650.

The Republic's internal problems cannot be fully understood without taking into account the extent to which rising tensions in Europe increased the sense of impending disaster. The Dutch seemed to be living in a world which grew more dangerous almost every day and such perceptions helped to fuel the fears and suspicions, verging on the paranoid, which characterised the religious and political disputes of the Truce years. The first major problem emerged at the same time as the negotiations for the Truce were being successfully completed. In March 1609 the death of duke Johann Wilhelm, the ruler of Jülich, Kleve, Berg and Mark, gave rise to a disputed succession which threatened to reopen the war with Spain almost before the ink was dry on the treaty of Antwerp, as the Spanish were drawn in to support one claimant and the Dutch the other. These territories just over their eastern border in the Rhineland were regarded by the Dutch as being of vital strategic significance and they could hardly remain indifferent to their future, especially when the candidate backed by the Spanish converted to catholicism to gain the support of the emperor. Tensions rose as Dutch and Spanish troops moved into the disputed territories. However, a compromise which divided the territories between the rival claimants was reached in the following year and the danger averted, only to resurface in 1614 when the agreement broke down and Spanish and Dutch troops again moved into the territories. Although the settlement was reimposed and a resumption of the war again averted, such instability in a region which the Dutch regarded as vital to their security meant that from its very start the Dutch could never be sure that the Truce would hold for its full term. If these Rhenish territories fell into the Imperial and catholic camp, the Spanish might well be tempted to take advantage of their improved strategic situation while the Republic was weakened by internal disputes.

One of the reasons why this succession dispute was so difficult to resolve was the increasing tension between catholic and protestant in the Holy Roman Empire. The Peace of Augsburg in 1555 had brought a halt to armed conflict over religion in the Empire and, perhaps unexpectedly, this peace had held for the rest of the sixteenth century, but in the first years of the following century the protestants began to feel that the settlement was being undermined by the actions of the catholics backed by the emperor. The treatment of Donauwörth, a small protestant Imperial city which was put under the Imperial ban and then forcibly brought over to the catholic camp in 1607–8, seemed deeply ominous. The creation of a Protestant Union and a Catholic League were institutional expressions of the rising tension between the confessions which was to play a major part in ensuring that the Revolt in Bohemia which broke out in 1618 would lead to the devastation of the Thirty Years War. The situation in the Holy Roman Empire contributed to the perception in the Republic that European protestantism was under increasing threat from a resurgent Catholic Church supported by the emperor and, of course, Spain. Seen from this perspective, the position of the Dutch Republic looked increasingly insecure.

This sense of the fragility of the Dutch situation was not helped by the assassination of Henri IV of France in 1610. Although he had converted to catholicism as the price of establishing himself firmly on the French throne, Henri had nevertheless continued with what might be called a protestant foreign policy, even after making peace with Spain in 1598. His death, however, brought a period of regency under the queen dowager, Marie de Médicis, and French policy became distinctly more pro-Spanish and markedly less friendly towards the Dutch. Oldenbarnevelt's attempts to resuscitate the alliance with France, which he saw as vital to the interests of the Republic in the long term, led to his supporting the French crown when it was faced with yet another Huguenot rising, but this backing of a catholic government against protestant dissidents did nothing to reassure his suspicious critics at home. A further cause for concern was the policy of England, the other key ally of the Republic's early years. Soon after his accession James I had made peace with Spain, and in succeeding years he became increasingly concerned to present himself as a great mediator, hoping to play the part of a peacemaker on a European scale. Given the increasingly dangerous situation which the Dutch felt themselves to be in, James's neutral policy seemed all too often to work in favour of Spain rather than the Republic. Various disputes over economic matters also soured the relations between the Dutch and England, while the attitude the English government adopted over the religious problems in the Republic only made this growing estrangement worse. While contemporaries could not predict the outbreak of the Thirty Years War and, even after it had started, it was to be some years before its gravity became evident, nevertheless the years between 1609 and 1618 were uncertain ones as far as the Dutch were concerned, and the deteriorating situation outside its borders undoubtedly added extra emotional force to the internal conflicts of the time.

The domestic struggles which came to a head in 1618-19 were in part a result of the disagreements between Oldenbarnevelt and Maurits and their respective supporters over the signing of the Truce. They reflected broader disagreements over foreign policy and, by extension, about the nature, purpose and true interests of the Dutch state. Such differences could in all probability have been resolved without any major disturbance to the political system; what made the internal situation so explosive was the addition of a doctrinal dispute which threatened to destroy the unity of the Reformed Church.

Maurits had opposed the signing of the Truce, and his stance gained widespread support for a variety of reasons. Distrust of Spain and the danger of passivity in an uncertain and threatening international situation led many to question the ageing Oldenbarnevelt's judgement (he was 62 in 1609). By the beginning of the Truce years, the *Advocaat* had been in power for almost a quarter of a century and the accumulation of experience and expertise had given him an extraordinary authority in the young Dutch state, but had brought him enemies as well as allies. His notorious impatience at opposition had perhaps only increased with age, and this helped to gain him a not wholly undeserved reputation for arrogance. Also, after so many years as effective head of the Republic, it would hardly be surprising if other individuals and institutions resented their exclusion from what they felt to be their proper share of power. Maurits's failure to prevent the signing of the Truce taught him that he needed to add a more influential political role to his military responsibilities, especially as leadership of the army threatened to become a less central part of the Republic's affairs with the ending of hostilities. The other crucial component of the opposition to Oldenbarnevelt was Amsterdam. Here again failure to prevent the signing of the Truce was the decisive moment, persuading the dominant faction among Amsterdam's regents that their voice was not being given its proper weight in the decision-making of province and state. More generally, the economic effects of the Truce were not uniformly favourable in the Republic, and those towns and individuals who felt themselves to be disadvantaged also began to turn against the *Advocaat van den Lande*. A more surprising, and decidedly more ominous, element in the opposition to the *Advocaat's* policies was the suspicion of a deliberate betrayal of Dutch interests that began to be voiced. Oldenbarnevelt's policies were coming to be seen – or at least presented – by some of his more extreme opponents not just as profoundly mistaken, but as conscious treason. That such implausible accusations should have been given credence by many – perhaps even in the highest circles[9] – is almost entirely due to the way in which the religious disputes of the period interacted with the disagreements over foreign policy to produce a situation which seemed to threaten to tear the Dutch state apart.

The conflict between the remonstrants and the contraremonstrants was as much about the nature of the Reformed Church as the doctrinal issues which were its overt manifestation.[10] The Reformed movement in the Netherlands had developed during the years of persecution ('under the cross') and exile, not as an officially created state church as had been the case in much of protestant Europe. Within a few years of the outbreak of the Revolt it emerged as effectively the official church of the new state: it was given the church-buildings for its own services and its ministers were paid out of the property of the old Church. (However, the ownership of both churches and property was appropriated and retained by the civil authorities at local and provincial level.) In the first decades of the seventeenth century the Reformed Church exhibited a fundamental ambivalence regarding both its identity and its aims: to a significant extent it still retained the ethos of a gathered church of saints which it had acquired during its years under the cross, but its consequent insistence on doctrinal rigour and strict congregational discipline contradicted its drive to become the church of the whole Dutch community. Similarly, it strove to retain as much independence from the civil authorities as possible, notably in the appointment of its ministers; it seemed it was unwilling to pay the necessary political price for becoming the official church of the Dutch state. In contrast many regents seem to have hoped that the Reformed Church would become decisively more flexible in both doctrine and discipline, and so prove capable of embracing a much higher proportion of the population than seemed possible for the existing church.[11] Faced with the task of governing communities which were religiously divided, many regents hoped that a latitudinarian church could supply that element of social cohesion which the old Church had provided in the past. As it was, the reformed were very much a minority in the Dutch population until well on into the seventeenth century. Although the Reformed Church was clearly the official church of the Dutch state, there was no duty of attendance at its services and there was no legal obligation on Dutch citizens to become members of its congregations – nor, perhaps, could there be while the Church retained the right to reject whomever they regarded as unworthy. Other protestants were in practice free to worship as they wished and, while catholic worship was formally banned, it was no crime to hold catholic beliefs.

At the beginning of the new century the position of the Reformed Church was still weak in a number of crucial respects: it had relatively few firm adherents and had only uncertain support from a regent group which was far from unambiguously committed to the calvinist cause. In these circumstances, the modest criticisms of its doctrines by Jacobus Arminius, professor of theology at Leiden, were seen as constituting a deadly threat to the integrity of the Church. The doctrine of predestination was coming increasingly to be regarded as the hallmark of calvinist orthodoxy, and Arminius's proposed modification of this in the direction of universal grace was seen as essentially heretical by his opponents – and, indeed, as the first step on a road which must inevitably lead to Rome. The remonstrants – as the followers of Arminius became known after their appeal (remonstrance) to the States of Holland for protection in 1610 – picked up considerable support in Holland especially from regents looking for a more latitudinarian official church for their communities. This political support was further encouraged by the readiness of the remonstrants to acknowledge the final authority of the civil power in religious matters much more unambiguously than the calvinists ever could. The remonstrant–contraremonstrant conflict was not a dispute over religious freedom, but a struggle within the Reformed Church with the doctrine and character of this church as its issue. The self-styled orthodox tried to suppress the arminians by calling a national synod of the Reformed Church which they believed, rightly, would be heavily weighted in their favour. The remonstrants naturally opposed this and in the end Oldenbarnevelt blocked the proposal, primarily perhaps on constitutional grounds: allowing a *national* synod to dictate on religious matters to Holland would have been an unacceptable infringement of the province's autonomy.

With no simple resolution available, the conflict between remonstrants and their opponents escalated, particularly at local level. There were serious clashes between church and civil authorities over appointment and dismissal of ministers in an increasing number of towns. In most cases – though certainly not all – these disturbances involved congregations dominated by contraremonstrants rejecting remonstrant ministers that town governments were trying to impose on them. What made this conflict so dangerous was its timing: it was gathering force in the first decade of the century and became particularly virulent after the Truce. A central concern was that the Republic was seen as essentially an alliance for the war with Spain; consequently it was feared that even a truce might allow the provinces to drift apart. Alongside the war, the Reformed Church was perceived as one of the most important forces holding the provinces of the Republic together, but the remonstrant movement – from this perspective – seemed likely to weaken and divide the church. In particular, as the remonstrant movement was much stronger in Holland than in the rest of the Republic, the fear was that the Church here would be taken over by the remonstrants while the orthodox calvinists remained in control in the other provinces, introducing a schism in the Reformed Church along provincial lines and thus breaking the religious link holding the Union together. In the atmosphere of distrust caused by disagreement over the signing of the Truce, it was only a short step to the suspicion that there was a deliberate plot to weaken the Republic fatally by undermining its internal coherence as well as lowering its guard against Spain.

There was a powerful popular movement in support of the contraremonstrants, perhaps fired in part by the association of orthodox calvinism with loyalty to the Revolt in the minds of many people. As internal tensions rose Maurits backed the contraremonstrants for, it would seem, political rather than religious reasons, and he moved decisively to their side in 1617 by demonstratively attending their services in the Cloister Church in The Hague which they had occupied. Oldenbarnevelt's attempts to force the contending parties to coexist in peace, and to protect Holland's autonomy from outside interference in religious matters, became less and less convincing. His position was perhaps decisively weakened by the opposition of a number of towns, led by the formidable Amsterdam, within his power-base, the States of Holland. The motives of this group of dissenting towns were a combination of distrust of Oldenbarnevelt's foreign policy, economic discontent, and an uncertain degree of contraremonstrant conviction. Dissatisfied with the support that remonstrant town governments were receiving from the army against unruly citizens – because of Maurits's unwillingness to act – the Sharp Resolution of the States of Holland in 1617 empowered the towns to raise their own troops (*waardgelders*), a move that was interpreted by Oldenbarnevelt's opponents as bringing civil war a significant step closer. In response, Maurits staged a coup in 1618, as meticulously planned and executed as one of his copybook sieges. First he suppressed the pockets of remonstrant strength outside Holland, notably in Nijmegen and the town of Utrecht, then he arrested Oldenbarnevelt and his closest collaborators, acting on a commission of dubious legality from the States General. In a series of *wetsverzettingen*, Maurits visited the voting towns of Holland in turn, purged their governments of remonstrants and replaced them with men he expected to be able to rely on. In 1619 Oldenbarnevelt was tried for treason and executed, while the synod of Dordt condemned the doctrines of the remonstrants and declared a strict predestinarian calvinism to be the true doctrine of the Reformed Church.

The crisis had been resolved with a minimum of bloodshed but at the cost of a considerable upheaval in the political system. From this point on until 1651 the successive princes of Orange[12] took the lead in the complex political system which governed the Republic. As head of the army, they were appointed by and subordinate to the States General; and as stadhouder in a majority of the provinces they were appointed by and subject to the respective provincial States. Nevertheless, using the power and influence which these offices gave them, they were able to build up an unchallengeable position despite their formally subordinate status. In other respects, however, remarkably little was changed by the crisis. Although Oldenbarnevelt had been tried and condemned in the name of a species of sovereignty for the States General, once the crisis was safely over provincial autonomy reasserted itself in practice. With the religious question settled, Holland could begin to unite again to use its financial strength to pursue its own political and economic interests. The defeated remonstrants suffered persecution for a number of years – a policy pursued by the victorious party with notable vindictiveness in some places – but in course of time they accepted their expulsion and were able to set themselves up as a separate church. Although this was not a welcome development as far as the Reformed Church was concerned, the remonstrants, once safely outside the Church, were not the subversive influence they had been when on the inside, and so could in the end be allowed to enjoy the same tolerance as other protestant dissenters.

1621–48: Consolidation

The final phase of the long struggle with Spain, starting with the end of the Truce in 1621, ran parallel to the Thirty Years War in the Holy Roman Empire, and the treaty of Münster with the Spanish which marked its official conclusion was part of the Peace of Westphalia which brought the latter conflict to an end. In retrospect the establishment of full Dutch independence in 1648 seems inevitable, but this result was by no means seen as a foregone conclusion either by the Dutch or by other observers at the time, at least in the first years after the re-opening of hostilities. Moreover, the vicissitudes of the war in the Empire are a reminder of the unpredictability of the overall situation for much of this period: a different outcome to the Thirty Years War could well have had far-reaching consequences for the Dutch. On the other hand, it is in this period that the Dutch Republic became an undisputed major power – and not just in Europe. The war with Spain had already spread outside Europe before the Truce, most importantly with the VOC's attack on the Portuguese position in the East, but the scale of the extra-European dimension to the struggle increased significantly in this final period with the founding of the West India Company in 1621, the subsequent opening up of a new front to the war in Brazil, and the rapid establishment of the VOC's predominance in

Europe's trade to Indonesia and much of Asia. The Republic became a world power while still struggling for its survival against the Spanish *monarchía*.

Despite the importance of such activities in the Americas and the East, the war on land in the Netherlands remained the most vital part of the conflict with Spain. While the Dutch could not perhaps have won the war on land, they could certainly have lost it there: no amount of success in Brazil or the Moluccas would have helped if the Army of Flanders had been able to break through the land defences of the Republic. So the primary effort had still to be devoted to this area, and the maintenance of a large and efficient army was essential. The number of troops in the Dutch army rose from about 50,000 at the resumption of the war to around 75,000 in the 1630s,[13] and had reached a temporary peak of perhaps 100,000 during the siege of 's-Hertogenbosch in 1629. The size of the army was allowed to drop somewhat in the final years of the conflict as the direct military threat from Spain decreased, but it still remained substantial. In addition to the effort necessary to defend and consolidate the Republic's land frontiers, the war at sea also demanded greater attention in these years as the Spanish reorganised and strengthened their naval presence in northern European waters.[14] The more important threat at sea, however, probably came from the Dunkirk privateers who developed into a major scourge of Dutch shipping and especially of the fishing fleet in these years. So, although the most spectacular Dutch naval success in European waters was the defeat of the Spanish armada of 1639 at the Downs, the main tasks for the navy were the convoying of merchant ships, the blockade of the Schelde and the Flemish coast, and the protection of the herring fleet in the North Sea.[15]

Though not its primary objective, certainly not in the case of the VOC, Dutch colonial expansion in this period was also part of the war effort against Spain, and in the end may have made a significant contribution to the final victory. The success of the VOC was the result of a combination of trading skill and force, and the target of Dutch attacks was principally the factories and trade of the Portuguese in the East. The capture of Malacca in 1641 was an important expression of Dutch supremacy in the region, but the effective absorption of the Moluccas though less dramatic was more important. The Portuguese were also the chief target of the West India Company (WIC), and the Dutch took over a large part of northern Brazil in the 1630s. Brazilian sugar formed the economic motivation for the attack, but the design of weakening Spain was always a very important consideration in the counsels of the WIC. In this case it may well have worked: the inability of the *monarchía* to protect Portuguese colonial interests from the depredations of the Dutch was an important element in the dissatis-faction with Spanish rule that led to the Portuguese revolt of 1640. So with the Dutch and the Spanish fighting each other directly or by proxy not only in the Low Countries, but in Brazil, the Caribbean, West Africa, India, Sri Lanka, Malaysia and Indonesia, if this was not quite a world war it was fought world-wide. Even in Japan it was the Dutch who undermined confidence in the Portuguese and established them-selves as the only Europeans permitted to trade with this country.

The serious domestic problems of the truce years prevented the Republic from getting more than peripherally involved with the Bohemian revolt which sparked off the Thirty Years War.[16] However, the logic of the victory for Maurits and the contraremonstrants seemed to be that they would wish to resume the war against the old enemy unless the Spanish were willing to concede the bulk of Dutch war aims. Spain accepted the necessity of continuing the struggle with the Dutch with a certain fatalism; while not expecting to be able to reconquer the rebel provinces, they hoped to be able to put enough pressure on the Dutch to gain significant concessions. Maurits, as if exhausted from the strains of the domestic crisis, adopted a largely passive defensive policy while the Spanish under Spinola gained a number of successes, most notably the capture of Breda in 1625. The Republic was aided by a subsidy treaty with France in 1624, but the crucial circumstance seems to have been the sheer expense of the Spanish campaign. Despite the propaganda triumph it gave them – recorded in the famous painting by Velázquez – the cost of taking Breda made it something of a Pyrrhic victory, and Olivares began to look for a less financially ruinous way of keeping pressure on the Dutch.[17]

The answer the Spanish found was to pursue a more defensive, and thus less expensive, strategy on land in the Low Countries, and shift the emphasis to economic warfare.[18] There were three main strands to this policy: to make the embargo on Dutch trade with Iberia more effec-tive, to bar the Dutch from trading with the Southern Netherlands, and to attack the Dutch Baltic trade. The last plan was the most ambitious and predictably came to nothing, but is a telling reminder of how closely connected the Hispano-Dutch war could be to the Thirty Years

War. The plan was only conceivable because of the successes of the Imperial army under Wallenstein in northern Germany in the middle years of the 1620s. A major port was to be captured and turned into the base for a Baltic admiralty which would be used to attack and destroy the Republic's Baltic trade, which was regarded as vital to its overall prosperity. In a way it was the Spanish/Imperial counterpart of the schemes to undermine the power of Spain by attacking its economic links with the Americas which attracted so much attention in England and the Republic in these years – and just as unlikely to achieve its aim. In the event, after the failure of Wallenstein to take Stralsund (1628) the scheme returned to the realm of more or less fantastic plots from which it had fleetingly emerged.[19] The other aspects of this economic strategy were more in touch with the possible and were certainly more damaging to the Dutch, especially when taken in combination with an intensification of the attacks on Dutch merchant ships and fishing boats by the armada of Flanders and the Dunkirk privateers. How effective all this was is hard to say: certainly the losses to the herring fleet were serious, and the number of merchant ships sunk or captured rose to disturbing levels, but it remains doubtful whether the Dutch economy suffered a great deal of damage overall. What is clear is that this economic strategy gave the Dutch the opportunity to turn to the offensive on the ground in the Netherlands.

The reversal of military fortunes in the Netherlands did not quite coincide with the death of Maurits and his replacement by Frederik Hendrik in 1625 – Breda fell to the Spanish soon after the latter succeeded to his half-brother's positions. However, Spanish financial problems and the consequent switch to the defensive meant that this proved to be their last great triumph in the Netherlands' theatre. In the next few years the Dutch were able to strengthen their strategic position both on their eastern border and in the south. Like his predecessor, Frederik Hendrik's talent as a military leader lay in careful planning and organisation rather than charismatic leadership in battle. The Dutch were operating on internal lines and so they could move troops and supplies to any area of the conflict along the inland waterways more quickly than the Spanish. Moreover, it was easier for Frederik Hendrik to disguise his intentions, as he could concentrate his troops at a central location and only reveal his hand at the last moment when they began to move. In these years he emerged as one of the leading generals in Europe, not in battle but through a series of the set-piece sieges which were his *forte*. In 1626 Oldenzaal was taken, and in the following year the more formidable fortress, Groenlo, contributing to a significant consolidation in the east. The first great triumph for Frederik Hendrik came, however, with the capture of Den Bosch in 1629 after a skilfully conducted formal siege which demonstrated to Europe his mastery of this branch of warfare, and three years later Maastricht followed. Breda was brought back under Dutch control in 1637 and this meant that – apart from a few minor adjustments – the Republic had found its definitive territorial shape. In particular, with Bergen op Zoom, Breda and Den Bosch in Dutch hands, more or less all of northern Brabant had become part of the Generality lands.[20]

Despite the alliance with France in 1635, this was the end of significant territorial gains by the Republic, in part at least because conquering more of the Southern Netherlands had little strategic point and could have led to severe political and religious problems. The aftermath of the taking of Den Bosch and Maastricht had made it all too clear what difficulties were involved in absorbing areas whose populations were almost totally catholic, and likely to remain so. The hopes still cherished by some that the inhabitants of such areas would rapidly convert to protestantism once restrictions on the preaching of the true word of God were removed proved illusory. The people of these areas had experienced the counter-reformation and when put to the test this proved remarkably effective in insulating them from protestant influences. (Despite over one hundred and fifty years of protestant rule, North Brabant remained as catholic when the Republic ended as it had been in 1629.) Moreover, these conquests gave a boost to the persistent campaign to give back to States Brabant (the Dutch-controlled part of the duchy) the membership of the States General which Brabant had relinquished in 1585.[21] The seven 'united provinces' had no wish to share power with another province, and further territorial gains in the south could only exacerbate this problem. Economically too, the merchants and manufacturers of Holland were not anxious to see the economy of the South revive. Amsterdam in particular was reluctant to see Antwerp rise again to become a possibly dangerous commercial competitor. The blockade of the Schelde was regarded as too valuable to be lightly relinquished.

Thus, after the middle of the 1630s the war ground on to little purpose but at great cost to both sides. A settlement proved elusive, however, until the Portuguese and Catalan revolts forced the *monarchía* effectively to give up its claims on the northern Netherlands. Both revolts can be directly attributed to the strains of long years of warfare – not least against the Dutch. In the case of the Catalans the revolt was a reaction to new financial demands coming from a Spanish state desperate to ease the fiscal burden which war was placing on Castile, and in this sense was a consequence of warfare. The Portuguese rising, however, arose more directly out of the war with the Republic, at least in part; the successful attacks of the Dutch on their trading empire in the East, and their conquest of the northern regions of Brazil brought the Spanish connection into disrepute. Not only had the rule of the Spanish crown failed to protect Portuguese colonial interests from the Dutch, it could be argued that it was only the link with Spain that had brought on these attacks in the first place.[22] Whatever the causes of these revolts, they immediately became the prime concern of the Spanish government. In the end the Spanish proved willing to make almost any concession in the Netherlands in order to free their hands to deal with the problems in Iberia itself. Negotiations dragged on for some years, partly because the Dutch were bound by their treaty with France in 1635 not to make a separate peace, and the French had their reasons for fighting on (as indeed they did until 1659). Finally, the Republic broke its treaty obligations to the French and made peace with Spain at the treaty of Münster in 1648. Spain – and by extension the emperor – finally recognised the full independence of the Dutch Republic and conceded all of the other points – including the closure of the Schelde – that the Dutch felt to be vital. The Eighty Years War had been won.

The treaty of Münster was part of the settlement which brought the Thirty Years War to an end, symbolising the degree to which the two conflicts had been intertwined in fact if not in legal fiction. The Dutch had never been formally at war with the emperor, but they knew, or feared, that a triumph for the Imperial and catholic side would be a disaster for themselves. Victorious Imperial forces could be expected to come to the aid of the – both catholic and Habsburg – Spanish in their war against the protestant rebels in the Netherlands. On the other hand, Spanish resources were continually being diverted to Bohemia, the Palatinate and elsewhere in support of the Imperial cause which inevitably relieved the military pressure on the Dutch to some extent. It was this strain on resources coming from a combination of the war with the Dutch and that in the Empire which finally broke the Spanish fiscal system and sparked off the Catalan and then the Portuguese revolts. For the Spanish, too, the war in the Empire was inextricably entangled with that in the Netherlands; the attempt to use the temporary Imperial dominance of north Germany to attack Dutch trade in the Baltic was intended to be, as we have seen, an integral part of their economic warfare against the Dutch.

After the Imperial victories in the 1620s, especially under the leadership of Wallenstein, the chances of eventual triumph seemed high, with the Edict of Restitution (1629) bringing considerable catholic gains in the Empire, and in Bohemia not only resistance to the Habsburgs but protestantism also being systematically crushed. From this perspective the intervention of Sweden and the spectacular victories of Gustavus Adolphus were a turning point of the war in the Netherlands as well as that in the Empire. The Imperial advance was turned back and, although stalemate soon followed after the death of the Swedish king, the likelihood of an eventual Imperial triumph had dwindled considerably. Similarly, the direct intervention of France in the Eighty Years War was also a major contribution to the defeat of Imperial policy in the Empire. A different outcome in Germany would have created serious problems, at the very least, for the Dutch and, by the same token, a Spanish victory in the Netherlands would have made it significantly more difficult to prevent an Imperial and catholic victory in the Empire. The securing of Dutch independence and the survival of German protestantism required that the Dutch succeed and the Austrian Habsburgs fail in their respective ambitions.

The formal recognition of the independence of the Dutch Republic by the rest of Europe as part of the Peace of Westphalia possibly also marked the peak of its power. In the later years of the century, the wars first with England and then with France would make it evident that the Dutch position was weaker in some respects than it appeared to be at the mid-century. For the moment, it was clearly a major power in Europe, and was also well on the way to building up a formidable position in the East Indies, though the weakening of the Dutch hold on Brazil was perhaps an ominous sign for the future.

In part the strength of the Dutch position lay in the weaknesses of others. The Holy Roman Empire was exhausted after three decades of war, and the Austrian Habsburg attempts to resuscitate the power of the emperor had failed. The centre of Habsburg power shifted decisively to the Bohemian and Austrian lands and the build up of a new state in this region would take time, especially as it was hampered by the permanent threat of the Ottoman empire on its borders. French power was drained by the continuation of the war with Spain and further weakened internally by the *Frondes*; only when these domestic problems had been solved and the indecisive war with Spain brought to an end (1659) would Europe begin to realise the formidable potential of the French state. After Münster, Spain was able to hold its own against France but, far from constituting a continuing threat to the Dutch, it was rather inclined to seek some form of alliance with them to help safeguard its position in the southern Netherlands against the French. For the Dutch, for whom the slogan *amicus non vicinus* (friend not neighbour) began to make sense where France was concerned, preserving the region from French encroachment was already beginning to emerge as a major foreign policy objective (though not, apparently, to the young Willem II), and so the aims of at least a powerful group of regents ran parallel to those of the Spanish in this respect. England also was in the grip of civil war and its aftermath at this time though, while this gave the Republic the upper hand in the 1640s, the wild fluctuations in English foreign policy which followed were soon to create serious problems for the Dutch.

Many of these advantages could only be temporary, and so the position achieved by the Dutch in 1648 was bound to be challenged in due course. It would take the Holy Roman Empire some time to recover from the devastation of the war, and in any case it contained no power either able or willing to do the Dutch much harm. The Austrian Habsburgs, although remaining a decidedly catholic power, were likely to align themselves with the Dutch in the case of a threat from France, as were the Spanish. However, its military performance in the later part of the Thirty Years War suggested that, when France emerged from its civil disorders, it would constitute a significant threat to the Spanish Netherlands, and thus to what the Dutch regarded as their interests. England was the greatest enigma: it was neither clear how powerful it was or could be, nor whether it was a natural ally or enemy of the Dutch. In any case, it seemed likely in 1648 that internal problems would prevent it playing a major role in Europe for some time to come. The Dutch had finally attained peace and independence, but their geographical situation together with conditions in Europe made it unlikely that they would remain undisturbed for long, particularly as their economic success aroused not only admiration but also jealousy.

Notes

1   Geoffrey Parker, *The Army of Flanders and the Spanish Road 1567–1659* (Cambridge, 1972), 241–3.

2   Robert Fruin, *Tien jaren uit den Tachtigjarigen Oorlog, 1588–98* (Amsterdam, 1861).

3   See, in English: Jan den Tex, *Oldenbarnevelt*, 2 vols (Cambridge, 1973).

4   J.I. Israel, *Dutch Primacy in World Trade 1585–1740* (Oxford, 1989), chap. 3.

5   Barry H. Nickle, *The Military Reforms of Prince Maurice of Orange* (Delaware, 1975); G.E. Rothenburg, 'Maurice of Nassau, Gustavus Adolphus, Raimondo of Montecuccoli and the "Military Revolution" of the Seventeenth Century', *Makers of Modern Strategy from Machiavelli to the Nuclear Age*, ed. P. Paret (Oxford, 1986).

6   Geoffrey Parker, 'Mutiny and Discontent in the Spanish Army of Flanders, 1572–1607', in *Spain and the Netherlands, 1559–1659* (London, 1979), 106–21.

7   H.L. Zwitzer, '*De militie van den staat*'. *Het leger van de Republiek der Verenigde Nederlanden* (Amsterdam, 1991), bijlage 1.

8   See, especially, I.A.A. Thomson, *War and Government in Habsburg Spain, 1560–1620* (Cambridge, 1976).

9   Maurits's entourage certainly made use of such suspicions, but whether they believed them or not is an entirely different matter.

10 See the argument in A.C. Duke, *Reformation and Revolt in the Low Countries* (London, 1990), 292–3.

11 See, for example, B.J. Kaplan, *Calvinists and Libertines. Confession and Community in Utrecht 1578–1620* (Oxford, 1995).

12 Maurits inherited the title from his older half-brother, Filips Willem, in 1618.

13 See J.L. Price, 'A State Dedicated to War? The Dutch Republic in the Seventeenth Century', in *The Medieval Military Revolution*, ed. Andrew Ayton and J.L. Price (London, 1995), 189.

14 R.A. Stradling, *The Armada of Flanders: Spanish maritime policy and European War, 1568–1668* (Cambridge, 1992), Part 2.

15 See J.R. Bruijn, *The Dutch Navy in the 17th and 18th centuries* (Columbia, SC, 1993), 19–28.

16 J.V. Polisensky, *Tragic Triangle. The Netherlands, Spain and Bohemia 1617–1621* (Prague, 1991).

17 J.H. Elliott, *The Count-Duke of Olivares* (New Haven, 1986), 235–6, and R.A. Stradling, *Philip IV and the Government of Spain 1621–1665* (Cambridge, 1988), 66–8.

18 J.I. Israel, *The Dutch Republic and the Hispanic World 1606–1661* (Oxford, 1982), 162–5, 204–23.

19 Golo Mann, *Wallenstein* (Frankfurt am Main, 1971), 499–505; M.E.H.N. Mout, ' "Holendische Propositiones". Een Habsburg plan tot vernietiging van handel, visserij en scheepvaart der Republiek (ca. 1625)', *Tijdschrift voor Geschiedenis*, 95e jg., afl.3, (1982), 345–62.

20 The Generality lands were areas, primarily northern Brabant and a strip of Flanders, which were part of the Dutch state. They were administered directly by the central government of the Republic, but not represented in the States General.

21 M.P. Christ, *De Brabantsche Saecke. Het vergeefsche streven naar een gewestelijke status voor Staats-Brabant 1585–1675* (Tilburg, 1984).

22 It is, indeed, doubtful whether the Dutch would have attacked Brazil had it not been regarded as part of the Spanish empire – the East was quite a different matter..

2

The Economic Miracle

THE DUTCH economy grew with a rapidity that was astonishing
to contemporaries. In only a few decades before and after the turn
of the seventeenth century, the Dutch appeared to come from obscurity
to economic dominance in Europe and, even more spectacularly, made
their presence felt as a major colonial power. It is hardly surprising that
this remarkable development was viewed not only with admiration but
also with envy, and it was felt by some that such a success could only
have been achieved by unfair means. In consequence, alongside a literature of praise for Dutch commercial virtues came a stream of criticism
concerning their immorality, ruthlessness and exploitation of the
vulnerable. The single-minded pursuit of gain which was seen, at least
in part, as the secret of Dutch success was a fundamental challenge to
the value-system based on honour and christian charity which still
informed the culture of the rest of Europe. Viewed with the advantage
of hindsight, the economic rise of the Dutch Republic in the early
seventeenth century is less surprising. The foundations had been
soundly laid in the previous century as part of a process which had
roots in developments in the later Middle Ages; so, in a great measure,
the economic boom was a logical development of pre-existing trends.
The ethical challenge presented by the Dutch was real, and it was
particularly disturbing, not so much because it confronted contemporary Europe with a rival social ethic, as through exposing a profound
contradiction within conventional morality. Pursuit of profit was
nothing new in the seventeenth century and was far from being
confined to the Republic, but the Dutch were perhaps more single-
minded and certainly more honest in the priority they gave to economic
concerns and so invited moralistic criticism. How far the Dutch themselves were able to resolve the contradictions in contemporary culture
over the proper way of living on this earth is another matter.

Whether as a result or as a cause of economic growth, the rapid rise in the population of Holland started well before the Revolt, and may indeed have been faster over the province as a whole in the first half of the sixteenth century than even in the early seventeenth. In the earlier period both town and countryside shared more or less equally in this demographic growth, while later it became more concentrated in the towns. In the other provinces, too, the demographic pattern of the early seventeenth century was already well established before the Revolt. Perhaps the most remarkable aspect of this development was the high proportion of the population which was already living in towns on the eve of the Revolt. By this yardstick Holland especially was at this point already in a rather different socio-economic world than the greater part of contemporary Europe. Similarly, the foundations of Dutch trading prosperity in the boom years were clearly laid much earlier, and in particular, as we have seen,[1] Dutch predominance in the trade with the Baltic – the *moeder negocie* or mother trade – dates back to the early sixteenth century. Moreover, the maritime region of the northern Netherlands as a whole shared in this burgeoning trade. Another pillar of the Dutch economy, the herring fishery, was also well developed before the Revolt. It was largely located in the ports of Holland and Zeeland, and its sixteenth-century peak was at least comparable in size to anything that came later in the Golden Century. The technological innovations such as improved curing methods and specialised fishing boats which boosted its development also ante-dated the boom of the early seventeenth century.

Developments in the manufacturing sector before the Revolt might be seen as contradicting this trend, as textiles were in difficulties and brewing well into its long and irreversible decline. However, even here the infrastructure was present which facilitated later growth: without the existing industries in Haarlem and Leiden the later explosive grown of textile production could hardly have been possible, and the towns had a wide range of artisan production for at least local consumption. Rather more immediately impressive was the development of ship-building in many of the Holland ports, in response to the needs of the merchant and fishing fleets, and this in turn stimulated related activities such as rope- and sail-making and the processing of the necessary timber. What were largely lacking at this stage were significant export industries, with brewing being forced back onto largely local markets and woollen textiles suffering badly from competition, particularly from the new types of cloth being produced in Flanders and Brabant. Taken as a whole, the manufacturing sector before the last two decades of the sixteenth century gave relatively little hint of the successes to come.

Fundamental changes were also well under way before the Revolt in the countryside, though here again the most obvious changes seem to have been restricted to Holland and to a lesser extent the maritime region in general. The salient points are the increasing agricultural specialisation, concentration on activities most suitable to the nature of the soil and the terrain, and production for the market rather than home consumption. There was an intense and continuing inter-relationship between the rural sector and the trading economy: for example, the shift away from grain production stimulated but was also made possible by the import of bread grains from the Baltic region to supplement local production. The increasing importance of dairy-farming and beef production was encouraged by the demand for food from the growing towns, and also by the access to more remote markets provided by urban merchants. Similarly the towns could not have grown as fast as they did without immigration from the countryside, while the switch to less labour-intensive types of farming created a surplus of labour which had to be absorbed in non-agricultural employment or move to the towns.[2] Capitalism, at least in the form of the penetration of market forces, had moved decisively into the rural economy even before the take-off of the last decade of the sixteenth century.

It is evident that these developments, though unspectacular, provided a sound basis for the rapid growth of the later period; the healthy trends in trade and fishing, and the profound changes taking place in agriculture were pointers to the future. Above all, perhaps, the rapid population growth and the extent of urbanisation, especially in Holland, were signs that a new form of society was emerging in the northern Netherlands. Not in the whole of the northern Netherlands, however: most of the key developments took place in Holland alone or, at most, were restricted to the maritime region. The demographic, economic and social developments in the land provinces before the Revolt were very different – but in this respect, too, they foreshadowed what was to be the pattern in the Golden Century.

The effects of the Revolt and the Eighty Years War

One of the most remarkable aspects of the rise of the Dutch Republic to economic predominance in Europe was that it took place during a long war which might have been expected, at the very least, to put a severe strain on its economy. The Dutch economic boom largely coincided with the Eighty Years War, but whether it happened because of it or in spite of it is a much more complex issue.[3] Opinion among contemporaries was divided, with perhaps the majority of traders and manufacturers pointing to the economic damage arising directly from the war such as the embargoes on trade with Spain and the depredations of Dunkirk privateers – not to mention the heavy tax burden to pay for a large army and navy – while others placed more emphasis on the advantages provided by the blockade of the Flemish ports, the closure of the Schelde, and the enormous opportunities which an attack on the Spanish colonial empire seemed to offer. It is worth taking into consideration the circumstance that, by the time the war with Spain came to an end in 1648, the period of rapid and uninterrupted growth for the Republic had come – or was coming – to an end as well, but it can be legitimately doubted whether there is much of a causal connection here. The war undoubtedly offered the Dutch economic opportunities they possibly would not have had in other circumstances, but without the disruptions and heavy taxation that the war brought with it Dutch economic growth might well have been even more rapid.

The short-term effects of the Revolt itself were unambiguously damaging to the economy of the whole of the Northern Netherlands and, perhaps, particularly to Holland and Zeeland but the worst was over, for these two provinces at least, by the second half of the 1570s. The shipping of the maritime region had already undergone some disruption in the years immediately before 1572 because of the activities of the Sea Beggars, but this was trivial in comparison to the effects of the risings of the summer of that year and the subsequent Spanish campaign to suppress the rebellion. From the autumn of 1572 to the summer of 1576 the war was fought in the provinces of Holland and Zeeland. From the fall of Haarlem in early 1573, Holland was effectively cut in two, and the countryside of both provinces was devastated by the actions of Spanish troops and the inundations which were widely used by the rebels as defensive measures. The flooding of large parts of South Holland to enable the sorely tested city of Leiden to be relieved by boat was the most famous example of the use of this tactic but such actions, albeit on a smaller scale, were an integral part of warfare in this region. For similar reasons the countryside of Zeeland suffered comparable damage during these years.

The effects of these critical years on the towns of Holland and Zeeland are less clear. While it remained on the Spanish side, Amsterdam's trade suffered severely through emigration and blockade by the rebels, but this situation may have benefited the economies of the leading ports of North Holland. Enkhuizen and Hoorn suffered relatively little from the direct effects of war and were well placed to take over a good part of Amsterdam's Baltic trade. Between 1574 and 1577 only 12 Amsterdam ships are registered as passing through the Sound, while in the same period no less than 2,155 ships from Enkhuizen and Hoorn were recorded, with another 890 for Medemblik.[4] Leiden, Haarlem and Alkmaar underwent major sieges, but the weakness of the Spanish naval presence in the Netherlands meant that the ports in rebel hands could continue to trade with relative freedom despite the war. The rapid Spanish reconquest of the rest of the northern Netherlands, i.e. the parts outside Holland and Zeeland, in late 1572 had the advantage that after the immediate impact of the passage of the victorious army these areas were largely exempt from the direct effects of warfare.

After the Pacification of Ghent and the effective withdrawal of Spanish troops from Holland and Zeeland in 1576, these provinces no longer had to see the war fought on their territory. Indeed, apart from minor incursions, they remained free from enemy troops for the rest of the war. The devastated countryside could start to make good the damage of the previous years, and this recovery seems to have been remarkably rapid.[5] The removal of actual warfare to the south and east also gave the trade of the maritime region more opportunity to flourish. The central problem in the period up to 1578 was that Amsterdam remained a Spanish stronghold in rebel territory, but in that year first the Satisfaction brought peace between the States and Amsterdam, and then the Alteration (effectively a coup) brought it fully over to the rebel side. From this point on Holland was united politically and able to develop economically as freely as conditions in the rest of the Netherlands and more broadly in Europe as a whole would allow.

From about 1579 to the end of the Eighty Years War in 1648 the question of the relation between war and the progress of the Dutch economy is more problematical. One of the great pillars of the Dutch trading system, the Baltic trade, was unaffected by the war until the 1620s, though the ability of the Dutch to sell the grain they bought in the markets of southern Europe was hindered by Spanish hostility, particularly in the case of Mediterranean countries. The Thirty Years

War brought a more direct threat and at times Dutch trade to the Baltic was seriously affected. From about 1624 the number of Dutch ships recorded as passing through the Sound fell dramatically. There was some recovery in the 1630s but the numbers remained well below those prevailing in the earlier decades of the century. An almost complete halt to Dutch trade to the Baltic in 1645 because of hostilities between Sweden and Denmark was a further reminder of its vulnerability. However, whereas short-term disruptions as a result of war are undeniable, they have to be placed in the context of much longer-term changes in the nature of the Baltic trade and decline of the Dutch share in it. Thus changes which would probably have taken place in any case muddy the waters and make it difficult to estimate the precise effects of the war. However, the immediate consequences in the middle years of the 1620s were clear and serious.

Persistent Spanish attempts to keep the Dutch out of the markets in Spain and its colonies hindered the overall development of their trading economy, though it remains unclear how effective these policies were. The embargo imposed in 1598 seems to have been distinctly leaky and, although Israel in particular has argued that Spanish economic measures against the Dutch from the middle 1620s onwards were more effective,[6] it can can be doubted whether these later measures were enforced with much greater efficiency. However, it does seem clear that Dutch trade with Spain and her colonies was made more difficult by the war than it otherwise would have been, and its rapid resurgence after peace was made in 1648 – practically forcing the English out of the Spanish market in only a couple of years – is an indication of the extent of the problems the war had caused.[7] On the other hand, it can be argued that it was precisely these Spanish efforts at embargo which gave the decisive stimulus to the start of Dutch overseas expansion. Antwerp had acted as the distributor for Portuguese spices and other colonial products in the years before the Revolt but, as Portugal had been brought into the Spanish *monarchía* in 1580, the conditions prevailing during the war made it difficult for Amsterdam, particularly after 1598, to take over the role Antwerp had been forced to relinquish. Attempts to establish direct Dutch trading links with the Asian sources of these colonial products and the founding of the VOC in 1602 were obvious responses to such problems. While it is probable that the Dutch would have attempted to gain direct access to Asian goods in any case, the difficulties that war put in the way of trading with the Lisbon spice market undoubtedly affected both the timing of these efforts and encouraged the flow of capital to back them. Later the setting up of the WIC was even more clearly a consequence of the war, though one that in the end met with considerably less success.

Another issue to be considered in assessing the effects of the war on the Dutch economy is the vulnerability of the Dutch merchant and fishing fleets to attack by warships and privateers. Throughout the war the privateers of Dunkirk and other southern ports were a major concern, but the Dutch navy's attempts to protect Dutch shipping by convoy and by blockade of the Flemish ports were never entirely successful.[8] Dutch merchant ships, especially those operating in northern waters, were highly specialised cargo carriers with small crews and limited armament, and thus presented a relatively easy prey. Even more vulnerable was the herring fleet, especially once it had its nets out to fish; convoying could hope to protect merchant ships, but when at work the herring fleet was too large and covered too great an area for warships to be able to protect it very effectively. The cost of sunk or captured ships was considerable and insurance rates rose in response. Also mutual aid societies were founded by sailors and fishermen throughout the maritime region to meet the costs of ransoming sailors imprisoned at Dunkirk and elsewhere. On the other hand merchant ships and fishing boats provided the privateers with so many victims because there were so many of them. Paradoxically, these losses to privateers were an indication of prosperity rather than a cause of decline, however much economic loss and personal suffering some people may have had to endure.

The Dutch economy continued to grow despite the war, but it cannot be said that it grew in the way or at the rate that it might have done if there had been peace with Spain, or even if the truce of 1609 had led to a lasting settlement. On the other hand, war of one sort or another was a normal part of European life in the early modern period – for the Dutch in the period covered by this study perhaps even more normal than peace – and so it should be treated as a part of the normal environment which shaped both the economic opportunities and difficulties for the Dutch Republic. Whether its influence was as decisive as some historians have argued is, however, a different matter.

The rise of the Dutch trading system

Trade, organised by Dutch merchants, financed by Dutch capital and with the commodities transported on Dutch ships, was at the heart of the economic success of the Republic: this was a commercial economy, and the other economic sectors were to a greater or lesser extent shaped by this fact. It was this aspect of the Dutch boom which most impressed contemporaries because it was the most visible: Dutch ships were to be found in all the ports of Europe, and Dutch traders and agents seemed equally ubiquitous – 'I think the Devil shits Dutchmen' a contemporary Englishman complained in a rather different context.[9] It was also the area where Dutch supremacy was most long-lasting – while the agricultural and manufacturing sectors were in trouble well before the end of the seventeenth century, trade maintained something near its peak levels well into the eighteenth century and even then the decline was neither great nor definitive.[10] It was indeed in trade that the basis of Dutch 'primacy' lay.[11]

The bed-rock of Dutch trading success was the trade with the Baltic region, particularly in rye and other bread grains. This is the conventional interpretation given by economic historians, and was also the view of contemporaries for whom it was the 'mother-trade' (*moeder negocie*). Recently, Israel has challenged this view of the importance of the Baltic trade to the overall success of the Dutch trading system, suggesting that on the contrary the move by Dutch merchants into the 'rich trades' was decisive in establishing Dutch trading supremacy.[12] There is an element of tautology in this argument as he defines trading primacy as taking a major part in these 'rich trades'. By this sleight of hand he underplays the importance of the so-called 'bulk trades', the most important of which was that in grain, for the Dutch trading system as a whole. Would the successful entry into the 'rich trades' have been possible without the experience and profits of the Baltic grain trade?

From the late 1570s until the middle 1620s more than 2,000 Dutch ships per year were registered for the Sound Toll; most of them medium sized – between 30 and 100 tons, though the proportion of ships larger than 100 tons grew considerably in the later years of the period.[13] The chief return cargo was grain, principally rye, partly for home consumption, but a significant proportion was either shipped directly to other destinations, or stored in Amsterdam until a favourable market

presented itself elsewhere in Europe. In many ways this was the archetypal Dutch trade: it involved large numbers of seamen and specialised
merchant ships; the Dutch market operated as a redistributive system,
buying in one part of Europe and selling in another; and it generated
considerable secondary employment, as a large work-force of lightermen, dockers and warehouse-workers was needed to unload, store and
reload the grain. The trading profits may not have been spectacular,
but the trade's contribution to general prosperity needs to take into
account the employment opportunities it created. A secondary but still
important element of the Baltic trade was hemp, tar and other naval
stores, and if the import of timber – though this was chiefly from
Norway rather than the Baltic – is also taken into account this branch
of the trade becomes even more significant. Supplies from Scandinavia
as a whole were essential for the development of the shipbuilding
industry as the Republic was almost wholly lacking in suitable timber.
The most important centre of the timber trade was Hoorn, and from
here wood could be easily shipped to the villages along the Zaan where
shipbuilding was beginning to flourish from the beginning of the seventeenth century. Both grain and timber were bulky commodities and this
circumstance encouraged the development of new types of ship which
were specially designed to be able to carry such loads efficiently. The
most famous Dutch cargo ship of the seventeenth century, the *fluit*
(flute), was first built in Hoorn in the last years of the sixteenth
century, and a version of this ship modified to carry timber efficiently –
including very long pieces for masts – was also produced.

Trade with the Baltic region, together with the Norwegian timber
trade, was the bread and butter of the Dutch trading economy, unglamorous but vital to its overall health. Without the profits, expertise and
experience gained through buying grain in the Baltic ports, ware-
housing it in the Republic and then selling it to areas of Europe with a
temporary or permanent shortage of food, it is at least doubtful whether
the more spectacular achievements of the Dutch trading system could
have taken place. The grain trade did not bring about Dutch trading
supremacy, but it made it possible.

The hallmark of the Dutch trading system as it grew and expanded
was its flexibility; Dutch shippers and merchants proved able to adapt to
the varying demands of dealing in most branches of trade and with most
regions of Europe. The salient features of the economy of the Republic
imposed their own logic on the shape of the developing trade. If the

radical transformation of agriculture in the maritime region caused a need for bread grains and this drew Dutch merchants to the Baltic, so herring from the expanding fisheries supplied an export article which was in considerable demand in that region. In turn the curing of this increasing catch of herring required large quantities of good quality salt, and Dutch traders were forced further and further afield to satisfy this demand. The success of the herring fishery thus stimulated a considerable geographical expansion of Dutch trade, eventually luring it to the New World in search of supplies of salt: first the Zeeland supplies were superseded by those from Brouage and the Vendée in France, then Portugal became a prime source and, as the conflict with Spain made trade with Iberia more difficult and unreliable, Dutch traders were forced to go as far as Punta de Araya (in modern Venezuela) for their salt.

The closure of the Schelde and the emigration of merchants and capital to the North in the aftermath of the Spanish conquest of Antwerp gave merchants based in the Republic the opportunity to take over the economic role which this city had played through most of the sixteenth century. In particular, Amsterdam was able to displace Antwerp as the distribution centre for colonial goods in northern Europe, especially spices from the Portuguese Indies. The immigrants from the South brought expertise, capital and contacts but the chief source of spices, Lisbon, and the Spanish supplies of colonial goods became less easy of access from the mid-1580s onwards. The various Spanish embargoes and limitations on Dutch trade may not always have been very efficient, but at best they made trade with Iberia considerably more difficult and less reliable than it might otherwise have been. This situation, as in the case of salt, lured the Dutch into colonial encounters, in this case to the East Indies for spices and the Americas for sugar – and silver. The distribution of Portuguese and Spanish colonial goods required, on the one hand, the building-up of a wide-ranging trade network in Europe north of the Alps, and the continuation of this branch of trade despite Spanish embargoes then pushed the Dutch into large-scale colonial adventures.

The grain trade similarly stimulated the development of Dutch trade to the Mediterranean and the Levant. Food shortages in Spain and Italy gave the Dutch, as the major suppliers of surplus grain, a foothold in the region – though Spanish enmity, together with the depredations of North African corsairs, meant that the trade had its own peculiar difficulties. The Republic was, however, able to establish diplomatic relations with the Ottoman empire at a comparatively early date, which helped to facilitate commerce with Levantine ports offering a wide variety of oriental goods, including silk. The development of Dutch manufactures both encouraged the expansion of trade and was made possible by it. Woollen textiles, for example, required the import of raw wool from Spain, England and elsewhere, and of semi-finished cloths as well. The latter trade threatened to cause a serious breach of relations with England when, in pursuance of a project of the London alderman, Cockayne, the English banned the export of unfinished cloths in 1614. The Dutch in turn banned the import of finished cloths from England and, as the English relied on the Dutch trading network for the distribution and sale of their cloths in continental Europe, this was a decisive move. (In any case, the English were unable, predictably, to build up a finishing industry of a sufficient size in the time required.) The linen industry of Haarlem was similarly dependent on imports for its raw materials, and both wool and linen textiles needed large markets for their products outside the borders of the Republic to sustain them which only the trading network could supply.

It can be argued that one of the chief reasons for the economic success of the Dutch was that they were parasitic on the weaknesses of other countries. As the general expansion of the sixteenth century slowed down and then reversed into a Europe-wide depression in the following century, the Dutch were able to turn the situation to their benefit and continue to expand, indeed achieve something like economic dominance.[14] Contemporaries, with their view of the international economy as a zero-sum game, certainly were inclined to see Dutch success as only being achieved at the expense of others, and both the English and the French tended to believe that their countries would only be able to make economic progress if the Dutch were humbled. However, it would be more realistic to suggest that the Dutch provided a service that the European economy needed at this stage of its development. It is some-what unfashionable to talk of the staple-market[15] but to a large extent the function of the Dutch trading system was indeed to act as a clearing-house for a wide range of commodities, buying in one place and selling in another. Evidently, European commerce still needed this sort of facility and the Dutch supplied it; the Baltic grain trade is a pre-eminent exam-ple of this service. Yet they had few natural advantages: they possessed practically no useful raw materials – unless North Sea herring can be seen as such – and only their geographical position can be regarded as a significant asset. They were well placed to take part in the north–south sea-borne trade route, possessed at least adequate harbours, and the Zuyder Zee and navigable rivers gave them access to a considerable hinterland in western and central Europe. Other qualities than mere position, however, are needed to explain the extent of their success.

In sharp contrast to the commercial system of Antwerp in the late fifteenth and early sixteenth century, the trade of the Republic was carried in its own ships, and the sheer size of this merchant fleet was impressive. Indeed, the number and ubiquity of Dutch ships was one of the more visible signs of the extent of Dutch economic pre-eminence; they seemed to be everywhere and in such large numbers that contemporaries were misled into wildly exaggerated estimates of how many there were. In fact, it seems that the Dutch merchant fleet probably contained around 2,000 sea-going ships by the middle of the seventeenth century,[16] though much depends on where the line is drawn on size – if smaller coasters were included then the total would be considerably higher. There were so many Dutch merchant ships because they did the job well: they were designed to carry cargoes – especially bulky ones like grain and wood – efficiently, and could be handled by relatively small crews, which enabled them to charge lower freight rates than their rivals. The *fluit* was the most successful merchant ship of the period; but its very suitability as a cargo carrier made it vulnerable, and Dutch merchant shipping made a rather easy target for privateers and warships. The number of Dutch ships and the great variety of routes they operated on also made it very difficult for the navy to protect them by convoy or other means. A less successful merchant marine would have been less vulnerable.

As Dutch economic growth gained momentum in the last years of the sixteenth and the early decades of the seventeenth century, the supply of cheap capital became an important element in Dutch trading success. Grain merchants could afford to store their rye in warehouses in Amsterdam until prices peaked just before a new harvest; wine traders could buy the grapes on the vine, taking the risk of a poor harvest but gaining favourable rates. The readiness with which investors provided capital for the VOC and, to a lesser extent, the WIC is one indication of the large amount of capital looking for good investments at this time, in the case of the former much of it from southern immigrants. Of more general importance, perhaps, was the way the system of *partenrederij* mobilised the resources of investors with only a limited amount of capital. Such people could take a small share in a trading venture and, indeed, could spread their investments in small amounts over a number of projects to minimise their risks. The founding of the Amsterdam Exchange Bank along with the adoption of technical innovations helped to regularise the financial side of international trade, and the Republic began to emerge as a major financial as well as commodity market in this period.

The importance of the expertise and experience of Dutch traders is hard to estimate, but it must have been considerable. Traders from the northern Netherlands had already built up a solid network of factors and other contacts in the Baltic and Scandinavian ports in the course of the sixteenth century, and the same is probably true of the east coast ports of Britain and the Atlantic ports of France. The fall of Antwerp brought to the North merchants who had knowledge of and contacts in more exotic branches of trade, such as spices, silks, and colonial goods in general. By the middle of the seventeenth century, Dutch factors could be found in practically every port in Europe and seem to have been almost as omnipresent as Dutch ships. The Dutch staple-market was built on information as well as contacts, and the prices of goods traded on the Amsterdam *Beurs* reflected knowledge of trading conditions throughout Europe – and as time went on the prices in Amsterdam came to determine the shape of trade to a considerable extent.

The more spectacular activities of the Amsterdam merchants make it easy to lose sight of the contribution of the other trading towns, but the role of Enkhuizen, Hoorn and even Medemblik in the development of the trade to the Baltic and Scandinavia should not be overlooked, and Rotterdam had a special position in trade with France (especially in wine). In fact, the towns of the maritime region acted to an extent as a single integrated system, almost like one very large urban agglomeration, though this has been relatively little investigated as yet.[17] From the perspective of the Republic as a whole, however, the expansion of trade was very largely limited to the maritime region, and some of the trading towns in the land provinces, such as the IJssel towns (Deventer, Kampen, Zutphen) lost their international roles to rivals in Holland. Even within the maritime region Zeeland proved unable to compete effectively with Holland in the first half of the century, and in Holland itself there were signs by mid-century at least that the smaller trading towns were beginning to lose out to Amsterdam. The imbalances of the trading economy which were to become so glaring during the Dutch decline were already apparent to some extent at the peak of its success.

The transformation of the rural sector

The evolution which took place in the economy of the Dutch country-side was as far-reaching as the dynamic expansion of trade, and closely integrated with it. As with other economic changes, it was the maritime region which saw the most fundamental changes in the rural economy, but the agriculture of the land provinces also was necessarily affected by the rapid advance of the market economy in the west. In particular, the powerful Holland market, linked to the international grain trade, formed the context in which farmers throughout the Republic had to work.

The transformation of agriculture in the maritime region was already well under way before the Revolt and, although the countryside of Holland and Zeeland had to deal with the depredations of troops and defensive inundations in the first years after 1572, the pace picked up again before the end of the century. The chief characteristics of this development were specialisation and market orientation. Farmers in this region (with the notable exception of Zeeland) increasingly moved away from arable, for which much of the available land was not par-ticularly suited, towards dairying and the fattening of beef calves – first for the growing urban market and then for export. Prices for butter, cheese, meat and other agricultural products had risen during the Europe-wide demographic growth of the sixteenth century, and re-mained healthy amid the continued population rise in the Republic until well into the second half of the seventeenth. This specialisation meant that the farmers had to rely on the market to supply them with the bread and other goods they were no longer producing for them-selves, and for services they no longer had time for.

Arable continued to be important in Zeeland, notable for an agri-culture centring on wheat, and the islands of South Holland but with a notably flexible response to market conditions.[18] Increasingly, farms in the maritime region were purely commercial operations, concentrating on a limited number of products which could be brought onto the market efficiently and aiming at maximising profits from their oper-ations. In the long term one effect of this process was to favour a growth in the average size of farms and the squeezing out of the small holder in the maritime region.[19] The power of the market also en-couraged greater concentration on non-food products such as madder and flax, and the rise of a market-gardening sector to serve the particular needs of the growing towns of Holland. The specialised production of tulips in Holland also dates from the early seventeenth century, and the notorious speculative bubble of the 1630s which saw the price of sought-after bulbs rising to crazy heights before the inevitable crash can be seen as emblematic of the power and ubiquity of the market in Dutch society in these boom years – as well as being a reminder of the endemic instability of early modern capitalism.

These changes in the rural sector were necessarily linked to the developments which were taking place elsewhere in the economy. The trade in Baltic rye, for example, supplied a substantial part of the demand for bread grains in the northern Netherlands and encouraged Dutch farmers to look elsewhere for their profits. The growth of the towns provided a ready market for a wide variety of rural produce, and at prices which began to bring noticeable prosperity to at least the larger farmers. Further, the developing trade network opened up substantial foreign markets, especially for high-quality butter, cheese and meat. Such influences were reciprocal, of course: the shift away from grain production increased the demand for Baltic rye, in the countryside as well as the towns, and agricultural products could supply at least some of the exports needed to help balance Dutch trade.

With these changes in agriculture came a marked diversification of employment in the countryside of the maritime region with a growing proportion of the rural population involved in non-agrarian activities. The increased penetration of the market into rural areas brought with it a growing need for transport services of various kinds; water was by far the cheapest and most convenient way of moving goods and people in this region, so the number of those involved in providing boat and barge services grew with the intensification of trade between town and countryside. Fishing was another important source of employment in the countryside of this region. River and lake fishing declined considerably during this period as a result of the large-scale drainages which were carried out, but fishing in the Zuyder Zee and North Sea remained a significant sector of the rural economy. At the beginning of the century some villages in North Holland were still significant centres of the herring fishery, but they steadily lost out to Enkhuizen and the Maas ports of south Holland in the course of the following decades. Nevertheless, service in the fishing fleet remained an important part of the employment cycle in rural areas. Artisan production to supply local needs also grew as farming became more intensive and specialised, while the prosperity of the rural sector encouraged the rise of a varied service sector in the villages as well.

The most visible rural transformation in the maritime provinces was physical: the large-scale draining of lakes and the reclamation of land from the sea. The late medieval period and the early sixteenth century had brought increasing problems in the control of sea- and river-water together with a series of damaging inundations leading to large-scale losses of land to the sea. In response, the local *waterschappen* (drainage boards) worked to improve the systems of dike maintenance, and the rising prices of agricultural products provided an incentive for investment in drainage schemes. Technical improvements in windmill design increased the available pumping power, and made the draining of large areas of water feasible. The result was that the Republic was able to increase its cultivable land by around a third during the early modern period, by far the greater part of this being drained before the middle of the seventeenth century, and possibly half of the total in the years between 1590 and 1650.[20] North Holland, formerly almost more water than land, was changed most radically; after the reclamations all the great lakes had gone, and communications by water became much more restricted and a cause of dispute both between towns and between towns and countryside.[21] Though leading to less spectacular physical changes, the drainage schemes were important in South Holland and Zeeland as well, and indeed the whole of the maritime region was affected to some extent. Besides the increase in available land, the re-clamation schemes made low-lying areas much more secure against the sea and considerably improved their drainage. In the process, however, the face of the Dutch countryside had been irretrievably altered.

Rural life in the land provinces presents a very different picture, but it also underwent considerable changes in this period, not least under the influence of the expanding economy of Holland. The power of the Holland market turned the eastern regions into something like its colonies, certainly affecting profoundly the circumstances in which the country people in this region had to live and work. Although it did not stagnate, the rural economy here developed in a rather different way from that of the dynamic maritime region. To an extent the response of the farmers – or perhaps peasants might still be a more appropriate description here – in Drenthe can be taken as typical: they diversified their activities rather than specialising, and their aim has been characterised as avoiding disaster rather than maximising profit.[22]

While powerfully affected by the opportunities and demands of the Holland market, and by competition from the efficient farming of the maritime region, the small free-holding farmer survived in this region, as did large numbers of smallholders. The influence of the market economy was felt in these provinces, but it failed to penetrate as deeply or to transform the economic structure as radically as it did in Holland.

The growth of manufactures and the importance of herring

A relatively high proportion of the Dutch population lived in towns and, even in the countryside a significant number of people were wholly or in part dependent on non-agricultural employment. The expansion of trade itself directly and indirectly brought increased employment opportunities: towards the middle of the century the trading fleet, together with the VOC, employed almost 30,000 men,[23] and the handling of cargoes in the ports provided work for large numbers of lightermen, dockers and porters. In addition, there were those involved in the internal transport system, moving goods and people along the rivers and canals. Another important source of employment was provided by artisan production of various kinds; manufacture was still labour intensive – literally handwork – with very limited inputs of non-animal energy, with the exception of the large-scale use of wind-power for sawmills. Also the fisheries and ancillary industries were important sources of employment. Although the import and re-export of goods through the staple-market was central to the success of the trading economy, manufactures and fisheries could also supply valuable export products which helped to oil the machinery of foreign trade.

The herring fishery was thus important as a source of employment and because it provided a crucial export item, as well as helping to feed the Dutch population. In terms of numbers of boats and men employed, most if not all of the growth of the fishery seems to have already taken place before the Revolt, with subsequent developments consisting chiefly of improvements in organisation and co-ordination between the various branches of the industry. Dutch success in the fisheries was by no means pre-ordained; the movement of the best herring shoals to the North Sea gave them the opportunity, but they were geographically no better placed to exploit this than many potential rivals, indeed less so than the Scots and the English. In the course of the fifteenth and sixteenth centuries, north Netherlands' fishermen had introduced a number of key innovations which gave them a decisive edge. A specialised fishing-boat (*buis*) came into use, and mother-ships began to sail with the fleet to enable the *buizen* to stay on the fishing-grounds longer. Also a new method of preserving herring was found in the fifteenth century, and curing began to take place at sea to improve the quality of the product. High quality was indeed the key to the export success of the Dutch herring business, and concern to maintain this edge over their competitors led to the use of the finest salt that could be found and to careful monitoring of the barreling process. It seems to have been agreed by contemporaries that Dutch herring were the best – which provided them with a market even in Scandinavia with its own sources of the fish. In fact, herring made a significant contribution to the development of the Baltic trade, providing an export item with a ready market there. Similarly, Dutch herring sold well in the Rhineland and northern France, where perhaps catholic religious practices increased the demand for fish.

There may have been as many as 500 herring *buizen*, almost entirely based in Holland, employed at the peak of the fishery in the early seventeenth century. This in itself must have provided employment for 6–7,000 men, though only for part of the year as the herring fishing was seasonal starting in late June and ending in December or early January.[24] However, if herring-packers and the coopers making the barrels in which the fish were packed are included then the work provided directly by the fishery rises considerably. Moreover, the indirect boost to shipbuilding and sail- and rope-making is impossible to calculate but must have been significant and, if the transport to various markets by barge and coaster is taking into consideration, then the overall impact of the fishery on employment opportunities rises again. There were other sea fisheries, especially cod, but the biggest growth in the early seventeenth century came in Arctic whaling, which rose from practically nothing to an important, if not always thriving, business. Initially this was open sea whaling but from about the 1640s onwards the right whale became increasingly difficult to find in open waters, which meant that whaling had to turn to the construction of specially strengthened ships which could follow the whales into the pack ice. The real expansion of whaling, however, belongs to the second half of the century. The importance of fresh water fishing as ancillary employment and as a source of food was considerable in the maritime region at the beginning of this period, but declined in the course of the century as a result of the drainage projects – there were losers as well as winners in the transformation of the Dutch landscape.

Artisan production was an important part of the economy of every town in the Republic, either for the satisfaction of local needs or to serve a broader market. Large-scale specialised production was rarer and only a few towns became major manufacturing centres. Within the general expansion of the Dutch economy, it can be said that certain older industries, such as brewing, which had been able to command a significant export market in the past, continued the decline which had already become evident in the early sixteenth century, while textiles recovered from their earlier slump to reach new heights in this period.

It seems to have been immigration from the southern Netherlands after Parma's reconquest of most of Flanders and Brabant in the 1580s, and especially after the fall of Antwerp in 1585, which gave the necessary stimulus to the troubled textile industry of the North. The newcomers were driven by religious motives or drawn by economic opportunities; they brought capital and expertise, and included entrepreneurs as well as skilled workers. Two main innovations seem to have been crucial: the introduction of new, lighter cloths made from mixed fibres (bays, serges, worsteds etc.) and a new organisation which brought the industry increasingly under the control of merchant–entrepreneurs rather than the skilled craftsmen themselves. The 'new draperies' had been the mainstay of the successful textile industry of the southern Netherlands in the previous century, where it had flourished outside the established urban centres at Hondeschoote and elsewhere. In the North, these developments were concentrated, as far as a significant export industry was concerned, at Leiden for wool textiles and at Haarlem for linen, helping here to compensate for the decline of the formerly powerful brewing industry. Textile production continued in other towns, but not on a scale to compare with these two specialised textile centres. Wool and linen textile manufactures were typical of the Dutch trading economy as they relied on imports for the raw materials and semi-finished cloths they needed, and the extent of their production could only be sustained by large-scale exports, as the home market alone could not have supported an industry of this size. A particularly good example of this was the branch of wool textiles that finished white cloths imported from England; this was a lucrative business and provided a service which, however, was not always appreciated by the English who came to regard it as a form of exploitation.

The processing of materials brought into the Republic by trade became important enough to require a term to describe it: *trafieken* referred particularly to the trades dealing with colonial imports such as raw cane-sugar and tobacco, and by the middle of the century sugar-refining had achieved some importance in a number of towns in Holland. In a way shipbuilding can be considered as a manufacture of this sort as, of course, it relied entirely on imported timber, and developed an important export market in the course of the seventeenth century. Fundamentally, however, the industry grew up to satisfy the needs of the Dutch merchant and fishing fleets, and its strengths were the advanced design of the ships it produced and the innovatory techniques involved in processing timber and in ship construction. Most of the port towns of Holland had some sort of a shipbuilding industry, and the VOC's shipyard in Amsterdam became the single biggest in the country, but the production of ships increasingly came to centre on the villages along the north bank of the Zaan to the west of Amsterdam. The *Zaanstreek* had quite good access to the sea and was particularly well placed to make the maximum use of windmills, particularly to power the local sawmills. Indeed, the lines of windmills were as characteristic of the developed industry of this area as the factory chimneys of a later time and place. Other manufactures that flourished in this period despite the Republic having no particular natural advantages in their respect were the clay-pipe making of Gouda and the potteries of Delft.

Although its economic importance is difficult to estimate, it would be wrong to exclude printing and publishing from a survey of significant manufacturing developments, as the industry not only satisfied the domestic demand for printed material of various kinds but also created a considerable export market. Indeed, the Republic can be seen as operating a sort of staple-market in ideas as well as in commodities, though the peak for this possibly came in the later seventeenth century rather than in this earlier period.[25] The reasons for the singular success of Dutch publishing are less than self-evident, though the high levels of literacy in the Republic, the sound basis provided by the early development of printing in the Netherlands – the northerners were even able to claim with a certain plausibility that printing was invented in Haarlem rather than by Gutenberg – and the need of a commercial society for information all must have played a part. Immigration from the South also made a significant contribution, personified by the move of the famous Elsevier firm from Antwerp to the university town of Leiden in the North. Although the tolerance of the Dutch civil authorities has been rather exaggerated in the past,[26] nevertheless the press enjoyed more freedom here than anywhere else in Europe. Books could be, and were, published in the Republic – or at least in Holland – which would have caused serious problems for authors, publishers and printers in other countries.

The ease with which money could be found to invest in the great reclamation projects of the period, together with the readiness with which a wide range of people subscribed to the VOC, not to mention the enormous sums the States of Holland were able to borrow to finance the war against Spain, are reminders that the availability of capital was one of the driving forces behind Dutch economic growth as well as one of its consequences. Helped by the foundation of the municipal Exchange Bank (1609) Amsterdam quickly became the chief financial market not just of the Republic but of northern Europe as a whole.[27] Capital was not only plentiful, it was also relatively cheap, and institutions existed which were able to mobilise it with some efficiency. The VOC itself was innovatory in its financial structure which helped to make it possible for quite small holders of capital to participate and, more generally, the *rederij* system mobilised savings by encouraging widespread investment in trade, fishing and whaling. The rudimentary Amsterdam stock-exchange facilitated financial ventures of a rather more elevated sort. Dutch capital drained marshes in France, exploited the iron deposits in Sweden and ran the monopoly of Austrian mercury. At home the money market displayed not a little of the volatility peculiar to capitalism, with the seventeenth-century equivalent of speculative futures-trading sometimes reaching heights which contemporaries found alarming if not immoral.

The foundation of a trading empire

Until the last years of the sixteenth century only Spain and Portugal had made much of an impact outside Europe. From this point on, however, the Dutch changed this pattern decisively, becoming not only the first non-Iberian country to found a substantial colonial empire, but doing so in a manner which pointed towards an essentially new form of exploitation by Europeans of the extra-European world. Neither Spain nor Portugal had been particularly strong economically at the time they established their colonial empires; whatever the reasons for their successes, they cannot be seen as expressions of economic power. In contrast, although the Dutch used military force and a variety of coercive techniques in the build-up of their colonial system, it remained essentially an extension of, and was made possible by, their trading strength in Europe. Unlike both their Iberian rivals, the Dutch became a great colonial power because of their economic success, not vice versa.[28]

It was in the East that the Dutch had their greatest, and most enduring, success as a colonial power. In the last decade of the sixteenth century a number of expeditions were launched by Dutch merchants to try to evade the Portuguese domination of the direct trade by sea in Asian products, in the first instance spices. Merchants in the Netherlands had long been accustomed to buying Portuguese colonial goods on the Lisbon market and acting as their main distributors to the rest of northern Europe. After Portugal had been brought into the Spanish system by Philip II in 1580, the uncertain Spanish policy regarding trade with the Republic with its unpredictably recurring embargoes made Dutch access to this market difficult and unreliable. One answer to this problem was to go to the source, which also promised much greater profits by cutting out the Portuguese middleman. It quickly became apparent that, besides the general difficulty of gaining a foothold in the East against Portuguese opposition, the various Dutch ventures were getting in each others' way as their competition in buying spices in the East tended to push prices up while similar competition when selling in Europe forced them down. The answer was a single company, given a monopoly by the States General to trade with the East.

The *Vereenigde Oost-Indische Compagnie* (United East India Company) received its charter in 1602, covering the area from the Cape of Good Hope eastwards. It consisted of a number of local chambers, based on the pre-existing companies, and directed by a central board, the *Heeren XVII*. Its initial finance was raised by selling shares, but the original intention had been to repay the capital invested along with any profits at the end of a given period. However, as the costs of building up the necessary military and organisational infrastructure in the East became apparent, the States General allowed the VOC to turn the money invested into fixed capital – in future the only way investors could get their money back was by selling their shares on the open market. Similarly, the monopoly – originally set at only twenty-one years – was successively renewed and became, in effect, permanent. The central aim of the company was to attack the Portuguese position in Asia and establish itself as the chief supplier of spices and other Asian goods to the European market. A particular target was the Spice Islands (the Moluccas and the Banda Islands) which were the sole source of cloves and mace. The most important spice, pepper, was grown much more widely throughout the region and its production and sale proved much more difficult to control.

Within a remarkably short period of time, the VOC had established a network of forts and factories (trading posts) from the Cape of Good Hope to Japan, with a headquarters and governor-general established at Batavia (modern Djakarta) in Java. The resources of the company meant that they could mobilise greater military and naval forces in the East than the Portuguese, and this was an important reason for their ability to oust the latter from their dominant position. However, the economic approach of the Dutch also gave them an edge. The Portuguese were as concerned with levying tolls on Asian trade from their strongpoints as with making profits from trade; in contrast the Dutch not only tried to control the flow of goods to Europe but also tried to defray their costs in the East by the profits from large-scale involvement in inter-Asian trade. A major problem for the Dutch as for other European traders in Asia was that there was no great demand for European goods, certainly nothing like enough to balance the cost to the company of the spices and other Asian products they were shipping to Europe. This trade imbalance had to be made good by bullion transfers, largely of silver; this was felt to be a bad thing theoretically and was expensive for the VOC in practice. The company's involvement in trade within Asia was intended to minimise the export of bullion, the policy achieved some success but was never able to bypass the demand for silver entirely. However, Japanese silver, acquired in return for Asian goods, did come to play a key role in the VOC's strategy, supplying nearly half its bullion needs in the decades after about 1630.

After some difficult decades due to the cost of establishing its position in the East, the VOC became the great success of the early seventeenth century, fatally undermining the Portuguese trading position and far outstripping the efforts of the rival English East India Company – not without the use of unfair methods in the eyes of the English. By the middle of the century the VOC had established a staging post at the Cape of Good Hope, had a strong position on both coasts of India, was near to controlling the trade of Sri Lanka, had taken Malacca in Malaysia from the Portuguese, and from 1639 was the only European power allowed to trade with Japan. Above all from their headquarters in Batavia they had effectively taken over the Moluccas and had gone a considerable way towards controlling the flow of spices onto the European market and thus the prices they would fetch there. This success was reflected in the share prices of the company and the dividends it was able to disburse. However, it was also becoming a major territorial power in Java, Sri Lanka, the Moluccas and elsewhere in Indonesia and, while this suited the dreams and ambitions of some among the company's leadership, others feared that the costs of maintaining this territorial position would ultimately undermine its profitability.

The promoters of a parallel company to trade to Africa and the Americas hoped that it could achieve similar success while striking an even more direct blow at the resources of the Spanish *monarchía*. Herein lies, perhaps, one of the chief reasons for the West India Company's eventual failure: the search for profit and the desire to contribute to the war against Spain were not easily compatible. The WIC's foundation was delayed by Oldenbarnevelt's desire to close the Truce with Spain and only after the expiry of the truce in 1621 could the company receive its charter. Those who invested in the company were happy with attacks on Portuguese and Spanish colonies as long as they brought profits, while the Dutch state looked on the WIC as a cheap way of fighting Spain but was likely to drop its support for the company if it became too expensive. The fundamental problem, however, was the nature of the situation faced by the WIC in the New World. The position of the Spanish and even the Portuguese here was much less vulnerable than the latter were in Asia: while Portugal's empire in the East consisted of a string of isolated forts and factories, Mexico, Peru and Brazil were consolidated territories and, in the case of the first two at least, were essentially invulnerable to attack from the sea. Similarly, in contrast to the highly developed economies of Asia, outside the Iberian colonies the Americas offered few opportunities for trade or profit – furs, timber and cod could not quite match spices and silk. The most obvious targets for the WIC were silver from the Spanish colonies and sugar from Brazil and the Caribbean. The sources of silver, at Zacatecas in Mexico and Potosí in Bolivia, were in remote, highland regions and so were out of reach. The only target for the Dutch was thus the Spanish silver fleet: the spectacular success of Piet Hein in 1628 produced an enormous windfall profit which kept the company optimistic, but it was never repeated.

In these circumstances, it is not surprising that the Portuguese in Brazil, where the sugar plantations were – necessarily – near the coast, became the WIC's chief objective. A major expedition in 1630 brought the capture of Pernambuco, and within a few years much of the sugar-producing area of northern Brazil was in Dutch hands. However, after the revolt of Portugal against Spain in 1640 the strategic significance of Brazil as a weapon against the Spanish disappeared – indeed purely politically there would have been considerably more point in helping the Portuguese rather than continuing the attack on their colony. So when the Portuguese colonists in Brazil revolted, the States General – or rather Holland – proved reluctant to provide aid on the scale the company needed. After the peace with Spain in 1648 the will to risk more resources in the attempt to shore up the WIC's position in Brazil was further weakened. At this point the imminent loss of Brazil left the company with only New Netherland, some Caribbean islands and a share of the slave trade. The northern colony, uncomfortably sandwiched between English possessions, offered the company furs and little else of immediate value as far as trade and profits were concerned. The WIC seems to have regarded the colonists in New Amsterdam and the other settlements of the colony with more than a little ambivalence; they provided little extra trade for the company, needed to be protected from the Native Americans, and their claims to self-government were a recurrent irritation. Curaçao provided a convenient base for trade in the Caribbean and also began to provide a modest supply of sugar but, apart perhaps from privateering, the slave trade was to become the company's most profitable business. The WIC came rather late to the trade, only getting a foothold on the African coast with the taking of Elmina in 1637, but in response to the demands of the Brazilian plantations and with a further base in Angola, slaving rapidly became a major part of the company's activities.

So by the middle of the seventeenth century, it was becoming clear that the WIC had failed – at least in comparison with the VOC. It was losing in Brazil, was uncertain what to make of New Netherland, and was otherwise limited to a precarious hold in the Caribbean. There was still political support for the company, notably from slave-traders and privateering interests in Zeeland, but it had rarely made a profit, its dividends had been meagre, and it now seemed unlikely that its commercial situation would improve significantly in the foreseeable future.

A parasitic economy?

As the general expansion which had marked the European economy in the late fifteenth and sixteenth century came to an end, and in some cases perhaps reversed, the new Dutch state took off into sustained growth. This chapter has tried to sketch out at least the main reasons why it was able to continue to expand while most of the rest of Europe slipped into depression. However, it might be argued that Dutch success came as much because of, as despite of this depressed economic environment; that they were able to exploit the weaknesses and problems of the surrounding economies. Some contemporaries certainly thought this way, and saw the whole Dutch boom as essentially parasitic, but this says more perhaps about the crudity of the economic thought of the time than about what was really going on.

The overall strength of the Dutch economy had roots deep into the sixteenth century if not earlier and its growth began during the general European expansion. If the Dutch economic take-off is dated to the 1590s, as argued by Israel,[29] then this is comfortably before the definitive down-turn of the European economy round 1620. The essential shape of the Dutch economy was established during the growth rather than depressed phase of European economic development. Certainly, the Dutch were able to take advantage of the problems of potential rivals: the effects on French economic growth of nearly forty years of internal disruption during the Wars of Religion are difficult to calculate but can hardly have been helpful, while the Thirty Years War had a devastating effect on large areas of central Europe at a time when the Dutch economy was expanding rapidly. Yet it would not be hard to argue, certainly in the case of the Thirty Years War, that the problems war caused the Dutch outweighed the opportunities it provided. For the Dutch at least it was obvious that, except in very specific circumstances, peace for themselves and the areas they traded with – which meant most of Europe – was their preferred environment.

The Dutch staple-market was as successful as it was because it performed a service which was needed at this stage in European economic development, and when this service could be dispensed with there would be little that the Dutch could do to maintain it. Again, Dutch manufactures processed imported materials and supplied their customers with products that were of a higher quality and relatively cheaper than any thing they could produce for themselves. Admittedly, textiles were highly competitive on the international market and Dutch success was a blow, for example, to producers in the southern Netherlands. On the other hand, the Dutch not only finished English white-cloths but also found markets for the finished product – the English textile industry needed these Dutch services as the Cockayne episode showed. By the same token the benefits the Dutch derived from providing these services would be threatened once they were no longer needed, and there would be nothing the Dutch could do about it. One of the more emotive issues, at least for the English, was North Sea herring; under James I and even later, when time could be spared from internal conflicts, England claimed that the fishing grounds were theirs and that, in effect, the Dutch were stealing their fish. Whatever the case in contemporary law, and no matter how strongly the English felt about the issue, this can hardly be taken seriously as a case of economic exploitation nor was it anything new. Fishing fleets from the northern Netherlands had been the major operators on the North Sea fishing grounds practically since the herring had migrated there over a century earlier; they had no natural advantages over their English rivals but had the technique and organisation to catch the fish and the market structure and skills to sell the herring once caught. There was nothing to prevent the English, or indeed the Scots, from making a similar use of this resource; certainly the Dutch would be able to do nothing to stop them, as the future would show.

One area where the accusation of exploiting the weaknesses of others does undoubtedly ring true is in the Dutch 'sea-borne empire'. Force was an unavoidable part of the establishment of colonies and extra-European trade in the early modern period, and the Dutch were as ready to use it as their Portuguese, Spanish, English and other European rivals, and with distinctly more success in these years, in Asia at least. Where they could, the Dutch used naval and military force not just to cut out their European rivals but also to enforce their will on Asians, as their ruthless conduct in the Moluccas and the Banda Islands shows.[30] However, while superior military power was a prime reason for their ability to push the Portuguese aside, it could not be the basis for the VOC's overall trading position in the East as their military and naval power fell far short of what would have been required to impose economic dominance in the East. Whatever the company's hopes and intentions may have been, their success was due more to diplomacy and trading skills than to force.

These are only examples, but they suggest that the Dutch succeeded in this period because they were able to perform services and provide goods that no other economy could. However, the need for just these services was unlikely to last. As the European economy recovered from the seventeenth-century depression and as rival economies also developed, the staple-market would be progressively eroded and Dutch manufactures hit by tariffs and competition. These changes in the international economy would inevitably signal the end of Dutch economic dominance.

Notes

1   See Introduction.

2   Jan de Vries, *The Dutch Rural Economy in the Golden Age 1500–1700* (New Haven, 1974), 237–8.

3   See Geoffrey Parker, 'War and Economic Change: the Economic Costs of the Dutch Revolt', in *Spain and the Netherlands 1559–1659* (London, 1979), 178–203.

4   Calculated from the data given in N.E. Bang and K. Korst, *Tabeller over skibsfart og varetransport gennem Oresund, 1497–1660* and *1661–1783*, 7 vols (Copenhagen / Leipzig, 1906–1953). Admittedly, Amsterdam's importance in this branch of trade was always under-represented in these records but, as the town remained in the Spanish camp in these years, it is unlikely that its merchants conducted much trade through skippers declaring other places as domicile, which is one of the problems in estimating the importance of the town's rôle at other times.

5   For a discussion of the resilience of the rural economy to the impact of war in this period, see M.P. Gutmann, *War and Rural Life in the Early Modern Low Countries* (Princeton, 1980), though this deals primarily with the area round Maastricht.

6   Jonathan I. Israel, *Dutch Primacy in World Trade 1585-1740* (Oxford, 1989), 130–6.

7   Israel, *Dutch Primacy*, 200.

8   R. Baetens, 'The organization and effects of Flemish privateering in the seventeenth century', *Acta Historiae Neerlandicae*, 9 (1976), 48–75; A.P. van Vliet, 'The influence of Dunkirk privateering on the North Sea (herring) fishery during the years 1580–1650', *The North Sea and Culture (1550–1800)*, ed. Juliette Roding and Lex Heerma van Voss (Hilversum, 1996), 150–65; R.A. Stradling, *The Armada of Flanders: Spanish maritime policy and European War, 1568–1668* (Cambridge, 1992), esp. appendix 11.

9   Sir William Batten, Surveyor of the Navy, reported by Pepys: *The Diary of Samuel Pepys*, ed. R.C. Latham and W. Matthews, Vol VIII (London, 1974), 345 (19 July 1667).

10   Johan de Vries, *De economisch achteruitgang van de Republiek in de achttiende eeuw* (Leiden, 1959), chapter II.

11   This makes Israel's title so apt, but also indicates the limitations of this work as far as the study of the Dutch economy as a whole is concerned: Israel, *Dutch Primacy*.

12   Israel, *Dutch Primacy*, chapter 3.

13   Bang and Korst, *Tabeller*.

14   See Jan de Vries, *The European Economy in an Age of Crisis* (Cambridge, 1979), chapter 1; for a different view of the seventeenth century, see Carlo Cipolla, *Europe before the Industrial Revolution* (London, 1976), chapter 10.

15   T.P. van der Kooy, *Hollands stapelmarkt en haar verval* (Amsterdam, 1931).

16   Jan de Vries and Ad van der Woude, *The First Modern Economy. Success, failure and perseverance of the Dutch economy, 1500–1815* (Cambridge, 1997), 404.

17   See C.M. Lesger, *Hoorn als stedelijk knooppunt. Stedensystemen tijdens de late middeleeuwen en vroegmoderne tijd* (Hilversum, 1990) for a pioneering study.

18   De Vries and Van der Woude, *The First Modern Economy*, 203–4.

19   J.L. van Zanden, *The Rise and Decline of Holland's Economy. Merchant Capitalism and the Labour Market* (Manchester, 1993), 39.

20   These estimates are taken from De Vries and Van der Woude, *The First Modern Economy*, 30–1.

21   Diederik Aten, *'Als het gewelt comt...' Politiek en economie in Holland benoorden het IJ 1500–1800* (Hilversum, 1995), chapter 3.

22   J. Bieleman, *Boeren op het Drentse zand 1600–1910* (Wageningen, 1987), 41.

23   De Vries and Van der Woude, *The First Modern Economy*, 406.

24   R. Willemsen, *Enkhuizen tijdens de Republiek* (Hilversum, 1988), 44.

25   C.G. Gibbs, 'The role of the Dutch Republic as the intellectual entrepôt of Europe in the seventeenth and eighteenth centuries', *Bijdragen en Mededelingen betreffende de Geschiedenis der Nederlanden*, 86 (1971), 323–49.

26   S. Groenveld, 'The Mecca of Authors? States Assemblies and Censorship in the Seventeenth-Century Dutch Republic', *Too Mighty to be Free: censorship and the press in Britain and the Netherlands*, ed. A.C. Duke and C.A. Tamse (Zutphen, 1987), 63–86; see also Groenveld, 'The Dutch Republic, an island of liberty of the press in 17th century Europe? The authorities and the book trade', *Commercium litterarum. Forms of communication in the Republic of Letters 1600–1750*, ed. H. Bots and F. Waquet (Maarssen, 1994), 281–300.

27   V. Barbour, *Capitalism in Amsterdam in the Seventeenth Century* (Baltimore, 1950).

28   C.R. Boxer, *The Dutch Sea-borne Empire* (London 1965) is still the best introduction to the subject in English, but see also the chapter on the Dutch in G.V. Scammell, *The World Encompassed. The First European maritime empires c.800–1650* (London, 1981).

29   Israel, *Dutch Primacy*, chapter 3.

30   Van Zanden, *Rise and Decline of Holland's Economy*, chap. iv.

3

Social Change

THE YEARS between the 1580s and the middle of the seventeenth century were a period of rapid economic growth and
change. These developments were so far-reaching that it has been argued
that a new type of economy – the first truly modern – took shape in
these years.[1] If this was indeed the case, then the implications for Dutch
society are profound, and even if the transformation was neither so
complete nor the shape of the Dutch economy quite so new as these
historians claim, nevertheless the rate of growth must necessarily have
brought significant social changes in its wake. Indeed, it might be
argued that one way of assessing the nature of the change which
occurred in the economy of the Republic is to look at its social consequences; the question underlying this chapter is the extent to which the
explosive economic growth of the period created a new form of society.

However, just as the roots of the economic developments of these
years must be sought in the earlier sixteenth century, if not before, so
the changes which can be seen in Dutch society also had roots deep in
the past. The transformation of the rural sector in the maritime region
of the northern Netherlands seems to have been well under way before
the Revolt, particularly in terms of patterns of employment and land-
holding; here the basic structure of society was beginning to be modified. On the other hand, the extent of change in the urban sector before
the Revolt is less clear: even in the more advanced regions the towns
remained on the small side, even by contemporary standards and certainly in comparison with the great towns of the southern Netherlands,
and their social structure looks to have remained relatively stable. In
the eastern provinces of the northern Netherlands changes in both
town and countryside before the upheavals of the Revolt were less
marked than in the west, but neither sector could be unaffected by
what was happening there. Even before its economic take-off in the
years after the Revolt, the growth of the Holland market, notably in

the case of grain, was already affecting the conditions in which both farmers and merchants in the eastern provinces of the North had to operate.

The sixty to seventy years of rapid economic growth up to around 1650 saw the consolidation of the processes which had already begun to transform rural society, but the emphasis in this period shifted to the spectacular development of the towns. Whereas up to the time of the Revolt demographic and social change seems to have been most rapid and most far-reaching in the countryside of Holland, after this point the population rise was increasingly concentrated in the towns, both large and small, of the province. Nevertheless, in the maritime region as a whole the rural transformation sign-posted in the early sixteenth century reached its apogee in these years and was reflected in the landscape itself. The massive drainage schemes and the fundamental changes to the environment which they brought about were the rural counterpart of a no less profound, though less immediately apparent, social transformation that was taking place in the urban sector of this region.

In the towns – most notably in Holland but similar developments are apparent throughout the maritime region – economic development was marked not only by population growth but also by physical expansion. City walls, and in some cases more modern defence-systems, confined the towns within their old limits, but neither the growing population nor the increased economic dynamism of these towns were easily contained within the existing urban space. The towns spilled over their medieval boundaries, necessitating the building of new housing and even the construction of new sections. It was in this period that the the centre of Amsterdam as it stands today, with its concentric semi-circles of canals, was planned and built, but this is only the most spectacular of the numerous planned urban extensions of the early seventeenth century.[2] Just as the great reclamations and the developments in agriculture were changing the face of the countryside, so the economic boom was changing the physical environment in the towns; and the society of the towns may well have been modified almost as radically as that in the countryside. If the towns had maintained much of their medieval social shape up to this point, such relative stability was at the very least called into question by the physical and economic developments of these years. To an extent it can be said that the changes were largely quantitative rather than qualitative, but the sheer size of the expansion in many of the towns implies that considerably more than a simple increase in numbers was involved. For the larger towns at least, a new form of urban society was in the process of being created.

It seems typical of what can now be called the Dutch Republic[3] that these years only intensified the differences between the two main regions of the new state. The rapid development and change which has been outlined in the last few paragraphs took place primarily in the maritime region, while the land provinces remained largely embedded in a distinctly different social world. The war with Spain also affected the two regions in very different ways. Holland, Zeeland and the greater part of Friesland were all but completely free of the most direct effects of warfare after the 1580s, while the land provinces as a whole remained subject to sieges, constant skirmishes and the movement of troops practically up to the end of the war in 1648. Nevertheless, the resilience of rural communities in this period should not be underestimated,[4] and the sharply differentiated social history of the two regions must be attributed to rather more profound causes than the accidents of military history, however damaging these may have been in the short term.

The towns of the land provinces failed to share in the explosive growth, either absolute or relative, of Holland and, indeed, a number of them declined in economic importance as compared to the later Middle Ages. The IJssel towns – Deventer, Kampen and Zwolle – which had in the past played at least a modest part in international trade as members of the Hansa now very largely lost this role to the Holland towns and were reduced primarily to local or regional market functions. In consequence, socially too they remained essentially much as before, though the presence of garrisons while the war lasted affected the social composition of the main centres significantly – and even after the end of the war the Dutch army was very largely based in the towns of the eastern provinces and the Generality Lands. These garrisons varied in size from time to time but nevertheless had a substantial impact on the demography, society and economy of these towns; this at least was a notable change from the past.[5]

The social structure in the countryside of the land provinces was not unaffected by the economic pressures and changes of the period, but it remained essentially traditional in nature in contradistinction to the radical changes which were taking place in the maritime region. Social groups which were rapidly disappearing from the countryside of

Holland, such as smallholding peasants, hung on in this region and even proliferated in some areas. The nature of farming was affected by the market, but the result was not to produce the specialised, market-orientated farmers of the maritime region. Similarly, the population of the region as a whole rose between the early sixteenth and the end of the seventeenth century but on a very much flatter demographic curve than was the case in Holland. There is a standing temptation to use the unfortunately loaded term 'modernisation' when dealing with the maritime region, but not with regard to the land provinces. Yet the impression of economic and social stagnation which colours the standard accounts is perhaps equally misleading. The rural sector of the land provinces too had its reclamations – particularly in peat regions – and responded positively to the economic challenges of the time; the changes which took place were different from those in the economically more advanced areas of the country, and probably less marked, but this was far from being simply a traditional society clinging to an established way of life.

Demographic growth and urbanisation

Although the population history of the northern Netherlands in the early modern period shows unfortunate gaps – the evidence for the sixteenth century is generally weak and as yet little is known about some areas – the overall pattern is reasonably clear. In the North as a whole (i.e. roughly speaking those provinces and areas which became part of the Dutch Republic) the population grew rapidly during the sixteenth century and this increase continued until about the last third of the seventeenth century; rising from around one million to just under two million in the course of these years. After this point stagnation and perhaps even a slight fall set in which lasted until the demographic curve began to rise again in the second half of the eighteenth century.

Within this general picture there were important regional variations, chiefly between the dynamic growth of the maritime region and the much less dramatic demographic history of the land provinces. The evidence is clearest for Holland, though even in this case there are disturbing gaps in the evidence: the best estimates available for this province suggest a population of ca. 275,000 in 1514, rising to 672,000 in 1622, and reaching a peak of about 883,000 around 1680.[6] Unfortunately, while the population of the province more than doubled in the century after 1514, the tempo of this growth remains unclear, and it is difficult to estimate how much of this growth came after the Revolt. Similarly, what can be traced of the demography of Friesland in this period suggests that its total population more than doubled between 1511 and 1660 (from ca. 79,000 to ca. 160,000) but, again, within this global picture very little is known about where or when this growth took place.[7] The evidence for Zeeland suggests that it followed the general pattern for the maritime region except that here the period of rapid growth seems to have come in the late sixteenth century and to have been rather brief, already coming to an end by the early seventeenth century and being followed by over a hundred years of stagnation.[8] Taking the economically buoyant western region as a whole, the years between the beginning of the sixteenth and the middle of the seventeenth century saw something like a three-fold rise in population. Although the timing of this increase is uncertain, and demographic growth was well under way before the Revolt, it is nevertheless clear that the population of the maritime region continued to grow from the 1580s to 1650. How much of the overall growth took place in this later period, however, is still too much a matter of informed guesswork for the comfort of the historian.

The demography of the land provinces appears to have been very different. Figures are available for only a limited number of areas within this region, and even here conclusions must remain to some extent speculative, but the picture they suggest is plausible and it seems likely that it is not untypical of the region as a whole. In Overijssel, the population seems to have increased from 53,000 in 1475 to 71,000 in 1675; in the Veluwe area of Gelderland the estimates are 36,000 in 1526 rising to a touch over 40,000 in 1650. If these figures are indeed indicative of the demographic pattern for the land provinces as a whole, it would seem that growth from the late fifteenth century to the middle of the seventeenth was modest at best and, in any case, a very stark contrast to what was happening in the maritime region. However, in these eastern areas growth continued, or better perhaps started, in the second half of the seventeenth century just as the western region came up against problems; and this growth went on into the eighteenth century, leading to a modest adjustment of the demographic balance between the two main regions of the country by the end of the Republic.[9] With regard specifically to the years between the 1580s and 1650 it is likely that there was little or no overall demographic growth in the land provinces. The war was an ever-present reality in this region for the greater part of the period, though quite how much this circumstance affected the demography of the region is impossible to say. The population of some areas and towns fell in these years, and it is hard to avoid the conclusion that warfare was partly responsible. On the other hand, what is known of the economic circumstances of the region suggests that even without war population growth here was unlikely to have been more than very modest.

States Brabant was again very different from the pattern established by Holland. There appears to have been significant growth in the early sixteenth century, but the population level attained by the eve of the Revolt does not seem to have been reached again until the last years of the Republic. Apart from the economic conditions that it shared with the land provinces in general, the effects of war in this archetypical frontier area were even more severe than elsewhere. Brabant continued to bear the brunt of Dutch involvement in land warfare in the later seventeenth century as well as during the Eighty Years War, though the demographic effects of this circumstance alone should perhaps not be exaggerated.

The demographic history of the towns shows a similar sharp contrast between the experience of the maritime region and the land provinces. In Holland in particular the century and a half after about 1500 saw a general increase both in the size of towns and in the degree of urbanisation, while in the eastern region the growth of the towns was relatively modest and the level of urbanisation rose only slightly. Between the 1580s and 1650 the contrast was even greater, as the towns of Holland grew even faster than before while those in the land provinces stagnated or even declined.

Holland in the sixteenth century was a province of many small towns, none outstanding by Netherlands' standards – certainly there was no town in the province which could compare with the size and dynamism of Antwerp. However, after the storms of the first years of the Revolt had been weathered, the towns of the province experienced a period of unprecedented growth; some grew faster than others but all shared to some extent in the general boom. Unfortunately, the earlier demographic history of these towns is still obscure, and the first clear picture comes as the result of a census held in the province in 1622. (Although it was held for tax purposes, the figures drawn from this census are considered to be reasonably reliable.[10])

The Population of the Holland towns in 1622	
Dordrecht	18,270
Haarlem	39,455
Delft	22,769
Leiden	44,745
Amsterdam	104,932
Gouda	14,627
Rotterdam	19,532
Gorinchem	5,913
Schiedam	5,997
Schoonhoven	2,891
Den Briel	3,632
Alkmaar	12,417
Hoorn	14,139
Enkhuizen	20,967
Edam	5,547
Monnikendam	3,990
Medemblik	3,983
Purmerend	2,556
The Hague	15,825

[*Source*: A.M. van der Woude, *Het Noorderkwartier*
(Wageningen,1972), vol.1, 114.]

After this point the total urban population of the province continued to grow, but the experience of the various towns began to differ sharply. In general, the larger towns went on expanding while in the smaller towns population growth slowed down or stopped, while in some cases the first signs of what was to be a long demographic decline were already becoming evident. Amsterdam was the most spectacular success in demographic terms reaching almost 200,000 by the 1680s. Relatively, Rotterdam grew even faster after 1622 rising to an estimated 45,000 by ca. 1675. The population of Dordrecht, in the past the premier trading town of south Holland, reached nearly 23,000 by the early 1630s but then fell back somewhat only to reach what was possibly a new peak in the last decade of the century.[11] By around 1675, Leiden had reached ca. 65,000, and The Hague had passed 20,000. In contrast, the population of the textile town Haarlem was possibly a little lower at this time than it had been in 1622 and none of the other towns had grown significantly. By this point Enkhuizen was well into the demographic decline which seems to have set in soon after its peak of the 1620s, and which was to halve its population by the early eighteenth century.[12] Hoorn too may have begun a similar decline about the same time. So whereas between ca. 1585 and 1622 urban growth seems to have been a general phenomenon in the province, after the latter date only a handful of larger towns was able to continue to expand significantly while the others at best held their position, and at least a few were already losing population. An exception to this generalisation is the peculiar case of the Zaanstreek: this agglomeration of manufacturing villages never formally became a town, but its collective population reached about 20,000 in 1622 and continued to grow after this point, reaching something like 24,000 by the middle of the century.

The demographic history of the towns of Holland up to 1622 is obscure through lack of surviving evidence, and even after this date the precise evolution of the population in most of them remains uncertain. Taking the period between the 1580s and 1650 as a whole, it seems likely that up to the 1620s the population of all the towns of the province rose quite rapidly but that in, or soon after, this decade the smaller towns ceased to grow while a handful of bigger cities accounted for the bulk of the subsequent population growth in the province. What is not clear is whether the stagnation in these less buoyant towns tipped over into actual decline by the mid-century. Normal urban death rates were high in this period and it took a combination of buoyant birth rates and considerable immigration to keep population figures up, never mind enable them to rise. Moreover, urban populations in this period were likely to undergo significant abnormal mortality from time to time through epidemic diseases, notably up to the end of the 1660s through recurrent visitations of bubonic plague, and the less resilient towns would have found it more difficult to make up such losses by immigration than the booming Amsterdam and Rotterdam. For these less successful towns, like Alice in the caucus race, it took all the running they could do to stay in the same place but, with minor variations up and down, it seems likely that they more or less kept up their numbers until at least the mid-century.

The situation was quite different for the towns in the land provinces and Generality Lands. Their continued exposure to the troubles of war together with fierce and growing competition from the dynamic towns of the maritime region meant that it was difficult for them to hold their own. A recent study of Deventer in Overijssel depicts a town living in a very different demographic environment than that of Holland. Although the evidence is open to interpretation, it seems that the population of the town fell between 1579 and 1600 from 8–10,000 to 4–5,000. Subsequently, numbers recovered somewhat and probably fluctuated between 6,000 and 8,000 until the end of the Eighty Years War.[13] It is perhaps significant that here the presence or absence of a garrison seems to have been a significant demographic variable – the population actually drops after the end of the war – underlining the contrast with the economically dynamic towns in the west. The other leading towns of Overijssel and Gelderland, together with 's-Hertogenbosch in States Brabant, seem to have shared similar experiences in this period; at best they held their own demographically, at worst they experienced a significant fall. The years which saw the towns of the maritime region grow in size and prosperity were much more difficult for those in the rest of the Republic, and the problems were not just caused by the circumstances of the war. Even after 1648 there was, demographically speaking, no significant upturn.

The demographic contribution of the rural sector of the Republic cannot be measured by population growth in the country areas alone; the population of the towns could not have been maintained, let alone been able to grow at the rate many of them did, without massive recruitment from the surrounding countryside. It is generally assumed that towns in this period had a negative demographic profile – that is, more people died than were born there – and thus needed a steady stream of immigrants to keep up their numbers. Even if the Dutch towns in their period of expansion had enjoyed an unusually favourable birth–death ratio, still the rapid growth they experienced would only have been possible through large-scale immigration. The movement of people from outside the Republic into the country, firstly from the southern Netherlands then particularly from the Holy Roman Empire, was a vital contribution to its demography in the seventeenth century though it is difficult to quantify. However, the primary source of population growth in the country as a whole as well as the towns was the country areas of the Republic.

Again it is necessary to distinguish between the maritime region and the rest of the northern Netherlands. Although evidence is rather thin, there is good reason to believe that population growth was particularly rapid in the first half of the sixteenth century for the countryside of Holland and that, after a probable pause during the first years of the Revolt, this rise continued well into the following century.[14] The rural population in the province as a whole doubled between 1514 and 1622 and continued to grow in North Holland, albeit at a much slower rate, until around 1650. Rural South Holland probably also showed some demographic resilience for a while after 1622, though the extent and timing of this is uncertain. By about the middle of the seventeenth century, however, this secular development had come to an end, signalling the beginning of a period of demographic stagnation for the countryside in general together with serious problems for some towns. This pattern probably holds true for the maritime region as a whole, though demographic growth seems to have been markedly less vigorous outside Holland. In Friesland the rural population rose from 60,000 in 1511 to possibly over 90,000 in 1689,[15] by which point it may well have already been past its seventeenth-century peak.

In the countryside as in the towns, the demographic curve in the land provinces was very different. For Overijssel, the Veluwe (in Gelderland) and Drenthe there is evidence for a steady, if modest, population growth during the sixteenth and early seventeenth centuries – interrupted for a longer or shorter period by the effects of the most acute phases of the war in these areas. In contrast to the western region, however, this growth continued and even picked up a little pace in the second half of the seventeenth century and into the next.[16] In States Brabant what little evidence there is suggests quite vigorous population growth in the sixteenth century but that here the demographic effects of the Eighty Years War were profound and long lasting, and population hardly regained pre-Revolt level before the end of the Republic.[17] A factor which is impossible to quantify but possibly important and certainly interesting is the amount of migration from the rural areas of the east and south to the dynamic towns of the maritime region in the period between the 1580s and 1650, pulled by economic opportunity and pushed by the circumstances of war. Such movement there certainly was, but whether it was considerable enough to effect the basic demographic pattern of these areas is uncertain.

Demographic history has a tendency to become a rather abstract series of more or less satisfactory or reliable statistics at the expense of the human reality underlying the figures. In the case of the Dutch Republic, and in this period of exceptional growth in particular, beneath the statistical surface was a population in movement. The strength of the Dutch economy in these years made it a magnet for immigrants both temporary and permanent from less economically favoured regions, and the particularly dynamic Holland also pulled in people from the rest of the Republic. There was a constant demand for domestic servants in the towns of Holland, and young women moved there not only from the countryside of the province itself but also from the land provinces and from even farther afield. A period of service as a servant, usually in a town, was a common part of the female life-cycle in early modern Europe: those going into such service usually intended to save up enough for a dowry and then move back to their home villages to marry.[18] A steady stream of women from the Rhineland territories of the Holy Roman Empire crossed the land provinces and the Zuyder Zee to find service in Amsterdam, and the almost insatiable demand of this booming city for domestic servants was also answered by a regular movement of farm girls from southern Norway.[19] Although most of these women intended their stay in Holland to be temporary, for many the move turned out to be permanent, in one way or another – these towns were, it must be remembered, not very healthy places. The Republic also drew in large numbers of migrant workers to supply the seasonal demand for labour in the countryside of Friesland and Holland,[20] and the army of the Republic also brought large numbers of foreigners to the country for more or less extended periods. It has been estimated that 40–60 per cent of troops in Dutch pay came from outside the Republic's borders and, given that the army rose to a peak of over 70,000 in the 1630s, they can be considered a not inconsiderable augmentation of the workforce. Some at least of these temporary migrants would eventually settle in the Republic.

Permanent migration to the Republic was an indispensable contribution to the Dutch demographic boom of these years. In the last decades of the sixteenth century the most important influx came from the southern Netherlands. As Parma conquered much of Flanders and Brabant in the 1580s, including the largest city, Antwerp, large numbers of committed protestants moved to the North.[21] Most will have hoped that a change in military and political fortunes would eventually allow them to return to home, but the Spanish grip on the South remained firm. This movement from south to north was strengthened by the economic success of Holland which drew people north for economic as well as religious and political reasons. The demographic impact of this migration is impossible to estimate with any accuracy, and it may well be that the qualitative influence on Dutch society was more important than sheer numbers. After this first wave from the

South, however, the neighbouring regions of Germany became the most important source of immigrants, and continued to be so for the rest of the seventeenth century. Amsterdam in particular needed immigrants to grow as fast as it did, and for much of the century something like 20 per cent of those marrying in the city had been born in Germany which gives some indication of the importance of this migratory flow.[22] The nature of the population movement changed as well: it is likely that the migration from the southern Netherlands was composed to a considerable extent of families moving together, whereas that from Germany was largely composed of single – chiefly young – men and women.

However, emigration was also important, and the total outflow included many former immigrants. It has been estimated that from 1602 to 1795 almost 1 million people left the Republic for the East on the ships of the VOC, with only around half of them ever returning. Perhaps a half of this million were originally from outside the Republic and rather less of this group ever returned from the East than was the case for Dutch-born emigrants.[23] There was a high death rate on the journey to Batavia, and the disease environment in tropical Asia was extremely unfavourable to Europeans, but the difference in return rate between the Dutch and others probably reflects the circumstance that, while most of the Dutch planned to return to the Republic if they survived, the non-Dutch were more likely stay in the East permanently through choice. Many of the settlers in New Netherland also were originally from outside the Republic, though the numbers involved in this case were very much smaller. The bulk of the emigration to the colonies came in the late seventeenth and especially the eighteenth century, and the demographic effects of such movements in the period up to 1650 must have been negligible.

These population movements from the countryside into the towns and of foreigners into the Republic – again chiefly into the towns of Holland – suggest an urban society in flux. The growing towns were having to deal with large numbers of newcomers from elsewhere in Holland, from other provinces within the Republic, and from the southern Netherlands and Germany. There seem to have been remarkably few problems in assimilating this mass of immigrants. Most, though not all, of the southern Netherlanders were Dutch-speaking, protestant and from an urban background, and so could fit quite easily into their new environment. It is possible that Germans from the Rhineland, too, did not have significant linguistic problems – David Beck, born and brought

94

up in Cologne, settled as a schoolmaster in The Hague in 1617 at the age of twenty-three and within a few years was writing his diary in Dutch.[24] Religion could cause difficulties: the uncompromising calvinism of many southerners seems to have been a disturbing element in the Dutch towns in the first decades of the century, and may have contributed significantly to the political crisis of these years; while many of those moving into the towns from the countryside were catholic, as were many of the immigrants from Germany. This could affect the religious make-up of a town but otherwise seems to have caused no trouble. Jewish immigration was less easy to assimilate, but the numbers were small up to 1650, and it was concentrated on cosmopolitan Amsterdam and consisted largely of sephardic Jews from Spain and Portugal. The larger-scale immigration of Ashkenazi from central and eastern Europe came later and created its own problems.

Urban growth and social structure

The growth of towns and increasing urbanisation brought a decisive change in population distribution in the maritime region and most particularly in Holland, but it did so on the basis of a relatively traditional pattern of employment. Unlike the next phase of European urbanisation, which was associated with massive increases in the new types of work in factories brought by industrialisation, the expansion of the Dutch textile industry which took place in the period from the 1590s to about the middle of the seventeenth century remained based on craft production. Manufactures in general were still just that – produced by hand. The Republic was still in the pre-machine era of production and the energy used for all purposes was mainly human and animal in origin, with the use of the wind to drive saw-mills and water-pumps making only a relatively modest addition to the power derived from muscle. Similarly, transport still depended on the use of animal and wind power – sail for ships and boats, horses for carriages and for towed passenger-barges. Thus two important economic sectors in urban society were the artisans, producing on a small scale to satisfy the needs of the local market in the first instance, and the providers of various transport services.

Within this traditional pattern of employment, however, there were significant changes of emphasis. The increase in prosperity together, perhaps, with a greater complexity of social interaction, led to both an absolute and a relative rise in the size and importance of the service sector in the towns. Education provided skills which were increasingly important in a commercial society, and provision expanded at every level from the teaching of basic literacy, through the Latin Schools for the sons of the urban elite, to the new universities and illustrious schools.[25] Medical needs too were met by a proliferation of practitioners of various sorts from university-trained medical doctors, through apothecaries and surgeons, to midwives, popular healers and quacks. The Reformation had initially reduced the size of the clerical element in the population by getting rid of monks, nuns and friars, but the persistence of a variety of protestant groups besides the official Reformed Church and the steady build up of religious provision for catholics in the course of the first half of the seventeenth century meant that the number of religious specialists rose again, though in a markedly different form than before. An increasingly commercial and prosperous society meant an expansion of the need for a whole range of legal services from university-trained lawyers to notaries. The towns were bigger and more complex than they had been, and literacy in particular became increasingly necessary for even modest social success. More perhaps than anywhere else in the Europe of the time, the inhabitants of the Holland towns lived in a print culture – and indeed printing and publishing, together with bookselling and the retailing of more ephemeral printed material became a significant part of the economic life of the towns, especially but not only in Holland.

Urbanisation, and the changes that went with it, was most evident in Holland, though the whole of the maritime region had to some extent similar experiences. If there was a new form of society emerging in the Dutch Republic, it was primarily in the towns of this province that it was most obviously to be found. However, even in Holland the towns were not homogeneous, differing considerably not only as regards absolute size but also in the nature and tempo of social change. The smaller trading towns experienced rapid growth in the early part of this period but then tended to suffer from competition from their larger rivals. The port towns of North Holland exemplify this pattern. Enkhuizen and Hoorn, followed at some distance by Monnikendam, Medemblik and Edam, prospered and grew until the 1620s on the basis of a healthy share of the Baltic trade, Enkhuizen's leading role in the North Sea herring fishery and Hoorn's dominance of the timber trade

with Norway. Associated crafts such as shipbuilding also did well in
most of these towns. After this point, the increasing dominance of
Amsterdam undermined their independent trading positions. While the
herring-fishery in Enkhuizen continued to thrive until well into the
second half of the century,[26] in other respects it became a subordinate
part of Amsterdam's trading system. Similarly, the prosperity of Hoorn
between the Revolt and the middle of the seventeenth century was
based on its specialisation in the timber trade rather than through
competing on a broader scale with its giant rival.[27] In South Holland,
Den Briel, Schiedam and even Dordrecht found it difficult to compete
with fast-growing Rotterdam. Although the latter was nothing like as
powerful economically as Amsterdam, nevertheless it far outstripped its
rivals in the Maas area. The population of Rotterdam more than doubled
in the half century after 1622 while the other towns of the area probably had difficulty holding their ground. Much the same might be said
of the whole province of Zeeland: in the late sixteenth century its
towns, notably Middelburg and Vlissingen, seem to have done quite
well, attracting a considerable part of the trade of Antwerp after 1585
and, initially, a significant share in the emigration from the South. This
early surge was not to last: it was already clear by the first decades of
the seventeenth century that even the leading towns of Zeeland were
losing out to their competitors in Holland, and resentment at this
relative failure was an underlying cause of the political tensions which
characterised the relations between the two provinces for much of the
seventeenth century.

The inland towns of Holland form another distinct category as far
as economic experience and social development during these years are
concerned. The extreme cases are the two great textile centres, Leiden
and Haarlem. Specialisation in the production of wool and linen cloth
created urban populations with a very different social profile from those
of the port towns. Although still based on craft techniques, control
over the various branches of the manufacture and preparation of cloth
was coming increasingly into the hands of merchant-entrepreneurs,
depressing the status of the weavers, fullers, dyers, etc.: these skilled
workers were no longer independent businessmen but were in the process of becoming little more than hired hands. Also a much higher
proportion of the total population was employed in one or other branch
of this manufacture in these towns. Delft and Gouda, too, were more
heavily dependent on manufactures than the port towns, though the

production of porcelain in the one and clay-pipes in the other appears to have remained much more in the hands of artisan-traders.

Amsterdam also constitutes an exception, not only through its size but also through the complexity of its economy. By the middle of the century it was about three times the size of the next largest town, Leiden, and contained almost a quarter of the total population of Holland. It retained the characteristics of a trading town, however, with large numbers of seamen, dock workers, porters and others involved in the manhandling of cargoes, as well as a very wide range of artisan producers to satisfy the needs of such a large agglomeration of people. In addition to being bigger, Amsterdam was wealthier than the other trading towns, though possibly The Hague had a higher average per capita income. This prosperity supported a richer crop of services than elsewhere, from a wide variety of churches and religious sects, through the most active theatre in the Republic, to a particularly lavish supply of prostitutes of various sorts.[28]

The Hague was another special case: formally it was not a town at all but remained a village, and was not represented in the States of Holland. It was much more of an administrative and legal centre than the rest of the Holland towns, being the seat of the States General, and also of what there was of an apparatus of central government for the Republic, of the States of Holland, and – not least – of the court of the princes of Orange. It was also the location of the two central courts of justice for Holland and Zeeland, the *Hof van Holland* and the *Hoge Raad*, and the staff of these courts together with the advocates pleading cases before them had a noticeable effect on the social mix of the town. In fact the commerce of the town was negligible and its manufactures were mainly to serve the needs of its wealthy inhabitants and visitors. The presence of foreign ambassadors with their entourages brought a unique element to the social mix, as did from the early 1620s onwards the court of the exiled Bohemian king, Friedrich of the Palatinate and his wife, Elizabeth (daughter of James I of England). In this way The Hague had more the social profile, albeit on a rather small scale, of other capital cities in contemporary Europe, than that of either the trading or the manufacturing towns of Holland. Zaandam, or rather the agglomeration of villages in the *Zaanstreek* which included also Westzaan and Oostzaan, was an agglomeration which reached the size of a largish town but without the commensurate political organisation or status. Also, as the service centre for the merchant and fishing fleets its heavy concentration on shipbuilding with its associated craft industries from saw-milling to the baking of ship's biscuits gave it a peculiar social shape.

Even within Holland, thus, the contrasts between the various towns were great, never mind the gap which separated them as a group from the towns in the east and south. There were enormous differences between the cosmopolitan Amsterdam and relative backwaters such as Purmerend and Schoonhoven. Nevertheless the life and society of the towns of Holland had certain common characteristics which make it possible to regard them to a certain extent as similar social phenomena. Indeed, it might be argued that the towns of the province taken together are better considered as a single entity: to a significant degree they acted as parts of a coordinated urban system with all of the constituent units performing separate functions within the whole. Excellent communications, by contemporary standards at least, particularly by water, facilitated such functional integration, but on the other hand the far-reaching political autonomy of the towns together with deep-seated commercial rivalries and clashes of interest undermine any picture of smooth and unproblematic co-operation. Whereas at a fundamental level the towns of Holland shared a community of economic and social interests, this was continually being obscured by more immediate conflicts; for much of the time competition and mutual jealousies were more obvious than co-operation.

With the partial exception of The Hague, all of the towns of Holland were dependent on trade in one way or another, and the availability of water transport and especially access to the sea was vital. Even the inland towns had relatively good communications with the sea: the Haarlemmermeer escaped the great reclamations and continued to provide Leiden with easy access to the Zuyder Zee, and De Rijp, in the centre of North Holland, was the home port of a considerable number of herring busses at least until the early decades of the century. Communication between the towns was considerably enhanced by the development of the *trekvaart* system for passenger transport: specially designed canals with towpaths for horse-drawn barges, providing what was eventually a dense network of regular services linking practically all the towns. The network did not reach its full extent until the second half of the seventeenth century, but the first important phase of *trekvaart* construction came in the period 1632–47.[29] These towns were open societies with mobile populations, and fishermen and sailors – and increasingly whalers – were a significant part of the urban population of the whole province and not just of the ports.

There were also other important similarities in the urban environment throughout Holland: the inhabitants of all but the very smallest of the towns were densely packed and socially mixed. There were richer and poorer quarters (*wijken*) in the towns, but it is equally characteristic that the side-streets and alleys (*steegjes*), where the less well-off and many of the poor lived, were often literally just round the corner from the houses of the wealthy on the imposing urban-canal frontages. Many towns have preserved a large part of their seventeenth-century centres more or less intact, so the visitor can still gain some impression of the urban physical environment in the Golden Age, though in a somewhat sanitised form. Contemporary townscape paintings, though not perhaps as purely realist as was once thought, can nevertheless, when used with discretion, give a lot of information about the physical aspects of life in the towns. Building land was clearly in fairly short supply, but more importantly canal frontage was precious and houses were built close together, typically with narrow fronts on the canal side but often extending quite deeply in the rear. On the main streets and *grachten* (urban canals) the façades were characterised by the stepped gables which were also typical of late medieval urban architecture in the Netherlands. A striking characteristic of almost all the towns was the presence of canals even, or especially, in the most prestigious of residential areas. The concentric semi-circles of canals which define the centre of Amsterdam today were created in the course of the early seventeenth-century expansion of the town. Terraces of new houses to provide suitably impressive accommodation for the more prosperous inhabitants of this booming town were purposely built along the new *grachten* with the frontages broken only by relatively narrow passages. Similarly in Leiden whereas the old main street with the town hall is canal-less, the prestigious Rapenburg with the newly founded university is a fine example of a *gracht*.

The demographic expansion of the towns of Holland meant that they began to fill up the space described by the lines of the medieval walls; new building, and even the creation of new quarters, became necessary. The most obvious example of this is Amsterdam, as it grew faster and further than any other town and required a number of extensions in the course of the seventeenth century, including the most famous in the second decade which produced the new centre much of which still survives.[30] It is significant of the perception the Dutch had of urban life that these new quarters were planned as areas to supply a variety of housing needs; it was expected that the rich, the not-so-rich and the far-from-rich would live almost cheek by jowl. Only in the extension of Leiden in the middle years of the century did the peculiar social profile of the town lead to the planned creation of a quarter consisting of small houses specifically designed for the masses of workers created by the boom in the wool-textile industry.[31] Another characteristic, at least of the larger towns, and one that is evident throughout the extensions and planned extensions of the period, is the continued concern for defence. The towns of Holland had not been exposed to direct attack since the 1570s but the Republic was at war till 1648 and the new forms of ditch and bastion defences designed to withstand cannon-fire which had replaced now-obsolete medieval walls, had to remain prominent features of any town with pretensions to autonomy. The traces of these large defensive structures can still be seen on the ground and in street names in many towns.

The growth of the towns put pressure on a whole range of inherited institutions as well as on the housing stock. For example, more people – and particularly a relatively larger middling group in the urban population – meant a greater demand for medical services. Towns appointed official doctors and midwives with considerable supervisory authority, but most medical needs were met by barber-surgeons and apothecaries, with only the better-off being able to afford the services of university-trained doctors. However, given the ineffectiveness – at best – of most of the treatments used by the best medical men of the time, access to a proper doctor was a privilege of questionable value. The more practical efforts of the barber-surgeons, who carried out physical operations on the body, and apothecaries, who prescribed herbal and other medicines, may well have been more useful or at least less dangerous. Doctors were professionals, surgeons and apothecaries craftsmen trained through apprenticeships, but medical care at child-birth was still provided by midwives, women with much experience but no formal training of either sort. Although contemporary paintings depict the unofficial healer as a male quacksalver, it is likely that women played a dominant role in the practice of popular medicine and the continuation of traditional ways of combating the multifarious dangers to health in the towns. The process of professionalisation which was to characterise health-care in the modern period, and was to exclude or reduce the role of women, had begun in the Republic in the first half of the seventeenth century but had as yet made only limited progress.

Rising populations also presented challenges of an unprecedented scale to the existing social welfare system. That care for the sick, the poor and the orphaned was a communal responsibility was a very powerful tradition in the Netherlands, and contemporaries prided themselves on the range and generosity of such social services. The most prominent foundations were the municipal hospitals, old peoples' homes and orphanages which as a matter of course tended to favour established citizens and the children of citizens over newcomers, not an unimportant bias considering the rate of migration into the towns in this period. New arrivals would have been among the most vulnerable of the inhabitants of a town, but were likely to find it more difficult to gain assistance. Poor relief in money or in kind was intended to supplement the resources of the poor and to help them over difficult times rather than support them entirely but such assistance, together with control over bread prices and the stock-piling of grain by town governments, does seem to have stopped people – as a rule – from dying from starvation in the midst of these prosperous towns.[32] A semi-official source of help for the poor were the deacons of the Reformed Church, whose resources were regularly supplemented by town governments. In most cases they only took responsibility for the poor among their own congregations, but in most towns of the province this had become a majority of the population before the middle of the century. There were also a wide range of private forms of charity which the lucky or astute could use to supplement their meagre receipts from elsewhere. The greatest strain on these ways of dealing with poverty probably came in Leiden and Haarlem, where they were inadequate to deal with the consequences of large-scale unemployment during the cyclical slumps in the textile trade.

The old were also a problem though, given the age-profile of the population, not an insuperable one. By modern standards relatively few people reached old age, certainly not in the unhealthy conditions of the towns of Holland, but on the other hand those who did so reached it earlier: to ask 'are you sixty' apparently had the implication not just of old age but of senility.[33] There were municipal old men's and old women's homes, and in many towns *hofjes* – a sort of sheltered housing – can still be seen as a visual reminder of the considerable private efforts that were made to deal with the problems of age and infirmity. However, the numbers that could have been housed in both public and private institutions combined was too small to have helped more than a tiny minority; most of the old continued to work as long as they could and for the rest relied on their own networks of family, guild, or neighbours for help. Orphans were a special concern of town governments: the *weeskamer* looked after the property and the interests of the children of deceased citizens, and town orphanages took care of those without family or other suitable guardians to bring them up.[34] The capacity of these institutions was again not great, but most children losing their parents probably found refuge within the extended family and the places available may well have been sufficient to house those who could not. The aim of the magistrates was not just to provide for the immediate physical needs of the orphans but also to give them sufficient education and training to enable them to earn a living when they grew up. While the expectations of the boards of governors were not pitched high – apprenticeship to a low grade craft for the boys and preparation for domestic service and preferably a respectable marriage for the girls – careful surveillance by the magistrates usually ensured that the regime in these municipal orphanages was humane.[35]

Educational opportunities also seem to have expanded to meet the demand in these growing towns, largely perhaps because most schools were private and thus self-financing, though needing to be licensed by the local authorities. The towns had an increasingly print-based culture, and the ability to read was coming to be a distinct advantage, though inability to do so was not necessarily a serious limitation in all fields of activity. The available evidence, though exiguous and difficult of interpretation, suggests that literacy was high in the towns and rising in the course of this period. In 1630 two thirds of the grooms and one third of the brides in Amsterdam could sign their names, but as reading was taught before writing in schools it may well be that distinctly more people – and perhaps especially women and girls – could read than could write.[36] Primary schools teaching reading, writing and arithmetic and little more would be all that the great majority of parents could aspire to for their children, but for the rather better-off there were schools – often known as French schools – which taught subjects useful in commerce, such as foreign languages and book-keeping. In the major towns there were also Latin schools which taught classical languages and literature, primarily Latin as the title suggests but with some Greek[37], to a handful of sons – not daughters – of wealthier citizens as a preparation for university entrance.

For most people, however, schooling was only a relatively small part of preparation for life; this was still a society where training for most jobs and activities was a matter of practice rather than theory. There was no institutional training for most of what adult women did and were expected to do: running a household, domestice service, or even work in the retail sector where women were so prominent. None of these tasks involved formal instruction but were learnt in the family, and by the example of more experienced servants and stall- or shop-keepers. This situation was not peculiar to women, however; most male occupations were also learnt through on-the-job training rather than school or academic qualifications. All skilled crafts were taught by apprenticeships lasting a varying number of years, some involving quite considerable outlays by parents or guardians. As a rule it can be said that the more prestigious crafts, and the ones likely to be most materially rewarding, required more expensive training, while those in less demand might have to provide apprentices with at least a modest wage during their training period. Although there was some schooling available in certain relevant skills, in the main commerce was also something that was learnt largely by practical experience. Besides working in the family business at home, it was a common practice in more successful merchant families to send sons to work abroad as factors in a port or trading centre, where they could not only be trained in the business but also learn another language and pick up valuable experience of the world outside Holland. Formal qualifications – apart from the master's certificate after apprenticeship – was only required for a handful of professions: medicine, law and, increasingly, the Church. While at the beginning of the century there was still room in the Reformed Church for 'Duitse klerken', ministers who lacked a university education (and thus, as the designation implies, did not understand Latin), half a century later only university-trained candidates were regarded as eligible for positions as ministers.[38] There was still some ambivalence, however, as although would-be ministers were required to read theology at university they did not have to take their degrees, but had to demonstrate their expertise and orthodoxy to a vetting committee set up by the Reformed Church not the university examination authorities. It might be suggested that most tasks in government and administration were similarly learnt by practice, and that this circumstance gave families with an established position an enormous advantage. Officials of the States General and the States of Holland in The Hague, or those attached to local government in the towns were typically able to found virtual office-holding dynasties, and undoubtedly the most likely route to an attractive administrative appointment was through the household and office of a family member or other patron.

Nevertheless, higher education was expanding, and a law degree increasingly became, if not a necessary, then a useful qualification for regents in the Holland towns. The proportion of regents with a degree, usually from Leiden and almost always in law, rose steadily in this period, though it was perhaps only in the second half of the century that it became something approaching the norm. Before the Revolt, there had been no universities in the northern Netherlands, though Leuven (Louvain) in Brabant had a European reputation. The university of Leiden was established in 1575 and Franeker in Friesland soon after, Groningen followed in 1614, Utrecht in 1636 and Harderwijk in Gelderland in 1648. In the last decades of the sixteenth and the early years of the seventeenth century the most urgent need these universities had to meet was the provision of trained ministers for the newly established Reformed Church, and theology remained one of the most important faculties, but rapidly the presence of prestigious humanists and the growth of medicine and law faculties changed the balance in these institutions, turning them into training schools for the professional and political elite.[39] Higher education was also available in some of the other towns in Holland in the form of so-called illustrious schools, which could provide a high level of instruction but which could not award degrees. The most famous was the Athenaeum in Amsterdam which initially benefited from being able to appoint notable scholars expelled from Leiden because of their remonstrant sympathies, and a remonstrant seminary which quickly established a considerable reputation was also founded there in 1634. Youths or young men from the most privileged sections of society could finish their education abroad, either by taking a degree at a foreign university and/or embarking on an early version of the Grand Tour, which in the Dutch case sometimes included England as well as the more obvious destinations, France and Italy.[40]

During the rapid economic growth of the period, and perhaps particularly when this boom began to falter in some towns towards the middle of the century, the economy was a central concern of the governments of the towns of Holland. The regents saw the promotion and preservation of the prosperity of their towns as one of their primary responsibilities as magistrates. This end could be pursued in two main ways: a town government could, usually in alliance with other towns, seek to influence the economic policy of the States of Holland and, by extension, of the States General; or it could use its considerable autonomous power to introduce and enforce ordinances to help the local economy. However, town governments regarded their duty as being in the first instance to protect the interests of their citizens, i.e. burgers, if necessary at the expense of mere inhabitants or newcomers. Burger status could most easily be inherited but could also be bought, and lists of new burgers provide valuable evidence about the extent and nature of immigration into the towns. A related concern was control of the craft guilds. Political turbulence and, in some places, the real power of the guilds was a major theme in the history of the Netherlands, but less in the north than in the south, and less in Holland than in, say, the town of Utrecht. By the seventeenth century, the guilds in the towns of Holland were firmly under the control of the local magistracy, and they had no political force and precious little independence; they did, however, represent important economic interests and their representatives were often listened to, even consulted, on economic matters. The guilds, however, were not just organisations for the collective protection of economic self-interest; they also had some of the character of friendly societies, providing help for the sick and proper funerals for the deceased. Perhaps most importantly for their members, they went some way to satisfying the need for a sense of belonging and identity in a world which was changing with unsettling rapidity, especially in the larger and more dynamic towns. Yet the very changes which made this sense of guild identity so important were also beginning to undermine the power of these medieval economic organisations. The power of the merchant-entrepreneur in the textile industry was in the process of destroying the economic independence of the weavers, fullers, dyers and other artisans, turning them in effect into little more than hired hands. Similarly in Amsterdam, the proliferation of new products and techniques meant that more and more of the urban economy escaped guild regulation of any effective kind.

An even greater priority of town governments than economic success was probably the maintenance of order, including the moral order.

One obvious aspect of this concern was the prevention and punishment of crimes against the person and against property, though the incidence of crime does not seem to have caused a high level of general anxiety at this time. In some ways this is surprising, as this was a society where physical violence was endemic: carrying knives seems to have been normal, and their use in quarrels, especially under the influence of drink, common. Not surprisingly in these circumstances, serious injuries and even manslaughter were far from unusual and were regarded with relative leniency by the courts. Especially in the larger and faster growing towns there seems to have been something of the atmosphere of a frontier society, and most of the towns of Holland were in some measure ports and displayed their typical turbulence – paid-off sailors, alcohol and knives were an explosive mix. Violent theft and crimes against property were more severely dealt with, and were inevitably common in the closely-packed environment of the Holland towns; branding, whipping, the pillory and banishment rather than imprisonment were the usual punishments – apart from the death penalty which was reserved for a limited number of crimes, such as murder and aggravated house-breaking – although how effective these harsh punishments were in limiting the incidence of serious offences is uncertain. A major problem was the erratic nature of law enforcement: in each town this was in the hands of the *schout*, but the resources available to this official were very limited – a handful of *onderschouten* was hardly enough to police a town the size of Amsterdam, or even Rotterdam or Leiden. The inherited system may well have worked adequately in the smaller towns but was badly strained by the conditions elsewhere. The authorities were dependent on the cooperation of the public for identifying and tracking down offenders, and to a large extent which laws were effectively enforced was a function of popular attitudes. The environment of the towns does, however, seem to have been inimical to the activities of criminal gangs operating on any considerable scale, in contrast to some parts of the countryside particularly in the east and south of the Republic.[41]

The comparative impotence of the police authorities is particularly evident in the case of prostitution, but in this case the practical limitations of the system of policing were also compounded by a deep-seated ambivalence. In the Netherlands – as in other towns of late medieval Europe – prostitution had tended to be regarded as a necessary evil and to be regulated by town governments. Indeed, in a number of cases it would seem that police officials were responsible for running what amounted to municipal brothels. Under pressure from post-Reformation morality in general, and in this period particularly from a Reformed Church which was attempting to impose its moral standards on society as a whole, such activities and the attitudes they represented were no longer acceptable, but the *schouten* and their subordinates still tended to see prostitution as something which could perhaps be regulated but never suppressed. Given their limited resources this was realistic rather than cynical, in port towns especially; where there were sailors there would be whores and there was not much anyone could do about it. According to a recent study of Amsterdam, there were periodic attempts to crack down on prostitution, but these came after the middle of the century and tended rather to change the ways in which whores operated rather than doing much to suppress the business as a whole.[42] Here street prostitution was supplemented by an impressively wide range of sexual services to satisfy a demand that was clearly not limited to sailors or visitors – though it would seem that the inns and *speelhuizen* (quasi-brothels with musical entertainment) where such services were available were becoming something of a tourist attraction in the course of the seventeenth century. It was only later in the century, however, that a guide to such places appeared in print.[43] Amsterdam was by far the biggest town in the province, of course, and had a substantial transient element in its population – seamen, merchants and a wide variety of commercial agents – but there was a demand in the other port towns for such services as well, if only at the rougher end of the trade, and The Hague possibly had a rather more sophisticated market, but the details of this are still unclear. As yet, no trace has been found in this century of homosexual prostitution, and indeed recent studies have cast doubt on whether homosexuality is a helpful analytical category in the Republic before the eighteenth century – but these are particularly murky waters.[44] There is some evidence for child-abuse, but no hint of its scale, and there is no sign of a commercial paedophile sex.

Despite the stigma – and dangers – of the job, there was no shortage of prostitutes: life in the Holland towns could be harsh, particularly for women on their own. Immigrant women, servant girls who had lost their place, the wives of absent seamen, could easily find themselves drawn into full- or part-time prostitution at one level or another, but it was seamstresses and others working in the less well-paid sectors of textile manufacture who were particularly prone to turn to prostitution. In the second half of the century around 80 per cent of prostitutes arrested in Amsterdam were born outside the town, and over a quarter outside the Republic;[45] before ca. 1650, when population growth and immigration were at their peak, these proportions may well have been even higher. The crime these prostitutes – and their clients – were regarded by contemporary society as committing was not always clear, but it seems that what might be called simple whoring was seen as less serious than adultery, i.e. when the client was married. Where such cases were concerned, the letter of the law imposed and the spokesmen of the Reformed Church demanded severe punishment, but in practice both the civil courts and the reformed consistories were more lenient than the public rhetoric on the issue might lead one to expect.[46] On the whole violence, drunkenness and whoring were activities that could, perhaps, be kept in check but not eradicated; the towns of Holland never came near to being the ideal godly communities of the proponents of the *nadere reformatie.*

Popular entertainments tended to overlap with crime or at least with behaviour that was unacceptable to the authorities and educated opinion in general. Inns and bars proliferated and were the most popular form of relaxation, but they also encouraged excessive drinking and violence. Also they were notorious as places where prostitutes came to find their clients, and the inns in Amsterdam where musical entertainment was on offer became notorious as little more than covert brothels later in the century.[47] Sadly, attempts to provide more respectable alternative entertainment, such as organ recitals in church, seem to have made little impact. The chambers of rhetoric – private associations for the composition and performance of dramatic works – continued to operate in the early decades of the century, but were losing more than a little of their cultural vitality, certainly in comparison to their religious and even political impact in the previous century. Newer forms of entertainment such as the theatre had to contend with determined opposition from the Reformed Church. The civil authorities were put under constant pressure to prevent the establishment of playhouses and actors, if members of the Reformed Church, were subject to discipline from their local consistory. Such general and individual campaigns ensured that only in Amsterdam, where the profits went to the orphans of the town, was there a significant regular theatre, the *Schouwburg*. Travelling players did, however, provide simple shows at fairs and on other occasions where crowds gathered, and many towns saw at least occasional performances.[48]

Fairs themselves were a regularly recurring source of popular and public pleasure, especially the annual *kermis*, which again attracted the criticism of moralists because of the excesses it undoubtedly encouraged. Indeed, eating and drinking too much on special occasions was characteristic of a society which for most people was still marked by long periods of short commons relieved by bursts of over-indulgence. Weddings – and often wakes too – were opportunities for eating and drinking as much and for as long as people could afford, but such immoderate behaviour was beginning to be seen as socially disruptive. Reformed disapproval of such behaviour was supported in a number of towns by local ordinances which sought to put some limits on these celebrations. Dancing was one of the activities at festivals, weddings and inns which brought these places and occasions into even worse repute. Quite why dancing was seen as such a threat to morality is not always clear, and even thoroughly respectable families continued to accept it as a perfectly proper social activity, but the belief that mixed dancing was a dangerous sexual stimulus was certainly an important consideration for its opponents, and it is true that the more boisterous forms of dancing, at a time when underwear of the modern sort was not worn, could easily lead to unambiguous immodesty. However, this was one of a whole range of popular activities that the moral reformers were never able to stamp out.

For the great majority of the population, even in the relatively prosperous towns of Holland, the ordinary pattern of daily life left very little room for play or any form of regular recreation. Hours of work were long and, as the contribution of children as well as women was essential to the economic survival of most families, they too had little time for unprofitable activities in their daily lives. Both boys and girls were expected to do work of some sort as soon as they were physically capable of doing so. Their work was not only a valuable contribution to the family budget, it was also an important part of their education: it was regarded as a moral activity just as idleness was seen as an invitation to sin, and also as a necessary preparation for adult life, especially if there was an element of training in what they were required to do.[49] There was regular relief from work in the rhythm of the week: the late medieval plethora of saints' days had been swept away as a consequence of the victory of protestantism, and was replaced by a renewed emphasis on the need to keep the sabbath holy and free for the worship of God. Thus, as Sunday became the only free day of the week, it is hardly surprising that the competition between church and pub became a marked feature of social life in both town and countryside. Besides the perceived duty of worshipping God, the moralistic literature of the period reveals a mistrust of leisure; disciplined endeavour was itself a virtue, and keeping busy preserved people from temptation. So not only had most people little time for recreation, they were taught from the pulpit and through pietistic tracts that play was at best a morally dubious activity. Of course, an underlying assumption of such moralists was that leisure was particularly dangerous for the mass of the population; the wealthier and better-educated sections of the population could be trusted, within certain limits, not to misuse their free time.

For most people then, games and entertainment only entered their lives at occasional and irregular times: weddings, family celebration, the annual feast of a guild or of the *schutters*, and most universally the local *kermis*. Some idea of what variety of games people played during their irregular breaks from labour can be gained from contemporary painting, though there is nothing quite as comprehensive as that which Pieter Breugel's painting *Children's Games* provides for the southern Netherlands of the century before. In the winter – and winters tended to be severe in the seventeenth century (a part of the 'little ice-age') – skating and forms of ice-hockey or curling were evidently very popular, and at other times of the year skittles and various ball-games. For members of the civic militia (*schutterij*), shooting competitions were a central element in their annual social gatherings; while they often seem to have been little more than an excuse for getting together to drink and eat too much, this might well be considered an important social rite, affirming their common identity. The rhythm of life for the better-off was very different. While the merchant or manufacturer, and even the lawyer, might themselves work hard, for their families leisure was an integral part of their lives. Of course, wives in upper-middle class families had quite complex households to run, and their children were expected to attain high educational standards – though the expectations with regard to girls were distinctly lower or, at least, very different than for boys – but there was still distinctly more variety to their social lives than the hard work relieved by irregular debauches typical of the lower orders. The availability of spaces where it could be played, of money to buy instruments, and of time to practise them, made music among family and friends a typical amusement of the wealthier groups in society; and private reading was becoming an increasingly common practice among those with the necessary time and education, as well as the money to buy books (which were relatively expensive).[50] A cultured man was expected to be able to write poetry as well as show a knowledge of ancient and modern classics, and the reading of plays seems to have been a favourite activity in the upper levels of society. The really well-off could relieve the tedium of their lives in town in the summer months, and perhaps escape more serious threats to their health at the same time, by moving for longer or shorter periods to the countryside. The *buiten* could be anything from little more than a garden outside the town walls, through a comfortable farm-house, to the fine country houses built – mostly later in the seventeenth or in the eighteenth century – along the Vecht by some of the wealthier Amsterdam citizens. It is, however, characteristic of even the richest families that they did not move permanently to the countryside: the town was the centre of their social and cultural, as well as of their economic and political lives.

Although one of the main themes of this book is the contrast between the maritime region and the land provinces, nevertheless the latter were strongly urbanised by the standards of contemporary Europe – only the comparison with Holland makes them appear a part of traditional society rather than of the new society that was emerging in the maritime region. In this period, one importance difference is that the proportion of the population which lived in the towns in the land provinces remained roughly stable, and there was certainly no increase in this ratio comparable to that which took place in Holland. There were substantial towns with proud histories in the east and south, but they displayed little or nothing of the dynamic which marked nearly all the towns in the maritime region.

The leading towns of the land provinces and Generality Lands – Utrecht,[51] Deventer, Kampen, Zwolle, Zutphen, Nijmegen, 's-Hertogenbosch – had in many cases a distinctly more impressive past than most of the towns of Holland, but from the late Middle Ages onwards they had been losing some of their old importance and in this period this relative decline was particularly evident. Whereas the towns of the maritime region were freed from the immediately damaging consequences of war within a decade of the start of the Revolt, those of the land provinces suffered from the direct and indirect effects of military action throughout the Eighty Years War. These towns were rarely free from at least the threat of attack from enemy troops, and the regular military operations in the region disrupted the trade routes on which they depended economically. The IJssel towns, for example, found it difficult to maintain the links with neighbouring areas of the Holy Roman Empire which were so important for their trade; at a time when they were already suffering considerably from the competion of Amsterdam and other Holland towns such interruptions were particularly damaging. It must be emphasised that these towns did not decline much if at all in absolute terms, but this period was undoubtedly a testing time for them. Consequently, their social and economic structure remained much as it had been before the Revolt, though the influence of what was happening in Holland can be seen in the development of educational, medical and social provision. In some ways it was easier for the governments of these towns to satisfy such social needs: they were certainly less prosperous than their counterparts in Holland, but a stagnant or even falling population perhaps presented them with rather less acute problems.

For the duration of the war, these front line towns became the homes of garrisons of soldiers for their defence and for some, such as Nijmegen and Maastricht, this status became permanent. The long-term presence of large numbers of troops in what were comparatively small towns had a considerable effect not only on their economies but also on their social and demographic structure. Here the inability to compete with the towns of Holland for extra regional trade, was compensated for to some extent by servicing the needs of the garrisons as well as by a greater emphasis on their role as intermediaries between their local areas and the national market. The chief towns in the Generality Lands while sharing many of the characteristics of those in the land provinces had another role as well. Breda, 's-Hertogenbosch and Bergen-op-Zoom were towns with protestant governments in overwhelmingly catholic areas; with their garrisons they were intended to help protect the country from invasion from the southern Netherlands, but they also had not a little of the character of fortresses controlling conquered territory.

Social change in the countryside

The transformation in rural society which took place in the course of the sixteenth and early seventeenth century can be considered in many ways as being even more far-reaching than the changes that can be seen in the towns. Whereas the late medieval social structure in the towns may well have been modified as a result of long-term economic developments but did not change out of all recognition, in the maritime region the changes in the countryside resulted in a social structure which was fundamentally unlike anything which had gone before. This process of change reached its culmination in the period between the 1580s and the middle of the seventeenth century, after which point the advent of very different conditions began to alter the direction of change in rural society. The situation in the land provinces is less clear cut: on the one hand it would be a mistake to see society as remaining wholly or even largely static, but on the other it is nonetheless true that change in this region was neither so radical nor so undeniably capitalist in its nature as it was in the west of the Republic.

The details of the process of change in the maritime region are difficult to trace, but the end result is becoming tolerably clear and marks the conquest of the rural economy by capitalism, with the economic triumph of the market bringing a fundamental restructuring of society. As agriculture became increasingly specialised in the products best suited to both the terrain and the market, a new articulation of society took shape in the countryside. A class of capitalist farmers developed, employing hired labour when they needed it and using the services of an increasingly numerous and varied service sector, and the relationship between these three social groups came to characterise the new social structure of the rural areas. There is evidence that the average size of farms grew in this period, and that the size of dairy herds in particular rose appreciably. Whether tenants or free-holders – and much of the land in this region was owned rather than rented, though there were considerable local variations – the farmers became effectively businessmen and their material prosperity grew markedly throughout this period. Part of the process of becoming more efficient economically was the switch from reliance on a permanent, 'family' work-force to wage-labour, both long-term and hired on a temporary or casual basis. In addition, a whole range of tasks which had in the past been carried out by the farm work-force were now delegated to outside specialists, and as a consequence a stratum of skilled workers serving the needs of the farming community emerged in the villages of the region.[52] This social sector was stiffened by carters and especially *schippers*[53] providing the transport services for passengers and, especially, goods that this market-orientated agriculture increasingly needed. At a rather more prosperous level, there was a generous sprinkling, for example in North Holland, of *schippers* of sea-going merchant ships. As a corollary to such social shifts as these, the number of smallholders fell to such an extent that one historian has traced the critical decline in the supply of cheap labour for the textile industry specifically to this phenomenon.[54] Beneath the level of the artisans, the class of people dependent on wage labour also expanded; they scraped a living for themselves and their families by combining a number of activities, some of them seasonal. Besides agricultural work, much of which dried up in the winter, fishing and the merchant fleet provided employment for a large number of men in the rural areas of the region, notably in North Holland and Friesland.

The impression of a quasi-urban social structure being formed in the countryside of the maritime region is strengthened by the availability of a wide range of services outside the towns. Partly, of course, this might be seen as a piece of sleight of hand through misleading definitions, as many of the villages in this region would have been considered towns in much of the rest of Europe. These large and economically diversified villages were, however, at the heart of rural life and were typical of its social as well as its economic organisation, rather than being an alien urban implant. Although the countryside along with the smaller towns was subordinate politically to the towns which were represented in the provincial states – except for the remnants of peasant self-government in Friesland, and even here the political system that gave a significant voice to the rural areas was being subverted by and in favour of urban notables[55] – the relative prosperity of these villages suggests that the rural sector was integrated into the economic system as a whole and shared in its general success. In the maritime region, at least, the countryside was not an economic colony of the towns: on the contrary, the modernisation of production techniques on the farms, the far-reaching specialisation within the rural economy, and the vital linking role performed by the larger villages, were essential to the success of the economy as a whole in this period.

Most of the great drainage projects in North Holland and elsewhere took place between the Revolt and the middle of the seventeenth century, and the new rural communities in the freshly drained polders were a spectacular example of the radical transformation of the Dutch countryside.[56] The polders were also typical in the way in which they exemplified continuity as well as innovation: the drainage projects for the Beemster, Schermermeer and Purmer, for example, may have been on a larger scale and required greater investments than any similar enterprise in the past but they were in the great Dutch tradition of reclaiming land from the water. Moreover, they were driven by the same motives as in the past: the combination of demand for more agricultural land, for more effective defences against the sea, and the need for better drainage of water from the rivers which emptied into the region. However, by the early decades of the seventeenth century the lure of gain was probably a more effective spur to investors than the fear of any recurrence of the disastrous floods which had been all too frequent in the previous century. The long-term and continuing buoyancy of agricultural prices, and thus rents, made these schemes attractive investments. It seems that much of the capital needed to finance these projects came from the towns of Holland and demonstrated a readiness to invest in the countryside as well as a relative oversupply of money looking for sound investments. The wealth of Holland, urban as well as rural, was instrumental in changing the face of the countryside of the province, and in the area north of the IJ the transformation was profound. Here the draining of the inland lakes, and to a lesser extent the reclamation of land from the sea, turned an area which had been almost as much water as land into a solid land mass with no large lakes and where the number of usable waterways was reduced drastically. The towns of the region were drawn into acrimonious disputes over the control of the remaining routes as they struggled to maintain their respective spheres of economic influence, and their access to the sea.[57] In Zeeland also land won from the sea substantially increased the agricultural acreage in this period, and the results for Zeeland-Flanders were even more spectacular.

Graft, a village on the Schermereiland in the middle of North Holland, is perhaps an extreme case of the economic diversity, even the urban nature, of the Holland countryside. It was unusual through its size: with over 3,000 inhabitants in 1622 it was one of the largest villages in Holland, and it maintained this level until around 1680 at least.[58] However, it does not seem to have grown much, if at all, after the 1620s and so seems to have followed a similar economic tempo to the towns in North Holland. Despite being about as far from the sea as it was possible to get in this area, Graft had very strong maritime links – as did the neighbouring De Rijp, another of the largest villages in the province. In 1680 about a third of the men of Graft were at sea, and it is estimated in 1635 that seamen possibly made up as much as half the male working population.[59] If the employment provided by the merchant fleet, fishing and, later, whaling was vital for the village in this period, it was not the only important economic link with the sea. Although neither ships nor fishing boats were built in the village, unlike De Rijp, Graft was heavily involved in the production of rope, sail cloth and fishing nets.[60] When *schippers* and hands working on canal boats and other inland water transport are taken into consideration, then not much is left of any direct involvement with agriculture in this particular village. Villagers owned land and were involved in dairy farming and cheese making, but such activities were not the economic and social heart of the village. Graft was clearly unusual through its size but in its pattern of employment, especially the strong links with the sea, it was typical of the villages of North Holland.

The non-agrarian character of many rural settlements in Holland is further exemplified by the villages of the *Zaanstreek* which were becoming the chief centre of the shipbuilding industry in the Republic during the first half of the century. The success of Zaandam and its surrounding villages dealt a fatal blow to the industry in the small towns of North Holland, although at mid-century both Rotterdam and Amsterdam were still formidable presences in this field. Apart from shipbuilding, people in the Zaan area found employment in a wide range of manufactures associated either directly with the construction and fitting-out of ships and boats or more generally with the needs of the merchant and fishing fleets. The ubiquitous wind-driven sawmills used to prepare timber for the shipyards were prominent visual symbols of the importance of manufactures in this area, but the timber trade supplying these mills and shipyards was also important. Similarly, the production of sails and sailcloth, rope and cables grew with the importance of the main industry, and the baking of ships' biscuits satisfied a rather different maritime need. The Zaan villages were, however, a special case by any yardstick and might be better considered as part of the urban sector, in social and economic terms in any case. On the other hand, it has been calculated that in the Noorderkwartier[61] less than 20 per cent – very roughly – of the adult working population were employed in agriculture during the first half of the seventeenth century;[62] even taking into account the towns of the area plus the *Zaanstreek*, this figure indicates that a substantial proportion of the undisputably rural population must have worked primarily in manufactures or transport and other services.

Another way of looking at the nature of rural society in the maritime region is through the availability and distribution of a wide range of services outside the towns. An investigation of the availability of such services (religious, economic, medical, legal, cultural and educational) in the various settlements of North Holland in 1811 showed that, whereas a more or less full range of such provision could be found only in the towns (plus Zaandam), thirteen villages were not far behind, and another nineteen (including Graft) ran these latter close. Even the remaining centres (with two exceptions) had significant religious, economic and medical services.[63] It seems likely that this picture was more or less typical of the rural sector in the maritime region as a whole. Admittedly this evidence is for such a late period that its relevance for the first half of the seventeenth century can be legitimately doubted, but North Holland had in fact become more rather than less agrarian, as well as distinctly less prosperous, in the century and a half after about 1650, and it is at least plausible to assume that most, if not all, of the services available in 1811 were already present during the years of prosperity rather than emerging in the later period of economic decline. Indeed, there may well have been some falling away in the facilities available: there were booksellers in six villages just after the middle of the seventeenth century, but later only Zaandam seems to have had one.[64] In this earlier period all villages had the services of a minister of the Reformed Church and many also had provision for the religious needs of local baptists and increasingly of catholics as well. Economic services were even more vital to the functioning of these villages in the seventeenth century than they were to be later, and must certainly have been present. For the rest, there were five schools in the banne Graft (a rural administrative division covering Graft itself and neighbouring villages or hamlets), two of these in the village itself, and the services of five barber-surgeons were available at one point, not to mention the indispensable midwives, and there was even an academically trained doctor in the village later in the century.[65] In addition to these educational and medical services, there was an orphanage and quite a respectable array of provision for the poor, so in this village at least all the services noted in 1811 were already present a century and a half earlier. Indeed, there seems little reason to doubt that a rich infrastructure of this sort was already in place throughout the maritime region by the middle of the seventeenth century.

North Holland was no doubt unusual even by Dutch standards: the geographical conditions and the nature of the agriculture of the area forced a high proportion of the population to find a living outside farming. In South Holland, and a *fortiori* Zeeland and Friesland the agrarian economy probably played a more important role, though still on a highly commercialised basis and with a relatively high percentage of the working population employed outside agriculture in comparison with most of the rest of Europe. Figures are lacking for Friesland in the seventeenth century, but in 1749 only about 44 per cent of the total working population was employed in agriculture, around a quarter in manufacturing and nearly 20 per cent in trade and transport.[66] These figures include the towns, but also some poorer districts with a heavier concentration on arable farming than most. Other districts had a more marked orientation to the sea, provided considerable numbers of *schippers* and sailors for the Holland merchant and fishing fleets, and in general displayed a social profile not dissimilar to that of their fellow (West) Frisians in North Holland. Comparable figures are lacking for Zeeland but what evidence there is suggests that the highly developed and market-orientated agriculture of the province played a more important part in its economy than the agrarian sector did in Holland. Similarly, the level of urbanisation, though high in contemporary terms, was significantly lower than for Holland, and may even have been in decline after an initial urban boom in the last years of the sixteenth century.[67]

South Holland had for centuries been more of a solid land mass than the north of the province, though still with much more extensive lakes and other areas of water than is now the case, and it was not without its own water-control problems. A greater proportion of the land could be used for farming than was the case in Holland north of the IJ, and agriculture here was highly commercialised, prosperous and just as closely integrated into the commercial economy of the province as was the case in the north. The evidence suggests that a rather higher proportion of the working population in the countryside here was involved in agriculture than in the north. However, this situation seems to have been the result of a considerably higher degree of urbanisation in South Holland and a consequently sharper division of labour between town and countryside. In 1622, almost 62 per cent of the population of South Holland lived and worked in the towns of the area (i.e. the twelve *stem-hebbende*[68] plus The Hague), as opposed to about 34 per cent in North Holland.[69] The level of urbanisation probably continued to increase – certainly in South Holland – until the middle of the century and even later. It should also be noted that even these remarkable figures are an underestimate as they do not include the smaller towns of South Holland; for the latter area, thus, the figure for the proportion of the population living and working on the land is somewhat inflated. The towns in the south of the province were large, numerous and politically powerful; they did not leave much room for the survival of any significant rural manufacturing sector to compete with that of the towns. There was no equivalent in South Holland of the *Zaanstreek*.

The whole of Holland was marked by a high population density by the standards of the time and by excellent communications. Not only were the towns practically within sight of each other, they were connected by an increasingly dense passenger-barge network. This was a system of horse-drawn boats using specially constructed and dedicated canals, operating to a fixed time-table, and enabling passengers to be transported more quickly and comfortably than they could be by road. The network was not restricted to Holland but it was far denser in this province than anywhere else in the Republic. The peak years for the construction of the new canals, the *trekvaarten*, were 1632–47 and 1656–65, so at least the first boom lay within this period, though the completion of the system had to wait till after the mid-century.[70] An oblique testimony to the importance of this new means of transport is the frequency with which pamphlets commenting on contemporary affairs used the device of a *schuit-praatje*, that is, a fictitious conversation between disparate characters on one of these passenger-barges. Another consequence of the density of settlement and good communications in the province is the absence of the large and very violent criminal bands which sporadically terrorised the countryside in other areas of the Republic;[71] apparently hardly any area of Holland was isolated enough to allow the activities of such gangs, and there were fewer and fewer places for them to hide out as the countryside of Holland was progressively tamed. In general terms this seems to have been true of the maritime region as a whole: the criminal bands found their most fruitful areas of operation in the east and, particularly, in North Brabant with its quasi-frontier status and oversupply of the human dregs of warfare.

A persistent theme of this section is the high degree of integration of the rural sector into the social and cultural mainstream of the maritime region.[72] Although Holland in particular can be regarded as being dominated by its towns – and this was certainly true politically – the countryside was no more a colonial territory of the towns in religious or cultural terms than it was economically. However, it did lack a full range of provisions especially of the rarer or more expensive cultural goods. Just as certain economic services could only be found in the towns so in education Latin Schools, let alone illustrious schools or universities, were only found in the towns. On the other hand, almost nowhere in the region were country people far removed from at least a small town and the services which it could provide and, as we have seen, communications were good and continued to improve during this period. The material benefits of the Republic's prosperity reached the countryside and were enjoyed by the more prosperous farmers and village notables; how far cultural goods followed the same route is less clear. The study of the spread of a print culture, for example, is only beginning even for the towns and perhaps lack of evidence means that not a great deal can ever be known about the penetration of printed materials into the cultural life of the villages and rural areas in general. It does seem that levels of literacy in the countryside were almost as high, if not as high, as those in the towns, but what was read by whom remains obscure. What can be said with some confidence is that the large numbers and wide distribution of printing presses in the Republic – no town of any consequence was without its printers, and even the smallest and least prosperous of towns appear to have had the use of at least one printing press – meant that people living in the countryside had relatively easy access to books and other printed materials.

In terms of religion, too, the countryside in Holland and the maritime region as a whole shared to a considerable extent the pluralism that was characteristic of the towns. The nature of Dutch religious pluralism and its social consequences will be discussed later in this chapter, the point here is to emphasise that there was no sharp or clear divide between town and country in this regard. There were differences: whereas the Reformed Church was uniformly dominant in the towns by the middle of the century, the religious geography of the countryside of this region was distinctly more patchy, with some areas moving strongly towards protestantism while others remained largely loyal to the old church. Decisions one way or another seem to have been made in the first few decades after the Revolt, influenced very strongly by local factors, after which the situation stabilised so firmly that the pattern established by the early seventeenth century was reflected in the religious geography of the region three centuries later.[73] However, although catholicism remained strong in some rural areas, it was not the case of a religiously conservative countryside facing a predominantly protestant urban sector; over much of the region the Reformation was at least as successful in the villages as it was in the towns, though by the standards of most of the rest of Europe this is perhaps not saying a great deal. At a time when in most parts of Europe the overwhelming majority of the population belonged to the dominant official church, this was practically nowhere the case in the Republic, and certainly not in the maritime region. Even in the solidly protestant Graft, the Reformed Church could only embrace about two-thirds of the population by the second half of the century, with the rest being shared almost equally between baptists and catholics.[74] How typical this situation is for the rural areas of the maritime region as a whole remains unclear: besides the concentrations of catholics which have already been mentioned there were also some areas of local baptist strength, notably in Friesland. Even where the membership of the Reformed Church was as high as it was in Graft, however, this still meant that upwards of a third of the population were dissenters of one sort or another, and so in this vital aspect of social experience life in the villages of the region was similar to that in the towns.

The situation in the land provinces was markedly different, though not perhaps quite as different in some respects as might have been expected. Only in comparison with the maritime region does it seem relatively traditional; in terms of the greater part of Europe, the region was highly urbanised and its agricultural sector very much geared to the market. In this period in particular the region as a whole could not avoid being profoundly affected by the proximity of the dynamic economy of neighbouring Holland. What distinguished the land provinces from the maritime region was their conservative and defensive reaction to the economic and social challenges of the time; traditional social structures and patterns proved distinctly more resilient here than elsewhere in the Republic. Smallholders continued to be an important element in rural society, and the social influence of the nobility – notably as regards its grip on political power at provincial as well as local level – remained much greater than in the maritime region, and indeed greater that its economic strength might seem to justify.[75]

It must not be forgotten that in the period from the 1580s to the middle of the seventeenth century the rural areas of the land provinces suffered even more than the towns from the effects of constant warfare. After the first decade of the Revolt, the maritime region remained almost entirely free from the direct effects of the war against Spain, but the land provinces had to suffer the disruptions caused by the movement of troops from both sides year after year, with the Twelve Years Truce as the only lasting remission from this constant pressure. So while in Holland the rapid commercialisation of agriculture could take place relatively undisturbed from the late sixteenth to the middle of the seventeenth century, the ability of farmers in the land provinces to compete was hindered by the effects of the war. Quite how disruptive this must have been is difficult to estimate: on the one hand, the essential resilience of the agrarian economy even in this region has been convincingly demonstrated; but the combination of almost uninterrupted warfare over such a long period of time with a set of economic factors which were hardly entirely favourable in other respects must have made things particularly difficult until the ending of the Eighty Years War. Especially hard hit in this respect was North Brabant as it formed the main border region between the Republic and the Spanish Netherlands, but on the other hand the area round Maastricht which came under Dutch control in the last decades of the conflict does not seem to have suffered too badly from the war in this period.[76]

Outside Holland, the proportion of the population living in towns by the second half of the seventeenth century was around 27 per cent,[77] which is low only by the standards of the leading province. In the Veluwe quarter of Gelderland urbanisation reached 32 per cent by the middle of the century, and in Overijssel 28 per cent by 1675, though if sixteen very small towns are included the figure rises to 43 per cent – but these latter with a total population of only around 10,000 were hardly even respectable villages by Holland standards, and are perhaps better regarded in this context as being part of the rural sector.[78] Whatever the precise figures might be, the contrast with the more developed areas is clear. Nevertheless, the region was not bereft of towns, many of them with a more impressive history than the majority of those in Holland. It is unclear whether the province of Utrecht should be regarded as one of the land provinces or not, but its capital, the city of Utrecht, had long been one of the largest towns of the northern Netherlands with a population of about 25,000 on the eve of the Revolt, and by the middle of the seventeenth century this had risen to 30,000. So it was a substantial town even by Dutch standards, but was largely lacking in the economic and demographic dynamism shown by the towns of Holland in this period. Stagnation, at best, marked the other leading towns of the region: Nijmegen with a population of about 12,000 in mid-century had just surpassed its pre-Revolt numbers; Zutphen with 7,000 at the same time had similarly more than held its ground; but Zwolle, Deventer and Kampen were all under 10,000 at this point and thus substantially lower than they had been in the middle of the previous century.[79] The towns of the land provinces in general were economically and demographically static at best, and the balance between urban and rural population in the region did not change significantly during this period.

Another marked contrast with Holland is the persistence, even proliferation, of smallholders scraping a living by a variety of means in some of the poorer areas of the region. Such impoverished cottagers later drew the textile industry to Twente (in Overijssel) and North Brabant in search of the cheap labour which had disappeared in Holland as a result of the agricultural changes. More generally, the pull of the Holland market encouraged what might be called defensive farming, the primary aim of which was diversification to avoid disaster rather than maximising profit. Also the mass of free-holding *eigenerfden* remained a relatively undifferentiated group compared to the polarisation that was taking place in the same period in Holland, and throughout the region they remained socially and politically under the thumb of nobles and rural notables. This is somewhat surprising, given that the economic power of the nobility in these provinces was not particularly impressive. In this predominantly agrarian region the nobles as a group did not own a great deal of land, yet in the period just after the Revolt the nobles and other local notables were able to consolidate their political dominance in these provinces to form what were effectively new oligarchies, and use this acquired position to their collective social and economic advantage. An extreme example of this process was the ability of the *ambtsjonkers* in Gelderland to control not only the political and judicial systems but also, and inevitably, tax-collection – to their own considerable advantage.[80] As far as the social position of the nobles is concerned, the sharpness of the contrast with the maritime region is blurred by the situation in Friesland and Groningen, where the political and social influence of the nobility – or rather quasi-nobility – in the country districts was considerable, and certainly much greater than in Holland. However, in Friesland the old nobility had to share power even in the countryside with urban oligarchs, and the *jonkers* in Groningen, although they controlled the States of the Ommelanden, had rather more of the character of a rural regent group than of a nobility rooted in a feudal past as was the case in Overijssel and Gelderland – and even in the province of Utrecht.

The land provinces were not homogeneous: there were important differences in agriculture and social arrangements not only between provinces but within them as well. Drenthe was notoriously poor and backward, but recent research has revealed a rather more nuanced picture. The economy of the province was almost purely agrarian, but was profoundly affected by the growth of the Holland market and responded flexibly to the opportunities it offered as well as to the problems it caused. Around the middle of the century, it seems that something like two thirds of the population were farmers and a further quarter smallholders, leaving room for only a rather small artisan or service sector in the countryside.[81] About 60 per cent both in number and in value of farms were in the hands of *eigenerfden*, and there seems at this time to have been relatively little differentiation socially within this group. In this small province the role of the nobility was distinctly limited, and there is also little sign of the polarisation between increasingly prosperous farmers and their work-force which characterised the rural sector in Holland. In Gelderland and Overijssel, the nobility owned a substantial proportion of the land, especially considering their small and falling numbers: in Salland and Twente (quarters of Overijssel) nobles owned nearly 30 per cent of cultivated land at the beginning of the century, and in the Veluwe the comparable figure was about 20 per cent around mid-century.[82] There were marked differences between these areas in other respects, however: the proportion of farmers owning their land varied greatly from area to area and was, for example, much lower in Salland than in Twente. The figures also make clear that even in the areas where leasehold was predominant, ownership of the land was far from being exclusively in the hands of the nobility; an important role was played by individuals and institutions from the towns of the region. In Groningen, in a curious development, rents were in the process of becoming fixed and nominal and leases effectively permanent, partly because the province itself had become the biggest landowner through taking over the property of the old church after the province went over to the side of the Revolt.[83]

In North Brabant a difference of quite another order needs to be taken into consideration. While there were pockets, and sometimes quite large pockets, of catholics in rural areas throughout the eastern provinces, in States Brabant the rural population remained loyal to the old church, or had returned to it by the time the Republic was able to take effective control of the area – which was only fully possible after 1648. So here a homogeneously catholic population was alienated from much of the political and social superstructure: they were governed by a tiny elite of protestants, the church buildings were taken over by the Reformed Church, and there was no legal or formal place for the priests and others who attended to their spiritual needs. However, for most of the first half of the century this northern part of the ancient duchy of Brabant was partly under Spanish control and partly disputed territory, only after the Treaty of Münster could the full consequences of the status of a Generality Land become apparent. The experiences of western and eastern parts of States Brabant in these years were significantly different: Breda was taken by the Dutch in 1590 and this effectively brought the surrounding area (the barony) under States control, and in general the western part of northern Brabant was within the sphere of influence of the States General before the Truce of 1609 – although it fell to the Spanish again in 1625 and was only retaken in 1637. In contrast, the Meierij of 's-Hertogenbosch, which covered most of the eastern section of what was to become States Brabant only began to be brought under Dutch control after 1629. Both areas had in common the disadvantage of being in the front line throughout these years, with significant disruptive effects on the social life of the whole area. The Lands of Overmaas (around Maastricht) which came finally into Dutch hands in 1648 also suffered the disadvantages of being a disputed territory of considerable strategic significance, and problems with competing jurisdictions continued here for a number of years after the settlement of 1648. However, while this area experienced difficult times in the 1630s[84] it was largely free of major military operations except when Maastricht was actually under siege, and seems to have recovered from the war quite quickly.

Although the countryside of the land provinces provides a considerable contrast to the dynamic agricultural sector in Holland, it would be misleading to give the impression of unchanging conservatism. It appears economically and socially traditional only in comparison with the altogether exceptional developments that were taking place in the maritime region; when set against the situation in most of rural Europe at this time, even these relatively conservative areas of the Republic show a considerable, and perhaps already decisive, break with the past. One way in which such developments can be illustrated is in the distribution of services at village level. Although more restricted in scope than in the countryside of North Holland, the range of services provided in many of the villages in the Veluwe, for example, is quite impressive by any other standard. Unfortunately, the available information on this subject comes from the middle of the eighteenth century, and can only be an uncertain indicator for the situation a century earlier. Standard services at this later date included a church with a resident minister, a school, and a range of economic specialisms, but medical facilities – i.e. the presence of an apothecary or barber-surgeon – were rare. Such evidence suggests that even in some poorer provinces of the Republic the country areas could expect to have a respectable supply of goods and services – an inn and a shop, along with a resident carpenter, miller, tailor, shoemaker, and blacksmith, while bakers, brewers, weavers and roofers were far from unusual.[85]

Village schools only provided elementary education at best, but many of the towns in the land provinces had Latin Schools of distinguished pedigree, and universities were founded in the region. Even if Groningen is set aside as belonging essentially to the maritime region, the university of Utrecht, founded in 1635 and soon with a reputation second only to that of Leiden, can be considered as being part of the land provinces. Harderwijk in Gelderland was founded just at the end of this period, in 1648, but never amounted to much – except perhaps as an institution where a doctorate could, in effect, be conveniently purchased – and the Generality Lands produced illustrious schools in Breda and 's-Hertogenbosch but neither can be said to have thrived. In general, it can be suggested that this region was becoming – if it had not already become – culturally subordinate to Holland, but it would be wrong to imply that their cultural identity had been swamped, and it would be rash to suggest that they failed to make their own distinctive contribution to the cultural life of the Republic.

In broader cultural terms, one aspect of society in which the land provinces and States Brabant showed distinctive characteristics was in witchcraft beliefs and, in particular, witchcraft prosecutions. Whatever may have been the case as regards belief in witchcraft, as far as prosecutions and convictions for witchcraft are concerned the contrast between the maritime region and the land provinces was stark in this period. There had never been many witchcraft trials in Zeeland, and in Holland such cases ceased in effect to be brought to court after the 1590s, as chances of gaining a conviction became remote after the *Hoge Raad* ruled that torture should not be used in such cases.[86] In Friesland, the *Hof* (central court of appeal) maintained a firm grip on the judicial system, and here too witchcraft trials and convictions were kept to a minimum. In the Ommelanden of Groningen, however, the independent judicial power of local notables allowed a small but vicious epidemic of prosecutions in the first half of the century, and Gelderland and North Brabant too proved susceptible to witchcrazes.[87] The disruption brought by the war to political and especially judicial processes in the land provinces clearly played a part in enabling suspicions of witchcraft to develop into prosecutions and convictions. Another contributory factor is that well-publicised campaigns against supposed witches in neighbouring areas of the Holy Roman Empire must have given a spur to existing fears and suspicions in these areas. Also the ending of prosecutions in Holland does not necessarily mean that belief in magic and witchcraft was less deeply rooted in popular perceptions here than elsewhere in the Republic; it indicates no more – but also no less – than that those in control of the judicial process were no longer willing to respond to accusations of witchcraft coming from below. It does not even mean that the social elite themselves had ceased to believe in the reality of witchcraft and magic, rather that they had come to believe that, in the main, those who were actually accused of such crimes were clearly innocent. So the disparity between the maritime region and the land provinces is possibly to a significant extent the result of different attitudes and actions among the regents, and the lawyers and doctors who advised them, rather than of more profound social or cultural factors.

Yet it might be tentatively suggested that the contrast between the two regions goes deeper than differences in the attitudes of their respective social elites. It is becoming clear that belief in magic and witchcraft persisted long after the end of the seventeenth century in at least parts of the land provinces.[88] On the other hand, in Holland it seems that the capacity of such notions to arouse anxiety and distress had declined significantly by the early seventeenth century. The patterns of belief, and even accusation, persisted but the social response was very different. Most cases involving witchcraft which came before the courts here after about 1600 were actions for defamation by the accused, which is a dramatic indication of how different attitudes in practice were in Holland – elsewhere in Europe such actions tended to be virtually suicidal, as they were all too likely to be transformed into a trial and conviction for witchcraft. Perhaps in some ways even more significant is the approach of the Reformed Church. In Amsterdam at least witchcraft accusations within the Reformed congregation were primarily regarded as disturbances to the harmony of the community of worshippers rather than as evidence of a satanic conspiracy against christianity; the consistory disciplined the accusers and tried to reconcile them with the accused, in no case did it press for the prosecution of the alleged witches, and the disciplinary measures employed were invariably relatively mild.[89] It is hard to avoid the conclusion that the root of the differences in such matters between the regions was social: the highly urbanised west, with an increasingly commercialised agriculture, had other things to worry about than whether it was a satanic spell that was preventing the butter from churning. While the land provinces were still to a considerable extent living in the enchanted world attacked later in the century by Balthasar Bekker, Holland had already moved decisively into a reality where trade cycles and international price levels were more important than the imagined spells of marginalised old women.[90]

The emergence of a religiously diverse society

The Dutch society which emerged in the course of the years between the 1580s and the middle of the seventeenth century was marked by a diversity of religious beliefs and practices together with a degree of religious toleration which was altogether unusual for Europe at that time. However, it must be stressed that even in the Dutch state toleration in particular was always a somewhat uncertain, even fragile, phenomenon: the rights of religious minorities were protected more by custom than by law, and there were distinct limits to its formal operation. A relatively tolerant society emerged as a result of a particular set of historical developments and through a series of pragmatic decisions by the holders of political power at every level; it was not chosen as a desirable state in itself, but as preferable to religious strife and, particularly, to religious persecution. The regents may well have preferred to have been able to live in a religiously homogeneous society; they certainly did not want a return to the bloody persecution of dissenters which had disfigured Spanish rule in the Netherlands. Yet the existence of an official church continued to be seen as necessary for political and social cohesion, and was indeed probably essential to the sense of national identity which was emerging in the Republic during these years. The Reformed Church became the church of the state, if not the state-church, the old church was regarded as an alien institution, and catholic worship continued to be formally proscribed.

The religious diversity of the Republic was most apparent in the towns, particularly those of Holland, but this religious pluralism developed in the context of the dominance both religiously and politically of the Reformed Church. Although in the early years after the Revolt there seems to have been considerable religious diversity among the regents of Holland and Utrecht,[91] and probably elsewhere also, gradually the grip of the Reformed Church on the political system grew more firm, and certainly after the crisis of 1618–19 political office at every level was confined – formally at least – to members of the official church. The civil authorities took over ownership and control of the property of the old church after the Revolt, but they employed it for the benefit of the Reformed Church: the churches themselves were devoted to reformed worship, and the revenues from land and other property were used to pay the salaries of the ministers of the new church. So the Reformed Church, with membership of the regent group confined to its adherents and able to use the buildings and revenue of the old church for its own ends, was in a strategically powerful position within Dutch society, especially after the triumph of self-proclaimed orthodoxy in 1619. If the leaders of the church did not always sound confident of their place in Dutch society, this was probably because of the enormous gap between the situation they had to live with and their ideal of what a true christian community should be. Confessional homogeneity was regarded, in principle, as the only proper relationship between religion and society in both protestant and catholic Europe at this time, and from the later sixteenth century onward the process of confessionalisation was increasingly making such conformity a reality for most states. In the Republic, the forces of confessional conformism may have been able to defeat and expel libertines and remonstrants from the Reformed Church, but they could not impose the beliefs and practices of the dominant church on society as a whole to the exclusion of all rivals.

One reason why a certain level of co-existence between different religious groups was possible in the towns of Holland was that the membership of protestant sects was not large enough to be a real threat to the leading position of the Reformed Church. Admittedly, up to the end of the sixteenth century the number of openly committed adherents of the new church in many towns remained quite small, but subsequently there was little doubt that it would be able to establish itself as the church of the majority of the population in Holland and in the Republic as a whole. It is significant that the critical religious conflict of the early seventeenth century concerned the nature of the Reformed Church, not whether it would in fact be the dominant church. Its chief rivals on the protestant side were the various mennonite groups, but while the strict congregational discipline which marked them proved attractive to many of the more zealous, it was also likely to set distinct limits on their possibilities for growth. The mennonites' division into a number of competing and often quarrelling sects similarly helped to restrict their influence on urban society. The catholics too were comparatively weak in the towns of Holland, and when reliable figures begin to emerge around the middle of the century they are nearly everywhere well below 20 per cent of the total population. In Amsterdam catholics formed about 20 per cent of the population in the later seventeenth century, in Rotterdam about 15 per cent, while in Haarlem around 1620 about 12 per cent of the population were active members of the old church – though this probably excludes many who at this early date were not fully committed but were more catholic than not.[92] Thus the dominant position of the Reformed Church was never really threatened either from the side of the protestant sects or from that of the old church. However, the religious situation, especially in the larger towns with their growing populations and large-scale immigration, remained confused and unstable for many years after the Revolt. The established pattern of religious loyalties had been shattered by the Revolt, and in its immediate aftermath only a minority of the population was either convinced calvinist or committed catholic. Only slowly did the mass of the urban population move definitively into one camp or the other; as late as the second decade of the century, as much as half the population of Haarlem seems not to have belonged to any church.[93] Given this apparent volatility it is not surprising that reformed leaders were far from complacent, and indeed seem to have been inclined to something like paranoia about the threats they saw as assailing their church from all sides.

If, in the end, the position of the Reformed Church in the towns proved to be relatively secure, the situation in the rural areas was much more varied, and took distinctly longer to resolve itself. In broad terms, it can be said that local and even regional diversity in the degree of conversion to the new and loyalty to the old church was very great, and that the eventual outcome was a patchwork of differing loyalties. While the Reformed Church became dominant in most areas of the countryside throughout the Republic, a combination of survival and resurgence made the Catholic Church the majority faith in some districts. States Brabant was the most prominent case: here the whole province, having undergone the Counter-Reformation while still under Spanish control, remained steadfastly catholic even after it came belatedly under Dutch rule. Elsewhere, catholicism survived in pockets – sometimes quite substantial pockets – in Gelderland, Utrecht and even in Holland. An explanation for this peculiar pattern of the religious geography of the Netherlands was put forward by Rogier in his authoritative history of Dutch catholicism in the early modern period: he argued that choice for or against the Reformation at the village level was taken at a very early date in accordance with a range of local factors and that these decisions once taken very largely determined local religious loyalties for the next three hundred years. While there is force in the central argument, there is also an apologetic element which oversimplifies the process of catholic survival and underestimates the lability of the religious situation at the village level for many decades after the Revolt. Catholic survival involved at least two processes: first there had to be a traditionalist resistance to religious change, but this could only come to anything in the long term if it could be turned into a conscious choice for a clearly defined catholicism. The general collapse of catholic pastoral care in the decades after the Revolt meant that it was only when the Holland Mission began to work effectively that the potential offered by this conservative reaction could be turned into a positive commitment to catholicism, and it was many years into the seventeenth century before this was the case. By the middle of the century the network of catholic missions was more or less complete, and it was at this point that the pattern of religious loyalties in the countryside can be said to have stabilised.

On the other side of the religious divide, the progress of the Reformation in the countryside was also a relatively slow process, especially in the east. In part this was a consequence of the war: much of Gelderland and Overijssel continued to be a major theatre of the war until at least the 1630s and this hampered the process of reformation at local level. Only as war receded could protestantism in its reformed state become a reality in many villages of these provinces. In States Brabant a combination of military and political circumstances prevented protestantism from making any headway before the middle of the century – and this turned out to be far too late. A more general problem facing the Reformed Church was the difficulty of finding personnel of an acceptable standard as regards learning and piety, particularly for some of the often unattractive and certainly less well paid rural parishes. In the early years after the Revolt the lack of university-trained ministers was acute, and many churches had to be satisfied with – at best – so-called *Duitsche clerken*, lacking in formal educational qualifications and not always theologically or even morally reliable.[94] Again the situation improved only slowly, but by the middle of the century the new universities were finally turning out enough candidates to satisfy the church's needs, at least with regard to theological training. Whether this successful professionalisation of the ministry was necessarily a good thing for either church or community is quite another matter; it certainly contributed to a renewed clerical dominance in the church which was more than somewhat at variance with the initial impulse of the Reformation. For many decades, however, it remained difficult to find even barely adequate ministers for many villages and this slowed up the process of bringing the reformed faith to the rural population in many parts of the Republic.

By the end of this period, the situation in the countryside would appear to have stabilised, though there may have been a continuation of the erosion of baptist strength. Mennonites were a significant force in a number of country areas, especially in North Holland and Friesland, but they seem to have passed their peak by the middle of the century. They are a reminder, however, of just how varied the religious situation often was, even in the countryside. Although villages tended to be predominantly either catholic or protestant, there were usually significant catholic minorities in protestant villages and vice versa, and frequently the presence of baptists further complicated the issue. Even in the thoroughly reformed Graft, as has been noted, fully one third of the population did not belong to the dominant church,[95] a situation not too dissimilar to that found in many of the towns of Holland. Nevertheless, it is probably true to say that by the second half of the seventeenth century rural life was distinctly more homogeneous in religious terms, especially in the land provinces, than was the case in the towns. In villages where the reformed were dominant, co-operation between religious and secular authorities could produce a situation that was more oppressive for minorities than either in most of the towns or in the areas of catholic dominance. In the latter, the protestant civil authorities often found it difficult to operate effectively against the interests of the catholic majority, and protestant minorities in States Brabant, for example, often found themselves the scapegoats for the structural conflict between the civil power and the population at large.[96]

More important than crude – and generally unreliable – statistics for an understanding of how religious pluralism worked in Dutch society is qualitative evidence about the relationships between the various religious groupings. Setting aside the often vicious nature of the conflict between remonstrants and contraremonstrants – which was essentially internal to the Reformed Church and profoundly affected by political factors – what is most striking about the Dutch situation is the relative absence of overt hostility between catholics and protestants, or between different protestant churches. This statement might seem at first sight somewhat surprising as at one level such hostility was very evident: the literature of religious polemic was a mainstay of publishing throughout the century, with the legal system very much favouring the champions of the Reformed Church over either catholics or radical dissenters. Nevertheless catholics and dissenters were able to publicise their views and, indeed, one prominent genre of the time was orthodox refutation of heterodox publications. It cannot be denied that the tone of such polemics hardly breathed toleration or indicated any genuine desire to understand the positions of opponents. Conventional thinking in Europe at this time still regarded religious unity as essential for the stability of society, and religious division as threatening the break-up of the state. To judge by the tone of religious polemic alone, this was indeed a society riven by profound and irreconcilable religious differences and must have been close to breakdown. This was, in fact, far from the case: underneath this surface turbulence and disharmony, the various religious groups appear to have co-existed with remarkably little friction.

One explanation for this lack of conflict might be that contact between the adherents of the various churches and sects with those of different beliefs was minimised, somewhat along the lines of the *verzuiling* (pillarisation) that became characteristic of Dutch society in the later nineteenth century. In such a system the members of the various 'pillars' (*zuilen*) – there were socialist and liberal as well as confessional *zuilen* – not only went to different churches but different schools and universities, voted for their own political parties, joined confessional trade unions and even – later and perhaps more in principle than in practice – listened to their own radio and watched their own separate television stations. It has recently been suggested that something like this radical separation of different confessional groups developed in the Republic in the course of the seventeenth century.[97] Were this the case, it might well help to explain why religious pluralism caused so little trouble. However, the available evidence does not provide much support for this suggestion.

Of course, the religious situation in the Republic was uncertain and labile for many years after the Revolt. This upheaval had destroyed the disciplinary system of the old church and, until the Reformed Church was firmly established as the majority confession, the religious loyalties of much of the population are obscure. Confusion, scepticism and even indifference were widespread, especially in the towns, and it was perhaps only towards the middle of the seventeenth century that a more settled pattern of religious commitment emerged. The catholic priesthood had disappeared from most areas of the new state, leaving the population with little or no pastoral guidance for thirty or forty years. The Counter-Reformation had made little impact on the northern Netherlands by the time of the Revolt and so, while many people may have regretted the loss of traditional religious practices, they would have had only an inchoate idea of what the old church stood for. Most people in this position would eventually end up in the bosom of the Reformed Church just because it was the official church, but the process seems to have been a slow one. The precise nature of the new church remained to an extent uncertain, or at least in dispute, until the synod of Dordt tied it to a particularly rigid version of calvinist orthodoxy. Up to this point there was some possibility that it would become a broad and inclusive church as far as both theology and ecclesiology were concerned. The victory of the dogmatic precisians over the libertines and the remonstrants also meant that it was unlikely that the church would ever be able to embrace the whole of the Dutch population. In the towns of Holland the situation was complicated by the large number of immigrants who arrived in the course of these years. Not all of the immigrants from the southern Netherlands were protestant, but most of them probably were and these brought a commitment to a fully realised faith that was somewhat alien to the religious atmosphere of the northern towns. However, immigrants from elsewhere in the Republic or from Germany may have been just as religiously unformed as most of the urban population they joined, and some were certainly catholic. It may well have been this mobility together with a lack of clear commitment among the urban population which damped down the likelihood of religious conflict – except within the official church.

This early fluidity slowly developed into a more well-defined pattern of religious allegiance as the century wore on, but the situation did not become entirely rigid. The baptists lost a lot of ground by the late eighteenth century despite their freedom from persecution; it seems likely that much of this decline took place before the end of the previous century but this timing remains speculative. The Reformed Church steadily increased its grip on the population as a whole in the course of the century; again the tempo is unclear and certainly varied from place to place, but the church was clearly much stronger in 1650 than it had been in the first two decades of the century. At the same time, the Catholic Church increased its active membership also. This process was largely a matter of the reintroduction of catholic pastoral care: the Holland Mission steadily built up its network of mission-stations to replace the old parish system and had almost complete coverage by the 1650s. This new institutional framework brought many of the previously uncommitted or indifferent back to the old church. (The total number of catholics in the Republic was, of course, also increased significantly by the addition of North Brabant and part of the Overmaas to its territory.) The religious life of the Republic was also continually being stirred by the emergence of heterodox groups of varying radicalism from the non-dogmatic collegiants to the quakers and the followers of Antoinette Bourignon, Jean de Labadie and other spiritual zealots around the third quarter of the century.

Such continuing religious instability was not conducive to the development of any form of *zuilensysteem* and, indeed, a wide range of common educational, cultural and even political institutions were shared by all denominations. All schools and universities came, at least nominally, under the aegis of the official church but there is no evidence for any widespread exclusion on religious grounds. It may have been irritating for catholic parents to have to send their children to a school which was at least nominally reformed, but they were not excluded from it by any religious test. In most villages there would have been only one school and it would have been attended by reformed, catholic and mennonite children. Richer catholics may have sent their sons to seminaries and catholic universities abroad, but below this level there was scant religious apartheid in education. Similarly, cultural life in the Republic did not run on separate confessional lines: indeed, it can be argued that this was one area where a distinctive Dutch character, superseding confessional differences, can be discerned. Publishing in general, literature more broadly, art and the theatre were all areas where reformed, catholics and baptists were engaged in a frame of reference which all held in common. The baptist Vondel remained at the centre of Dutch literary life after his conversion to catholicism, and his plays continued to be staged in the Amsterdam *Schouwburg*. The uncertainty that continues over whether or not Vermeer was a catholic suggests just how relatively unimportant the question was for the nature and quality of his art.

It is true that the values of the Reformed Church were in significant ways privileged above all others; this was not a society where all religions were equal. There were, for example, distinct limits to the extent that views directly challenging the beliefs of the orthodox reformed could safely be published. The Reformed Church was the official church and there was an intimate, though not always smooth, relationship between it and the civil authorities; and members of the church came to have a monopoly on political and public office. This was not the case in the early decades after the Revolt but catholics and dissenting protestants were steadily squeezed out of the regent group and, after the political defeat of the remonstrants, the political elite was restricted to the ranks of the reformed. However, if catholics and baptists were excluded from political power, so were the vast majority of the reformed as well. The Republic was an oligarchy and all outside the regent elite – reformed as well as catholic and baptist – were in more or less the same boat politically. Moreover, it was the regents, despite being exclusively recruited from members of the Reformed Church, who held the theocratic instincts of that church in check and ensured a certain level of toleration for both dissenters and catholics. Both in practical and ideological terms – to a significant extent the nascent Dutch identity was not only protestant but specifically reformed – the orthodox calvinists were a privileged group in Dutch seventeenth century society, but the systematic favouring of one religious group above all others is not the same as pillarisation.

It may well be true that there was a growing tendency towards endogamy in the separate religious groups; this would not be surprising, especially as the confessional picture became more stable in the middle years of the century. The available evidence is suggestive but inconclusive. Nevertheless a more persuasive picture is provided by the various confessions living together cheek by jowl under and through common institutions. Only the Jews in Amsterdam with a whole range of social and educational institutions separate from those of christians,[98] would seem to constitute a distinct pillar in Dutch society – together perhaps with the protestants in States Brabant.

Rather than being the result of an early version of *verzuiling*, religious toleration in the Republic can be seen as a consequence of the beginnings of a process of secularisation, or at least of what looks like a rejection of the confessional state.[99] Despite the victory of a narrow interpretation of reformed theology at the Synod of Dordt in 1619, the Republic was never a calvinist state in any more than a very limited sense. Nor was the Church able to impose its concept of the godly community on society as a whole. The practice of the regents with regard to dissenters and catholics implied that there were other – secular – priorities for the civil authorities at all levels than the imposition and preservation of religious purity. Whether such attitudes are traced to the indifference to dogma typical of erasmian humanism, to a reaction against the horrors of the religious persecution of the Spanish period, or to a pragmatic response to the difficult problems that they faced in having to deal with a religiously diverse population, the result was that prosperity and internal peace were consistently given priority over the pursuit of unity in religion.

It might have been possible to bring the great majority of the population of the Republic into the new church if it could have been constructed on the lines of a broad church. The so-called libertines in Utrecht (in the 1580s and 1590s) have been seen as aiming at a church which could embrace the whole urban community, while their calvinist opponents insisted on doctrinal purity and disciplinary rigour.[100] Many of the regents who supported the remonstrants at a rather later stage were similarly hoping to promote social and political stability through a church which would be inclusive rather than exclusive. The calvinists on the other hand were trapped by their own recent history as a persecuted church of true believers: their years 'under the cross' led them to demand high standards of their membership in both what they believed and how they lived their lives. As long as such strict standards were enforced, the Reformed Church was going to find it difficult to become much more than a puritan sect.

The Reformed Church was, indeed, caught between two aims which in retrospect appear incompatible: to remain a church of the godly and become the church of the majority of the Dutch population. The movement for a *nadere reformatie* which gathered force in the 1620s and 1630s was striving to achieve a closer approximation of a truly godly society both by means of greater personal piety and through imposing the moral values of the pious on the rest of the community. On the other hand the practical necessities of nurturing a reformed community in Amsterdam led to an unmistakable decline in the standards of congregational discipline in the course of the seventeenth century.[101] Although the zealots of the reformed community had a considerable influence on the civil authorities at all levels from the States General through the provincial states to town and village magistrates, it cannot be said that they were able to harness them for their own purposes. As has been argued, when push came to shove the regents in the main proved to have other priorities than the promotion of the godly society. Moreover, whatever the success of the *nadere reformatie* at a personal level in intensifying the spiritual life of a select band of believers, its ability to affect the mores of Dutch society as a whole was minimal. Indeed, the only way in which the Reformed Church could become the church of the majority was by lowering its standards and, in effect, ceasing to be a gathering of saints.

It is possible that at the village level and in some of the smaller towns something approaching a calvinist society could be created – though it remains to be demonstrated that this was ever the case – but this was a much more difficult task in the larger towns and in the biggest towns of Holland, especially Amsterdam, it was altogether impossible. The conditions were simply unpropitious for the creation of a religiously homogeneous society. At the beginning of this period, during the first decades after the Revolt, membership of the Reformed Church was tiny, the multiplicity of baptist and other protestant sects already large, and a majority of the population was probably more catholic than anything else. During the struggle for survival against the Spanish, Oldenbarnevelt and his supporters did not want to stir up unnecessary domestic problems – indeed, they tended to blame religious fanatics for many of the setbacks the Revolt had had to face. In addition, the cosmopolitan atmosphere of the trading towns and the high level of immigration made a heavy-handed approach inadvisable, and it was commonly argued that toleration attracted economically desirable immigrants to the Republic. There was also the problem caused by the printing press. Nowhere in Europe were presses so thick on the ground as in the Republic: this was especially the case in Holland, and here also the decentralisation of political authority meant that it was difficult to exercise effective central control over what was published.[102] Add to this a pervasive distrust of clericalism among the regents and a more general revulsion against the recent severe persecutions which were still lively in the collective memory, and the likelihood that this vigorous and varied society might be turned into a northern Geneva seems remote.

Dissenting protestants may have made up only a rather small proportion of the overall population of the Republic, but they were both visible and vocal. The membership of the various mennonite groups may well have already begun to fall towards the end of this period, but baptists were no longer generally seen as a threat to the social order. They had gained a reputation as industrious, with strict moral standards, and consequently trustworthy in business; they thus tended to be seen as in many ways model citizens, especially of a commercial society. The remonstrants, after their defeat at Dordt, eventually set up as a separate church. Their numbers were never great, and in this respect they were never a threat to the official church, but the new church attracted a notable proportion of its membership from the better-off and the better-educated. Its strength lay in the Holland towns and here it developed a certain social cachet – although serving regents could not be open members. The remonstrant seminary in Amsterdam acted as the academic spokesman of this highly respectable dissenting voice in Dutch society and, in general, the contribution of remonstrants to the cultural life of the Republic was out of all proportion to their numbers. The collegiants were another dissenting voice with a considerable presence intellectually in the middle years of the century. They had no fixed membership and so were and are difficult to define, but this again was a grouping which was particularly attractive to adventurous spirits within the educated elite. The peculiar circumstances in the Republic enabled such groups to gain relatively unfettered access to the printing press; although there was censorship on religious and political grounds, it was far from watertight, and in any case the bounds of the permissible were certainly wider than the defenders of religious orthodoxy found acceptable.

Although visitors perhaps exaggerated the extent of religious diversity to be found in the Republic, the presence of mennonites, remonstrants and others profoundly affected Dutch society in both town and country. Daily experience of living in harmony with members of different confessions or at least no more inharmoniously than with members of their own church – contradicted powerful inherited attitudes and assumptions. Such preconceptions did not die, and they were encouraged by religious leaders on the orthodox side, but they seem to have been submerged under the necessity of living and working together. Of course, protestant dissenters could be seen as unthreatening in part because, besides being for the most part eminently respectable, there were not too many of them. The catholics certainly failed the latter test: not only were there a lot of catholics, for most of this period no one could be sure just how many of them there were – nor, possibly, could many people themselves be absolutely sure whether they were catholic or not. One of the elements in the situation which eased the strain – or limited the threat – of catholic numbers was that a large proportion of them were in the Generality Lands and in country areas in the east well away from the centres of political power. The catholic presence in the voting towns of Holland was considerable but, as has been seen, perhaps not so large as to alarm the protestant majority. There was friction, on the other hand, between the new protestant authorities and the catholic majority in States Brabant though the extent of this only became clear in the later part of the century. There were also violent reactions even in Holland to clumsy enforcement of the laws banning catholic worship in areas of catholic strength in the countryside,[103] but there is little or no evidence of real problems in the towns. There does not appear to have been any significant hostility between protestants and catholics, and the civil authorities mostly chose to turn at least a partially sighted eye to clandestine catholic worship.

The new catholic organisations were also to some extent convenient for the regents: the network of missions produced a framework which enabled the catholics to look after their own poor, sick and aged, thus reducing the burden on public poor relief and welfare systems. In some towns municipal poor relief was effectively in the hands of the Reformed Church, and in all towns the civil authorities, staffed exclusively by calvinists (at least after 1618), worked closely with the Church in the provision of help to the poor. In these circumstances, the Catholic Church feared that, at best, the catholic poor could be discriminated against by protestant authorities and, at worst, that they would come under pressure to convert. This gave catholics a strong incentive to provide for their own, but in any case a separate welfare system was a vital expression of confessional soldarity for them as well as for calvinists.[104] For their part, the civil authorities were in the main only too happy to have the responsibility for the welfare of a substantial – and often poor – section of the population taken off their hands, even if this meant giving a sort of semi-public recognition to catholic institutions.

In what sense, then, can this be seen as a calvinist society? The Reformed Church was the official church of the Dutch state: it took over the existing church buildings, its ministers were paid by the civil authorities from the income from secularised church property, and its members had a monopoly of political office by the third decade of the century at the latest. When the seven provinces came together in the *Grote Vergadering* (Grand Assembly) in 1651, they declared that the three elements which held the Republic together were the Union, religion and the army (*Unie, Religie, Militie*). Thus, along with the political union between the provinces and the army which defended that union against foreign enemies, the religion the provinces had in common – and, of course, by this was meant the Reformed Church – was seen as a vital unifying element. This was a realistic position to take for, although loyalty to the reformed faith did not unite all the people of the Republic, it did unite the ruling elites throughout the country; there were considerable differences between the provinces but this at least they held in common.[105] By the second half of the century over a half — and possibly as much as two-thirds by the end — of the population were members of the official church; more importantly, the proportion of reformed in the towns, and especially in the politically crucial towns of Holland, was markedly higher than in the country as a whole. Where it mattered politically, the Reformed Church was dominant: in the regent group in general and in the voting towns of Holland.

Ideologically, too, the reformed were able to a considerable extent to put their stamp on the Dutch sense of identity. It is a curious circumstance, given that so many of the Dutch were catholics or protestant dissenters, that the related ideas of the Revolt as a calvinist uprising and the Dutch people as essentially reformed took such firm root in the course of the seventeenth century. The attitudes and perceptions of the reformed section of the community to a significant extent shaped public life in the Republic. The civil authorities were always extremely sensitive to the prejudices and susceptibilities of the Reformed Church and, for example, routinely banned publications which it found offensive. The unremitting hostility of the Reformed ministry to the catholics helped to ensure not only that anti-catholic legislation remained in force but that, on paper at least, it was steadily made more rigorous. Yet appearances were often deceptive, and the impact of the Reformed Church on Dutch society was far more limited than at first seems to be the case. Not only was the influence of the non-reformed section of the Dutch population considerable — and very resistant to reformed pressure — but more fundamentally a pervasive secularisation modified and to some extent undermined the religious vision of the purpose of social life. Secular values were coming to dominate public life by the end of this period, not least in the evident preference for toleration over religious purity; the Dutch Republic was never to become the Geneva of the north.

Change and continuity

The comparatively rapid changes discussed in this chapter so far are one aspect of Dutch society in these years, but there is another which was just as important though it has not perhaps attracted quite the same attention as the former. Alongside the new there was the old; innovation was balanced by the persistence of inherited attitudes, customs and manners. In the end these are as much cultural as social in nature but the distinction between the two, although useful analytically, is artificial. Ways of thinking, feeling and perception find their expression in social action of one sort or another, indeed are what gives social life its meaning and coherence for individual actors; conversely, social formations, actions and experiences also shape the ways in which people experience the world. The Dutch in the seventeenth century were caught between change and continuity, between innovation and tradition, and only by realising this can a fuller understanding of the society of the period be gained.

The changes discussed here can be viewed in two main time-frames: the long sweep from the late Middle Ages to the second half of the seventeenth century, and the shorter burst of very rapid development between the Revolt and about 1650. The longer-term economic transformation produced profound and irreversible effects on the society of the northern Netherlands, and the length of time involved enabled social attitudes and cultural forms more or less to keep up with structural change. There were inevitably stresses involved in adjusting to such far-reaching developments: indeed, the Revolt itself might well be seen as stemming in a great part from a disequilibrium between the priorities of the Habsburg political system and a society with very different needs. Similarly, although it has become distinctly unfashionable to suggest such links, nevertheless it is clear that the weakening of loyalty to the established church and the progress of the Reformation in the Netherlands before the Revolt were inextricably linked to the processes of economic and social change which were affecting the whole region so powerfully in the course of the first half of the sixteenth century. Revolt and Reformation were certainly two very considerable disruptions to social continuity, but at a more fundamental level the process of adaptation to change seems to have gone rather more smoothly, encouraging a somewhat sentimental nostalgia for times past rather than any profound sense of alienation.

The more explosive period of development between the Revolt and the middle years of the seventeenth century is a very different matter: both the scale and the pace of change were of a different order than before, and the problems of adjustment for individuals and groups were consequently markedly greater. In these circumstances, it would not be surprising if there was a considerable lag betwen the changing situation and a relative conservatism in cultural and social attitudes and perspectives. In other words, while on the one hand a new form of society was being rapidly created in the Republic, or at least in Holland, more traditional attitudes and perceptions remained powerful. This uneasy conjunction between a largely capitalist economy and a culture which was to an important extent still entrapped in pre-capitalist ways of understanding the world gives the Golden Century much of its particular flavour. In Dutch seventeenth century society the magical universe confronted capitalist materialism, and the conflict between the old Europe and the emergent new is the key to an understanding of many social and cultural phenomena which fail to fit the stereotypes too often used to explain the Dutch Golden Age.

Both more people and a high and growing proportion of the population of the Republic were living in towns in this period, though this phenomenon was much more marked in the maritime region than in the land provinces. However, urbanisation was already well developed before the Revolt, so this expansion of the towns was in the main an intensification of a well-established trend rather than a fundamental change in the structure of society. The scale of urban life changed as the towns became larger, but this explosive urban growth was largely restricted to Holland and even here was perhaps limited to the largest and most successful towns. In this case, the element of continuity was strengthened by the relatively stable economic structure of the towns: despite their sometimes massive expansion, their inhabitants continued to do the same sort of work in the same sort of conditions as before. Craft production was still dominant in most economic sectors and where entrepreneurs were converting craftsmen to mere employees, as in the textile industry in Leiden and Haarlem, this process had already started before the seventeenth century. It seems that town life, while on a larger scale, remained very similar to what it had been before the post-Revolt boom.

The rise in size of the towns in the maritime region was significant, of course, as was the increase in prosperity which accompanied this growth. Although detailed comparative studies are lacking, it seems that one major effect of growth and increased prosperity was an expansion of the middling groups in society, not just in numbers but more importantly as a proportion of the total population. Relatively prosperous traders and merchants were an important part of this middling group, but a growth of the service sector – education, law, medicine, transport, food and drink – also made a significant contribution to its expansion. What is well established is that as far as Holland is concerned the wealthiest citizens of the biggest towns were much richer than their counterparts had been in the previous century; but it is also clear that members of the economic elite in Amsterdam, say, were rich on an altogether different scale from the most prosperous people in the smaller towns of the province. The leading families in Edam, Monnikendam, Purmerend, Gorinchem and Den Briel among the voting towns of Holland had a distinctly different life style from that enjoyed by the richest citizens of the bigger towns, and in general social life in these and other small towns even in this province may not have changed all that much between 1550 and 1650. At the other end of the social scale there was a proliferation of unskilled and semi-skilled employment in the docks of the port towns and in transport more broadly, but only in the great textile towns did the growth of a proto-proletariat upset the inherited balance of society. In Leiden and Haarlem the increasing control of the cloth industry by the merchant-drapers depressed the status of skilled workers such as weavers, fullers, shearsmen and dyers to hired labour which was, moreover, extremely vulnerable to the cyclical downturns which plagued the industry. Here the strength of the guilds had never been very great, and elsewhere the years of expansion appear to have weakened the ability of such craft organisations to enforce their own regulations.

Population growth also encouraged the creation of new social organisations or at least the development of existing institutions in different ways. The disappearance of the charitable foundations of the Catholic Church placed a heavy burden on municipal provision rather than on the Reformed Church, though the latter played its part as far as its own members were concerned at least. On the whole it would seem that municipal provision for the poor, sick, orphaned and old was adequate to the demands made on it, though the system was likely to teeter on the verge of collapse from time to time – in these prosperous years enough funds to deal with the most pressing problems at least were usually found somehow. As far as most recipients were concerned, public welfare provision was intended to be supplementary to the support given by family, craft organisation, or personal networks; for the poor, or for broad swathes of the economically vulnerable in hard times, life was a matter of getting by through a combination of earnings where possible and an accumulation of small-scale hand-outs and practical assistance from a variety of sources. The public welfare system of the larger towns, however exemplary by the standards of the time, could never have coped if it had been expected to supply all the population's welfare needs; the inhabitants of the towns were dependent on a range of grass-roots institutions and informal social sub-systems for mutual aid. Towns were divided into quarters (*wijken*) and sub-divided into neighbourhoods (*buurten* or *gebuyrten*). The town militias (*schutterijen*) were organised and recruited on a *wijk*-basis, which gave some expression to *wijk* solidarity, but just how widespread the *buurten* system was and quite how it worked remains obscure. In some towns at least there was a more or less formally constituted neighbour-hood organisation with an elected head responsible, among other things, for the maintenance of good order. It is not clear to what extent this system survived the rapid growth of the towns, and the even more rapid turnover of the urban population in the boom years of the early seventeenth century.[106] In the land provinces the difficulties of the towns in this period came not from rapid growth but from the economic stagnation or decline associated with the disruptions of war which continued almost to the mid-century. Here the social and economic structures remained stable, except for the effects of the decline of long distance trade and of certain manufactures. In the towns of this region, continuity was distinctly stronger than change, though it was more a desperate clinging to a past that was rapidly disappearing than a confident reliance on an established position.

In large areas of the Dutch countryside, mostly in the maritime region, change was an even more dominant theme. Whereas an economic structure based largely on craft production persisted in the towns, the intrusions of the market were in the process of replacing what was left of a traditional rural society with one with most of the markers of a capitalist system. The increasing importance of specialised production for the market was squeezing out the smallholder and smaller farmer. An important supplement to the income of the poorer rural households had been fishing and wild-fowling but the great drainages and recla-mations of the period very largely cut away this prop. A class of rural labourers emerged which was mainly dependent on paid work, and this was complemented by the consolidation of a stratum of capitalist farmers, both free-holding and tenant. A fairly wide range of transport and other services was provided by an increasingly significant service sector. Together these developments were well on the way to trans-forming the social structure in the countryside by the middle of the seventeenth century. Although the main lines of these changes had been evident from at least the beginning of the sixteenth century, in the shorter term the pace accelerated during this period and the concentration of the great drainage projects in these years was both a consequence of and a further boost to this process.

Rural society in the land provinces was more conservative socially, but could not avoid changes in response to economic pressures, chief among which was the growing power of the Holland market. Seen in the long term, both the economic position of the nobles and the proportion of the land owned by them were declining, and the free-holding *eigenerfden* were growing stronger, though this fundamental social shift was to an extent disguised by the concentration of political power after the Revolt in the hands of a noble oligarchy, which tended to become even more exclusive by the middle of the century, in most of these provinces. Here too there are some signs of the emergence of a rural proletariat in the form of cottagers with far too little land to support a family and thus dependent on whatever paid work they could find. In this region the war was an ever-present reality throughout most of this period, and this meant even more disruption to the rural economy than to that of the towns. Yet, this was neither a backward nor a stagnant region, and the resilience of the agriculture of the Lands of Overmaas in the face of recurrent warfare is a reminder of its underlying social and economic potential. Nevertheless, the period between the Revolt and the middle of the seventeenth century, which brought an unprecedented boom to Holland and rapid growth to the rest of the maritime region, presented the land provinces and North Brabant with persistent economic problems and it was all they could do not to fall too much below the position they had reached at its beginning.

Family life, courtship practices and marriage were relatively little affected by the short term changes of the period, but the longer term social transformation was inevitably much more disruptive of traditional patterns of behaviour. Indeed, some at least of the developments which have been regarded as emerging in the early modern period, or even as essentially the product of the economic miracle of the seventeenth century, may well have had their roots in the later Middle Ages. Urbanisation, the penetration of the market into every nook and cranny of the economy, and the long-term impact of the Reformation combined to put in question customs and mores which had evolved in a distinctly different society. One of the more prominent developments was the rise of the conjugal family to dominance in both the towns and the maritime region more generally.[107] Here in particular, however, the timing is uncertain, and the true extended family has been progressively relegated to a time when the lack of demographic evidence gives room for speculation; as soon as demographic materials emerge they indicate something that looks more like the conjugal family than anything else. However, such analyses are primarily and unavoidably concerned with patterns of residence, and say little about the sense of family, how far the awareness of family connections went, and how strong such ties were. A quasi-modern pattern of residence does not necessarily mean that the sense of family and its obligations had already become as attenuated as it was to become only much later.

The predominance of the conjugal family was associated with the development of a peculiar marriage system in western and northern Europe, whereby couples only married when they were economically in a position to set up a separate household. This tended to make age at marriage very sensitive to economic circumstances. When reliable evidence for the average age at marriage in the Republic starts to become available, usually only for the later years of the seventeenth century, it is already high and also rising. For men the age at first marriage in the second half of the century was roughly between 25 and 29, and for women very slightly lower. This failure to use a considerable portion of women's potential fertility kept the birth-rate down and, in combination with high infant and child mortality, severely restricted the rate of natural increase of the population as a whole. The high level of urbanisation probably increased the death rate because of the unhealthy living conditions in the towns, and possibly lowered the birthrate – though this may have been an illusion caused by the high numbers of young people who were drawn to work in the towns but who returned to the countryside to marry and have their children. In this demographic regime, slight changes in the mean age of marriage – of women specifically – could have a dramatic effect on long-term population trends. However, in the main reliable evidence only becomes available for the time – after the middle of the seventeenth century – when the population was already beginning to adapt demographically to less favourable economic conditions. The earlier population growth, both in the long term and during the shorter boom between the Revolt of the middle of the century, must have been made possible by rising fertility or falling mortality (or a combination of both, of course). There is no evidence for any significant fall in mortality, nor any reason to believe that the northern Netherlands were any more healthy in the sixteenth century and early seventeenth century than in the periods before or after.[108] Consequently it seems inescapable that more favourable economic conditions encouraged or allowed a somewhat earlier average age at marriage during the period of growth in the sixteenth century, and thus a robust natural increase of the overall population, and that a continuation of this natural increase was supplemented during the shorter-term expansion from the end of the sixteenth to the middle of the seventeenth by a significant wave of immigration.

The central importance of family and kinship ties for the individual was challenged and to some extent weakened by the religious and social upheavals of the period. The economic changes in the countryside and migration to the towns, sometimes over a considerable distance, must have weakened the bonds of family both for those who moved and those who remained. In addition, the growth of protestantism and the establishment of a religiously pluralist society in the Republic not only rendered the link between community and religion problematic, but also made religious choice more a personal than an inherited, family-determined matter – at least for a time. Yet it would be a mistake to underestimate the resilience of the family even under such pressures. Distance was rarely an insuperable obstacle in the Republic, certainly not in Holland, and only service with the VOC seems to have caused men to disappear entirely from the ken of their relatives. Families often moved together, and this was true also of wider kin groups, and ties of kinship were perhaps particularly important for the migrant faced with an uncertain future in an unfamiliar environment. It was certainly difficult, even in the towns, to find a replacement for family support in hard times. The effects of religious change were perhaps more corrosive but only in the short term; after the brief flurry of religious choices in the first decades after the Revolt, patterns of confessional loyalty stabilised and the second generation in the main stayed with the choices their parents had made. Religion became again something one was born into, determined by family and background, and only for a small number of exceptional individuals was it still a personal choice – though the relatively open nature of Dutch society made it much easier for such people to take their own road than was the case elsewhere in Europe.

Traditional courtship practices proved to be resistant to the efforts of both religious and political authorities to suppress what they regarded as either immoral or disorderly, often both. Urbanisation and the economic modernisation of the countryside in almost half the Republic, however, was more corrosive of inherited customs, which were already coming to be seen as curious and even 'folkloric' by educated observers in the towns. Although the evidence comes from a slightly later period, it is worth noting that States Brabant showed a particular attachment to such practices as the Low Countries' version of the French *veillée*. Unmarried women and girls would gather together in the evenings to spin, weave and the like, with the young men of the village joining them in a variety of ways determined by strict local rules.[109] Neither the catholic clergy nor the protestant ministers of the area approved of such practices but the latter lacked all authority with the overwhelmingly catholic population of the countryside, and the former were weakened by their unofficial status. As far as the civil authorities were concerned, there was a whole range of regional customs that they may well have disapproved of but could not act against without further alienating the people they governed who already questioned their legitimacy (as protestants and, often, as outsiders).

More generally, the campaign against popular customs which the educated elite regarded as immoral, disorderly or just uncivilised already had a long history in the various provinces of the Republic. There is evidence from the late Middle Ages onwards of attempts to suppress those aspects of popular culture which looked too much like excuses for licence or violence, notably carnivalesque ceremonies and charivaris. They persisted in the countryside but were more easily suppressed in the towns, though their disappearance here only seems to have opened up the way for other practices to take their place. By the seventeenth century the *kermis* had taken over as the occasion for the sort of behaviour among the populace as a whole which almost automatically brought condemnation in sermon and moralising tract. Despite centuries of propaganda, at the end of this period the Dutch everywhere still ate too much and danced too much at weddings, and displayed far too much freedom of association between the sexes – even bundling seems to have continued in many places. This latter custom, or rather group of related practices, which caused the moralists particular distress, was a semi-public ceremony in which courting couples spent at least part of the night together in or on the young woman's bed, though with – in theory at least – strict limitations on the nature and extent of the sexual activities which were permitted.[110] Also this was by modern standards a violent society – at least at the level of popular behaviour – men carried knives and used them particularly under the influence of drink. The faster-growing Holland towns had a relatively mobile population with large numbers of recent immigrants drawn by booming economic conditions, and who were probably only imperfectly integrated into urban society. The institutions developed to maintain public order in the much smaller towns of an earlier period came under great strain in these years of expansion. On the other hand the middling groups in the towns grew as fast if not faster than the unskilled or casual sectors, and it was this section of society that was beginning to internalise the values of order, discipline – especially self-discipline – and considerably more restrictive sexual mores. Nevertheless, violent behaviour in particular was more a normal part of burger life than the conventional picture might suggest, and rioting – usually led by the lower ranks of the middle classes – was a common form of what might be called the informal politics of the time, and could take on horrifying forms as it did with the murder and ritual dismemberment of Johan and Cornelis de Witt in the tense summer days of 1672. This particular incident, however, was a product of a hysterical reaction to the invasion of that year with a French army apparently about to overwhelm the defences of Holland, and was in its extreme nature wholly untypical: politically inspired violence against the person was relatively rare in the Republic, mobs usually attacking property rather than people. It was perhaps only after the end of the century that the civilising campaign had any real impact on sexual mores, and it seems to have taken even longer for it to have any effect on the levels of violence let alone on the consumption of alcohol in the Republic. The introduction of tea and especially coffee in the later seventeenth century may have had a greater 'civilising' effect – on the levels of violence if not on sexual practices – than a century of sermons.

Dutch society in the period of rapid growth between the late 1580s and the middle of the following century was caught between contradictory forces and in consequence suffered from a persistent ambivalence that has perhaps been underplayed. Historians have differed over whether a new type of society emerged in these years which embodied a decisive break with the past in cultural terms as well. It has become almost an orthodoxy in recent years to emphasise the persistence of traditional moral and social values, and in particular the way that religion continued to form the basis for contemporary conceptions as to the nature and purpose of society. An alternative interpretation has tended, in contrast, to stress the process of secularisation that was clearly starting to affect profoundly the nature of public life in particular. As is so often the case, the answer is that both these views of Dutch society are true, though the relative weight of the traditional and the secular varied greatly from place to place, and also between various social groups. The rapid economic growth of the period was indeed producing a new form of society, but conservative instincts remained strong. There seems to have been a marked difference in tempo between economic and cultural developments, and the emergent capitalist society was informed by a culture which at all levels was to a great extent still devoted to other and older values. Dutch society, and most particularly that in Holland, was torn between two value systems; the social stress which resulted from this ambivalence was not as great as it might have been if the ground had not been prepared at least to some degree before the Revolt. Society in the northern Netherlands had already undergone considerable change in the late Middle Ages and early sixteenth century, and at a less frenetic tempo than in the later boom period. This more measured pace of development had allowed attitudes and perceptions to adjust to the changing situation to such an extent that it could well be argued that seventeenth century culture was essentially the culture of the late medieval town writ large. The late medieval towns were even in the Netherlands to an extent alien islands in a largely aristocratic culture,[111] but the process of urbanisation meant that the towns became steadily more important and by the seventeenth century they were the dominant voice, at least in the maritime region of the Republic. Holland in particular was an urban society with even the rural areas taking on urban characteristics.

Yet even in Holland the tension between two contrasting worlds was evident, with important consequences for the religious history of the period. The strength of the new might be sought in the degree of support for the Reformation. However, only a minority in the Republic were committed to one of the various forms of protestantism by the beginning of the seventeenth century so it can be argued that the eventual choice for the Reformation was the expression of the political needs of a ruling clique rather the expression of powerful social forces. Setting aside the overestimation of the extent to which the civil authorities could be independent of broader social forces which this argument involves, it might be suggested that the lack of commitment to the old church which was also evident at this time is an even more important pointer to the changing needs and perceptions of a broad swathe of the population of the region. Most significant of all was the ability of the Dutch after the Revolt to live in a religiously pluralist society with relatively little conflict between the confessions – the only violent and dangerous division took place within the Reformed Church. Catholics, reformed and a rich variety of dissenting protestants lived side by side in the towns and even in the villages of the maritime region with remarkably little friction. The towns in particular proved to be an environment where the public or private exercise of a number of confessions caused few mutual problems. In the villages the reformed took over all the existing churches which created problems for the other confessions at first – the parish church was usually the only building suitable for worship in a village, and it was also the most powerful symbol of communal solidarity making the reformed take-over a threat to the sense of community. Friction seems to have subsided quite quickly, however and, though villages were divided along religious lines, a substantial degree of communal solidarity seems to have been maintained. Nevertheless the desire for the sort of communal identity which confessional unity could bring remained powerful. In a sense the remonstrant controversy was a clash between two contrasting routes to religious unity, and in the wake of the contraremonstrant success at Dordt there was an attempt to stamp the Republic more firmly with a reformed signature. This failed, but the need to have an official religion was never seriously questioned and the Reformed Church became the religion of the state and of the ruling elite. The Republic was a protestant, indeed a reformed, state and this was an important element in Dutch identity in the seventeenth century, despite the fact that this was to a significant extent a fiction. Within a pluralist society an atavistic yearning for religious unity remained powerful – and would keep catholics from a full place in national life for centuries to come.

Similarly, capitalism was not entirely successful in displacing the established system of moral values: to an extent it could be a smooth continuation of the commercial morality which developed in the towns before the Revolt, but its implicit values had never gone unchallenged and did not do so in the seventeenth century. A case in point is the question of usury. This was a concept developed for an economic and social system where the lending of money at interest was regarded as the unchristian exploitation of the weak. In the capitalist world of the Republic, lending and borrowing were vital parts of business — which is not to say that the poor were not still the victims of unscrupulous moneylenders. Yet many theologians and moral thinkers until well into the seventeenth century were still living in the pre-capitalist moral world, as is shown by the adverse reaction to the publication of Salmasius' treatise on usury in 1638.[112] The torrent of sermons and tracts stressing the moral dangers which were felt to accompany the economic boom of the period are in part, of course, conventional christian warnings against wealth and too great a concern for the things of this world, but they also can be seen as reflecting a pre-capitalist moral system. On the other hand, of course, as Weber and others have argued, the insistence on a disciplined life of service to God's will and a condemnation of idleness and waste could provide a religious ethic compatible with capitalism.[113] The constant tension between purism and accommodation, conservatism and innovation which marked the Reformed Church in this century — gomarists against arminians and later voetians against cocceians — can in an important sense be seen as an expression of a fundamental ambivalence towards the new society that was emerging in the Republic in this period.

Despite the persistence of cultural forms which were rooted in a very different society, in the end it was clear that toleration would successfully resist the pressures for confessionalisation, commercial values would prove acceptable, and in general that the forces of innovation would prove to be stronger than those of tradition. Dutch society was able to adjust to the rapid changes of the years between the Revolt and the middle of the seventeenth century because the ground had been thoroughly prepared. The new society of this period was to a large extent the urban society of the pre-Revolt years writ large. The commercial towns of the Netherlands in the late medieval period developed both a trading practice and a commercial ethic which fore-shadowed that which triumphed in the seventeenth century. In the rural sector too, the intrusion of the market had been modifying practices and perceptions for over a century before the take-off of the Republic's economy. So in a sense much of what appears as innovation in attitudes and perceptions, and in culture generally, was building on a powerful indigenous traditon, and Dutch cultural ambivalence stems not from the struggle of innovation versus tradition but from the clash of two conflicting traditions in the northern Netherlands.

Notes

1   Jan de Vries and Ad van der Woude, *The First Modern Economy. Success, failure, and perseverance of the Dutch economy, 1500–1815* (Cambridge, 1997).

2   E. Taverne, *In 't land van belofte in de nieue stadt. Ideaal en werkelijkheid van de stadsuitleg in de Republiek 1580–1680* (Maarssen, 1978).

3   Though some parts of the Republic, such as most of States Brabant, did not
 ‑   come definitively under its control until the very end of this period.

4   See M.P. Gutmann, *War and Rural Life in the Early Modern Low Countries* (Princeton, 1980).

5   The importance of the garrison to the life of the town is one of the themes of the recent study of Bergen op Zoom under the Republic: Charles de Mooij, *Geloof kan bergen verzetten* (Hilversum, 1998).

6   De Vries and Van der Woude, *The First Modern Economy*, 52.

7   De Vries and Van der Woude, *The First Modern Economy*, 53.

8   Pieter Priester, *Geschiedenis van de Zeeuwse landbouw circa 1600–1910* ('t-Goy-Houten, 1998), 56.

9   De Vries and Van der Woude, *The First Modern Economy*, 54–5.

10   Hubert Nusteling, *Welvaart en werkgelegenheid in Amsterdam 1540–1860* (Amsterdam/Dieren, 1985), 15–16.

11   Hubert Nusteling, 'De bevolking: van raadsels naar oplossingen', *Geschiedenis van Dordrecht van 1572 tot 1813*, ed. Willem Frijhoff, Hubert Nusteling and Marijke Spies (Hilversum, 1998), 80–2.

12   R. Willemsen, *Enkhuizen tijdens de Republiek* (Hilversum, 1988), 99–100.

13   Paul Holthuis, *Frontierstad bij het scheiden van de markt. Deventer: militair, demografisch, economisch*, 1578–1648 (Deventer, 1993), 106–9.

14   A.M. van der Woude, *Het Noorderkwartier* (Wageningen, 1972), I, 111.

15   J.A. Faber, *Drie eeuwen Friesland* (Wageningen, 1972), II, 413–15.

16   De Vries and Van der Woude, *The First Modern Economy*, 54–5.

17   De Vries and Van der Woude, *The First Modern Economy*, 56.

18   See Olwyn Hufton, *The Prospect Before Her. A History of Women in Western Europe*, vol I 1500–1800 (London, 1995), 70–98.

19   S. Sogner, 'Popular contacts between Norway and the Netherlands in the Early Modern Period', *The North Sea and Culture (1550–1800)*, ed. Juliette Roding and Lex Heerma van Voss (Hilversum, 1996), 185–98.

20   J. Lucassen, *Naar de kusten van de Noordzee. Trekarbeid in Europees perspektief 1600–1900* (Gouda, 1984).

21   J. Briels, *Zuid-Nederlanders in de Republiek 1572–1630. Een demografische en cultuurhistorische studie* (Sint Niklaas, 1985).

22   Hubert Nusteling, *Welvaart en werkgelegenheid*, 44.

23   De Vries and Van der Woude, *The First Modern Economy*, 75.

24   David Beck, *Spiegel van mijn leven. Haags dagboek 1624*, ed. S.E. Veldhuijzen (Hilversum, 1993).

25   There could be no more than one university per province but, in addition to Leiden, some of the larger Holland towns had institutions which provided a similar level of education but could not award degrees.

26   Willemsen, *Enkhuizen*, 55–7.

27   C.M. Lesger, *Hoorn als stedelijk knooppunt. Stedensystemen tijdens de late middeleeuwen en vroegmoderne tijd* (Hilversum, 1990), 97–9, 177–8.

28   Lotte van de Pol, *Het Amsterdams hoerdom. Prostitutie in de zeventiende en achttiende eeuw* (Amsterdam, 1996).

29   Jan de Vries, *Barges and Capitalism. Passenger transportation in the Dutch Economy (1632–1839)* (Wageningen, 1978), 26–9.

30   Taverne, *In 't land van belofte*, 147–54.

31   Taverne, *In 't land van belofte*, 223–34.

32   A.Th. van Deursen, *Plain Lives in a Golden Age. Popular culture, religion and society in seventeenth-century Holland* (Cambridge, 1991), 59.

33   J. Steendijk-Kuypers, *Volksgezondheidszorg in de 16e en 17e eeuw te Hoorn* (Rotterdam, 1994), 107.

34   Anne E.C. McCants, *Civic Charity in a Golden Age. Orphan Care in Early Modern Amsterdam* (Urbana/Chicago, 1997).

35   Willem Frijhoff, *Wegen van Evert Willemsz. Een Hollands weeskind op zoek naar zichzelf 1607–1647* (Nijmegen, 1995) gives a fascinating account of an orphan brought up in the orphanage of the small town of Woerden who made good by becoming a minister of the Reformed Church.

36   Van Deursen, *Plain Lives*, 122–4.

37   The offically prescribed curriculum in Holland is outlined in E.J. Kuiper, *De Hollandse 'schoolordre' van 1625* (Groningen, 1958).

38   G. Groenhuis, *De predikanten. De sociale positie van de gereformeerde predikanten in de Republiek der Verenigde Nederlanden voor ± 1700* (Groningen, 1977), 169.

39   On the social rôle of the universities, see Willem Frijhoff, *La société néerlandaise et ses gradués, 1575–1814* (Amsterdam, 1981).

40   A. Frank-Van Westrienen, *De Groote Tour* (Amsterdam, 1983); for an example, see Lodewijck Huygens, *The English Journal, 1651–1652* (Leiden, 1982).

41   Florike Egmond, *Underworlds. Organized crime in the Netherlands 1650–1800* (Cambridge, 1993), 188–9.

42   Van de Pol, *Het Amsterdams hoerdom*, 222–4.

43   Van de Pol, *Het Amsterdams hoerdom*, 52–7.

44   Theo van der Meer, *Sodoms zaad in Nederland. Het ontstaan van homoseksualiteit in de vroegmoderne tijd* (Nijmegen, 1995); D.J. Noordam, *Riskante relaties. Vijf eeuwen homoseksualiteit in Nederland, 1233–1733* (Hilversum, 1995).

45 Van de Pol, *Het Amsterdams hoerdom*, 103–4.

46 See the discussion in Manon van der Heijden, *Huwelijk in Holland. Stedelijk rechtspraak en kerkelijke tucht 1550–1700* (Amsterdam, 1998), 263.

47 Van de Poll, *Het Amsterdams hoerdom*, 274–84.

48 Ben Albach, *Langs kermissen en hoven. Ontstaan en kroniek van een Nederlands toneelgezelschap in de 17e eeuw* (Zutphen, 1977), 19–22.

49 Van Deursen, *Plain Lives*, 125–6.

50 See on 'book culture', Marika Keblusek, *Boeken in de hofstad. Haagse boekcultuur in de Gouden Eeuw* (Hilversum, 1997).

51 Utrecht and Groningen are difficult to place in the simplified division of the Republic into maritime and land regions. For a combination of economic and social factors, it seems on balance most appropriate to regard Utrecht as part of the land provinces and place Groningen in the maritime region, but such choices have an unavoidable element of the arbitrary about them.

52 This specialisation and its consequences were first explored by Jan de Vries, *The Dutch Rural Economy in the Golden Age 1500–1700* (New Haven, 1974), esp. 224–35.

53 Owner/operators of boats or ships.

54 J.L. van Zanden, *The Rise and Decline of Holland's Economy. Merchant Capitalism and the Labour Market* (Manchester, 1993), 39.

55 This process, however, only became unmistakable in the second half of the century, see J.A. Faber, 'De oligarchisering van Friesland in de tweede helft van de zeventiende eeuw', *Afdeling Agrarische Geschiedenis*, Bijdragen 15 (Wageningen, 1970).

56 Van der Woude, *Het Noorderkwartier*, 1, 50–2.

57 Diederik Aten, *'Als het gewelt comt...'. Politiek en economie in Holland benoorden het IJ 1500–1800* (Hilversum, 1995), chapter 3.

58 A.Th. van Deursen, *Een dorp in de polder. Graft in de zeventiende eeuw* (Amsterdam, 1994), 15–18.

59 Van Deursen, *Een dorp in de polder*, 102; Van der Woude, *Het Noorderkwartier*, II, 370.

60 Van Deursen, *Een dorp in de polder*, 103.

61 As defined by Van der Woude, this comprised only a part, though in area about a half, of North Holland.

62 Van der Woude, *Het Noorderkwartier*, II, 277–8.

63 Lesger, *Hoorn als stedelijk knooppunt*, appendix F.

64 De Vries and Van der Woude, *The First Modern Economy*, 519.

65 This was no less a person than Bernard Nieuwentijt of considerable contemporary fame as a scholar (Van Deursen, *Een dorp in de polder*, 73, 112). See also Rienk H. Vermij, *Secularisering en natuurwetenschap in de zeventiende en achttiende eeuw: Bernard Nieuwentijt* (Amsterdam, 1991).

66 J.A. Faber, *Drie eeuwen Friesland. Economische en sociale ontwikkelingen van 1500 tot 1800* (Wageningen, 1972), I, 101.

67 Priester, *Zeeland*, 70–4.

68 I.e. those with representation in the States of Holland.

69 Van der Woude, *Het Noorderkwartier*, I, 111.

70 Jan de Vries, *Barges and Capitalism. Passenger transportation in the Dutch economy (1632–1839)* (Wageningen, 1978).

71 Florike Egmond, *Underworlds*, 188–9.

72 A related point is made from a rather different angle by De Vries and Van der Woude, *The First Modern Economy*, 507ff.

73 L.J. Rogier, *Geschiedenis van het katholicisme in Noord-Nederland in de 16e en 17e eeuw*, (Amsterdam, 1964³), 338–9.

74 Van Deursen, *Een dorp in de polder*, 25

75 J.L. Price, 'The Dutch Nobility in the Seventeenth and Eighteenth Centuries', *The European Nobilities in the Seventeenth and Eighteenth Centuries*, vol.1, ed. H.M. Scott (London, 1995), 82–113.

76 Gutmann, *War and Rural Life*.

77 De Vries and Van der Woude, *The First Modern Economy*, 61.

78 De Vries and Van der Woude, *The First Modern Economy*, 67–8.

79 Israel, *Dutch Republic*, 332.

80 S.W. Verstegen, *Gegoede ingezetenen. Jonkers en geërfden op de Veluwe 1650–1830* (Zutphen, 1990), chapter 2.

81 Jan Bieleman, *Boeren op het Drentse Zand 1600–1910* (Wageningen, 1987), 132.

82 De Vries and Van der Woude, *The First Modern Economy*, 531.

83 De Vries and Van der Woude, *The First Modern Economy*, 548–9.

84 Gutmann, *War and Rural Life*, 85–6.

85 De Vries and Van der Woude, *The First Modern Economy*, 514–15.

86 Johannes de Waardt, *Toverij en samenleving. Holland 1500–1800* (The Hague, 1991), 121–6.

87 See Willem Frijhoff and Marijke Gijswijt-Hofstra (eds), *Witchcraft in the Netherlands: from the fourteenth to the twentieth century* (Rotterdam, 1991), for a valuable survey.

88 Willem de Blécourt, *Termen van toverij. De veranderende betekenis van toverij in Noord-Oost Nederland tussen de 16de en 20ste eeuw* (Nijmegen, 1990).

89 Herman Roodenburg, *Onder censuur. De kerkelijke tucht in de Gereformeerde gemeente van Amsterdam, 1578–1700* (Hilversum, 1990), 206–8.

90 See De Waardt, *Toverij en samenleving*, 207–8. Bekker published his *Betoverde Wereld* in 1691.

91 For the town of Utrecht in these years, see B.J. Kaplan, *Calvinists and Libertines. Confession and Community in Utrecht 1578–1620* (Oxford, 1995)

92 J.L. Price, *Holland and the Dutch Republic* (London, 1994), 84.

93 J. Spaans, *Haarlem na de Reformatie. Stedelijke cultuur en kerkelijk leven, 1577–1620* (The Hague, 1989), 104.

94 For the general problem, see Groenhuis, *De predikanten*, 163–5.

95 Van Deursen, *Een dorp in de polder*, 25.

96 For an example, see G. Rooijakkers, *Rituele repertoires. Volkscultuur in oostelijk Noord-Brabant 1559–1853* (Nijmegen, 1994), 201–3.

97   Simon Groenveld, *Huisgenoten des geloofs. Was de samenleving in de Republiek der Verenigde Nederlanden verzuild?* (Hilversum, 1995), 71.

98   See R.G. Fuks-Mansfeld, *De Sefardim in Amsterdam tot 1795* (Hilversum, 1989)

99   See below, chapter 4.

100   Kaplan, *Calvinists and Libertines*, chapters 1, 2.

101   Roodenburg, *Onder censuur*, 387–8.

102   See the contrasting approaches of H.A. Enno van Gelder, *Getemperde Vrijheid* (Groningen, 1972) and S. Groenveld, 'The Mecca of Authors? States Assemblies and Censorship in the Seventeenth-Century Dutch Republic', *Too Mighty to be Free: censorship and the press in Britain and the Netherlands*, ed. A.C. Duke and C.A. Tamse (Zutphen, 1987), 63–86.

103   See, for example, J.J. Poelhekke, 'Het geval Zijdewind', in *Geen blijder maar in tachtig jaer. Verspreide studiën over de crisis periode 1648–1651* (Zutphen, 1973), 106–52.

104   Cf. Charles H. Parker, *The Reformation of Community. Social Welfare and Calvinist Charity in Holland, 1572–1620* (Cambridge, 1998), chapter 4.

105   Price, *Holland and the Dutch Republic*, pt. iii, chap. 2.

106   For an introduction to this somewhat mysterious organisation see Herman Roodenburg, 'Naar een etnografie van de vroegmoderne stad: de "gebuyrten" in Leiden en Den Haag', *Cultuur en maatschappij in Nederland 1500–1850: een historisch-antropologisch perspectief*, ed. P. te Boekhorst, P. Burke and W. Frijhoff (Meppel/Heerlen, 1992), 219–43.

107   Donald Haks, *Huwelijk en gezin in Holland in de 17e en 18e eeuw* (Assen, 1982), 219–22.

108   Especially considering the frequency of epidemics of the plague throughout the growth period, L. Noordegraaf and G. Valk, *De gave gods. De pest in Holland vanaf de late middeleeuwen* (Bergen, NH, 1988), 43–7.

109   Rooijakkers, *Rituele repertoires*, 307–17.

110   P. Zumthor, *Daily Life in Rembrandt's Holland* (London, 1962), 122–4.

111   For which Johan Huizinga, *The Waning of the Middle Ages* (London, 1924) is a classic introduction.

112   C. Salmasius, *De usuris liber* (Leiden, 1638).

113   Max Weber, *The Protestant Ethic and the Spirit of Capitalism* (London, 1930). This is a much misunderstood work, for a discussion which is particularly helpful to the historian, see Gordon Marshall, *In Search of the Spirit of Capitalism. An essay on Max Weber's Protestant ethic thesis* (London, 1982).

PART TWO

Apogee and the Portents of Decline, 1648–1713

4

A Bourgeois Society?

B Y THE middle years of the seventeenth century the Dutch Republic had reached the height of its economic success: the period of explosive economic growth and dramatic social change was over, and for at least two decades the Dutch were able to enjoy relative social stability together with continuing, though much more modest, economic growth. Later in the century clear indications of what was to turn out to be a long-term decline were to emerge, but for a brief period the Dutch economy remained strong and Dutch society had a breathing space in which to adjust to the rapid changes in society which it had experienced in the previous century or more. The Treaty of Münster in 1648 which brought peace with Spain and the French invasion in the *rampjaar* (year of disaster) of 1672 can be taken as convenient political markers indicating the approximate beginning and end of this relatively short period of prosperity and social retrench-ment. These years were a plateau between the increasingly precipitous ascent of the sixteenth and early seventeenth centuries and the descent, at first quite gentle then distinctly steeper, of the last quarter of the seventeenth century and the whole of the eighteenth.

In this period the Dutch were able to enjoy very nearly a quarter of a century of respite from the political and military pressures which dogged them for the greater part of the century. Even in these years, however, the two wars with England (1652–4, 1665–7), although they did not constitute a real threat to either the independence or the pros-perity of the Republic, brought severe though short-lived economic disruption. The first half of the seventeenth century had been dominated by the continuation of the struggle for independence against Spain and, while in retrospect it is tempting to see the outcome as inevitable, until perhaps as late as the 1640s it was far from clear to contemporaries that the Dutch would win. Similarly, after the shock of the French invasion of 1672, which brought the troops of Louis XIV to the borders of the province of Holland and seemed for a moment to have brought an abrupt and violent end to the independent existence of the Republic, the threat which France appeared to represent to the vital interests of the country dominated the rest of the century. Between these two phases came a period when there was no apparent fundamental threat to the interests of the Republic. After 1648, Spain was at first absorbed in the continuation of its war with France (until 1659) and by the middle of the 1660s it was Spanish weakness rather than strength which created problems for the Dutch. At first, France was not only taken up with the war with Spain but also by the internal problems caused by the Fronde. However, in the course of the 1660s after the ending of civil strife in France and with the beginning of the personal rule of Louis XIV, the dangers to Dutch interests posed by French ambitions became increasingly apparent. In particular the war of Devolution (1667-8) showed that the Spanish were unable to defend the southern Netherlands effectively against France, and from this point onwards the latter came to be seen as a threat not only to the interests but perhaps also to the very existence of the Republic – as the events of 1672 demonstrated with some force. The comfortable certainties of the previous decades were swept away, and Dutch self-confidence was seriously shaken.

Internally, too, the Republic achieved and maintained a greater degree of stability during these years. It would seem that the sense of unity between the provinces had grown over the years, and that by the mid-century the union had come to be accepted as both more natural and more necessary than it had appeared in the uncertain first decades of the century. The double crisis of 1650, when Willem II first attempted a coup against the States of Holland and Amsterdam, and then died suddenly leaving only a posthumous son, was overcome with remarkable ease, certainly compared to the dangerous rifts which had opened up in Dutch society during the Truce crisis earlier in the century. It is true that the resolution of the conflict would almost certainly have been considerably more difficult if the prince had lived, but it must also be stressed that the Republic was a much more solid political institution by this point than it had been thirty or more years earlier. The *Grote Vergadering* (Great Assembly) which met in 1651 after the prince's death in the previous November declared a common loyalty to the union, religion, and the army, as the three pillars of the Dutch state. The following decades also demonstrated that the Republic could be governed effectively without a prince of Orange as stadhouder of the majority of the provinces and captain general of the army, despite the challenges of the time which included two naval wars with England. No inner necessity, only the quite exceptional circumstances of 1672 brought the regime down.

Thus, after the rapid social change of the earlier years of the century, these decades provided an opportunity for consolidation. The growth of the towns and the social transformation in the countryside – especially, but not only, in the maritime region – had very largely come to an end. The population of the largest towns in Holland – Amsterdam, Leiden, Rotterdam, The Hague – continued to grow throughout this period, but elsewhere demographic expansion seems to have ceased. Similarly, what more or less reliable statistics there are suggest that the Dutch economy had peaked by the 1640s and that, from this point on, it was characterised rather by trying to preserve the gains already made than by further expansion and change on the lines of the previous half century or more. This general picture of a relatively prosperous society seeking to hold on to what had been attained and to come to terms with the far-reaching social changes of recent years is not entirely deceptive, but nor is it the whole truth.

Any attempt to give a global picture of the Republic in this period runs the risk of giving a misleading appearance of homogeneity to a society which remained as diverse in this period as it had been earlier in the century. Quite apart from the continuing contrast between the experiences of the maritime region and the land provinces, distinct differences within the former area were beginning to emerge. Even in Holland itself, while the larger towns continued to grow, others had ceased to expand economically and not a few were already experiencing serious economic difficulties. Enkhuizen had probably peaked as early as the 1620s, while by the middle years of the century Hoorn was facing structural problems partly caused by competition from Amsterdam in the Baltic trade.[1] Indeed, the whole of the Northern Quarter of the province of Holland may have already entered the economic turndown by this time: certainly, its demographic *élan* seems to have evaporated before the second half of the century.[2] In South Holland, too, Haarlem had almost certainly ceased to grow by around 1640 and the economies of the smaller towns seem to have been rather less buoyant than before. However, in this area both urban and rural sectors remained relatively prosperous and only hindsight lends prominence to the sparse indicators of future problems. In Holland – and the same is probably true *mutatis mutandis* of the maritime region as a whole – while only a handful of the largest towns continued to grow with anything like the same economic vigour as before, for most towns and much of the countryside overall economic expansion may have come to an end but an equally general decline was far from evident. Only in the Northern Quarter is a general recession apparent (though more evidence might bring Zeeland into this category also) and even here the problems of the leading trading towns, Hoorn and Enkhuizen, were made to seem more prominent because of the contrast with their earlier spectacular success.

The economic and social rhythm of the land provinces was significantly different. The war with Spain had caused considerable economic damage in both North Brabant and the eastern provinces during most of the first half of the century, and for these areas the years after the Treaty of Münster were a period of modest recovery which brought the overall level of economic activity back to something like the pre-war situation. However, this still meant that these areas had very largely lost out on the economic miracle which the maritime region had experienced during the war, and the gains of the later century could in no way make up for this. Also, when the towns of the eastern provinces emerged from under the shadow of military activities, they found that the much greater economic strength of the towns of Holland especially had changed irrevocably the economic world in which they had to live. Towns such as Deventer, Zwolle and Zutphen which had had important trading links with western and northern Germany in the not-too-distant past found that much of this commerce had been captured by Holland and diverted into the Baltic trade of Amsterdam especially. The coming of peace enabled these towns to rebuild their economies and their positions as local or even regional markets, but their international role had very largely disappeared.

The countryside of Gelderland, Overijssel and North Brabant had suffered even more severely from the war, with the agricultural economy regularly disturbed by the passage of troops, the demands for contributions, and all too often by the depredations of marauding soldiers. Although in the final phase of the Eighty Years War the troops on both sides were kept under a control that was strict by contemporary standards, the constant threat or reality of military action in the region was a considerable burden on its agriculture. Even if it can be argued that the rural economy in such areas was much more resilient than the more lurid contemporary and later accounts might suggest, the constant demand – from both sides – for forage for the cavalry and draught horses alone must have had a significant and unpredictably disruptive effect on farming. In consequence, it is hardly surprising that the demographic curve in this region is markedly different from that of the countryside of Holland. Whereas the population in the latter had virtually ceased to grow and may well have already started to decline – almost certainly so in North Holland – by the mid-century, in the eastern provinces the end of the war with Spain marked the beginning of a period of slow but steady population growth that was to continue at least until the end of the Republic. North Brabant showed a similar pattern of demographic recovery after about 1648, but this seems to have been disrupted by the wars with France after 1672, as military activities during these conflicts directly affected this province more than any other.

The quarter century after the Treaty of Münster was one of relative peace for the Republic, marked by a peak of prosperity for the maritime region and a measure of economic recovery for the land provinces. Socially, the rate of change had slowed down and this circumstance makes this a suitable point to assess just what sort of a society had been created by a century and a half of economic growth and demographic expansion.

An established oligarchy

The third quarter of the seventeenth century saw the political triumph of the regent oligarchy: the absence of a stadhouder[3] and almost twenty years of political dominance by that epitome of regent virtues, Johan de Witt, allowed the regents to rule largely without challenge or external restraint until a combination of the French invasion of 1672 and the never-robust Willem III surviving to adulthood brought the house of Orange back to power. So, with the political system simplified to a significant extent, the nature of the regent regime can be seen most clearly during these years. For rather different reasons this period also displays the oligarchy as a social group in a form very close to the ideal-type: before this period the years of rapid growth – and intermittent political upheaval – had facilitated change in both the nature and the composition of the oligarchy, while afterwards the long economic decline was also to affect the regent group profoundly. As a consequence perhaps only in this short breathing space between tumultuous growth and inexorable decline can the regent elite be seen at the peak of its power and vitality.

Even at this time, and perhaps especially so, the nature of the oligarchy in the Republic as a whole remained fundamentally ambivalent, both in its social origins and in its image of itself. There were two main components of the oligarchy of the Republic: although the ruling groups – primarily the members of the town councils or *vroedschappen*, although the precise composition of the regent group varied from town to town – in the towns of Holland can be regarded as the archetypal regents, the political elite outside the leading province also included nobles and rural notables – the latter less clearly noble but with many of the same social pretensions and attitudes. However, it was not just the division between what one might call regents proper and the nobles of the land provinces which makes the nature of the oligarchy uncertain; the regents were also caught between a burgher – or even bourgeois – identity and a quasi-noble sense of family tradition and inherited status. In addition, the regent group was rather different in different parts of the country: the Holland regent was not the same as a regent of Nijmegen or Deventer, but also an Amsterdam regent was a very different animal from his counterpart in, say, Edam. The dominant oligarchy took on various forms in different parts of the Republic, and it remains uncertain whether – at this stage at least – it constituted in any very meaningful sense a single distinct and coherent social group.[4]

The first stadhouderless period (1650–72) allowed the regent oligarchy to consolidate its position in the Republic and particularly in Holland, politically as well as economically the key province. The dominance of the regents had been established in the course of the Revolt and the first half of the Eighty Years War, but had been to a certain extent challenged by the rise to leadership in the Republic of the princes of Orange after what was effectively a coup by Maurits in 1618. The power of, successively, Maurits, Frederik Hendrik and Willem II was based on distinctly different institutional foundations from that of Oldenbarnevelt, but perhaps more importantly the systems employed by the Orange stadhouders and the people they worked with had a significantly different social composition than that which had characterised Oldenbarnevelt's regime. Of course, they could not hope to carry out their policies without the support, or at least the passive acquiescence, of the regents of the leading towns of Holland, but the centre of government had become a quasi-princely court rather than the States of Holland, and the stadhouders' power rested to a considerable extent on the manipulation of the political influence still exercised by the nobles in the land provinces. The death of Willem II, and Holland's decision not to appoint a successor as stadhouder of the province, brought political authority and the initiative in the exercise of power firmly back to the regents. Johan de Witt showed no reluctance to work with nobles in various offices in Holland and elsewhere when it was convenient to do so, and he had to accept the reality of noble influence in many of the other provinces, nevertheless the foundations of his control of the politics of the Republic lay in the States of Holland and behind them the oligarchs of the voting towns of this province. The social base of his regime was even more of a contrast to that of the princes than had been the case with Oldenbarnevelt: De Witt embodied the rule of the Holland regents and during his period in power there was no effective challenge to their domination, either in social or political terms, of the Republic.

The return of the house of Orange, in the person of the young Willem III, to the leadership of the Republic in 1672 brought with it a shake up of the ruling elite but no significant change in its social composition. The *wetsverzettingen* during the late summer of that year changed the personnel of the town governments of Holland and Zeeland[5] but the fundamental structure of oligarchic rule remained intact. Like his father and grandfather before him, Willem worked through his control of the politics of the land provinces, and some of his most prominent collaborators were nobles – such as Bentinck, Dijkvelt and, later, Keppel – which gave his regime a different surface appearance to that of De Witt. The basic reality of Dutch politics, however, had not changed: the state could not be governed without the co-operation of the States of Holland which was the institutional expression of the power and interests of the regents of the province. In more general terms, however dictatorial the personal style of Willem III was, he had to work with and through the established oligarchy at provincial and local levels, i.e. the regents in the more inclusive sense. He could exploit differences between the provinces, manipulate the ambitions of needy nobles, and take advantage of factional clashes within the towns, but political power remained with the same social groups as before.

The regent elite of the towns may not have been entirely homogeneous, but it did share a range of common characteristics and it is very much a matter of perspective or interpretation whether the similarities or the differences should be seen as most significant. The oligarchs of the voting towns of Holland can be seen as the fullest development of the type of the regent, though this meant that they were far from representative of the Republic as a whole. The Holland regent group also is difficult to characterise as it changed significantly in its nature in the course of the century. In the early years of the seventeenth century, the families which had come to power during and just after the Revolt were firmly in place, but their bourgeois (or burgher) roots were still clearly visible. The great majority of regent families had risen through trade and manufactures and at this stage most were still actively involved in the businesses and trades which had brought them to social prominence. Later in the century, there was a marked tendency for established regent families to retreat from any immediate involvement with trade or manufactures and to become something like professional politicians, living on a combination of investments and the – legitimate or illegitimate – profits of office. New families were brought into the elite through occasional upheavals such as the *wetsverzettingen* of 1618 and 1672 or, less spectacularly but regularly, as a result of demographic attrition within the regent group. To some extent such newcomers served to maintain a proportion of active merchants in the *vroedschappen* (town councils) of the province. However, the fact that new families continued to be able to break into the oligarchy in one way or another did not stem the trend towards the regent group becoming largely composed of *rentiers*, as the social group from which new regents were recruited – in broad terms the upper bourgeoisie – also seems to have begun to drift away from trade by the second half of the century.[6] The regents of Holland as a group were probably considerably richer at the end of the century than they had been at the beginning, but as investors in loans to the States of Holland and holders of shares in the VOC rather than as active traders to the Baltic or as textile entrepreneurs.

One element that remained constant was the tendency towards endogamy in the regent group. The oligarchies of the towns were self-recruiting, usually through co-option, and for a regent to strengthen relations with other regent families through marriage alliances was a sensible strategy. Factions at the local level are probably better seen as groupings of families rather than of individuals, and inter-marriage helped to form and maintain such connections. The result was that at any given time the regent group of a town would display a dense set of relationships between families which at first sight gives an almost caste-like appearance. However, approaching the regent elite from this direction is to a significant extent misleading: regent families did inter-marry, but not exclusively so, and there were good reasons for marrying outside the narrow confines of the established group. For one thing, the regent group was too small in any single town to make total endogamy possible as well as desirable. In most towns membership (which was for life and by co-option) of the council or *vroedschap* defined the regent group, and numbers were universally small. The Rotterdam *vroedschap* had 24 members, that of Amsterdam 36, the *veertigraad* of Leiden had (naturally) 40 members as had the council in Gouda, and that of Haarlem had 32. In the voting towns of Holland membership of the governing councils varied from 14 to 40, and these numbers did not rise with the demographic expansion of the towns. The size of the regent group is larger than these figures might suggest because there were restriction on fathers and sons and brothers from being members at the same time, so there were some limits to the extent to which a small number of families could dominate the group. Nevertheless such a very restricted number of families was too small to provide a healthy choice of marriage partners, and so marriage outside the narrow regent circle was both usual and inevitable.

Political considerations could also encourage the establishment of connections with families which were outside the regent group but in other respects qualified for entry to it. Generally, brothers- and sons- in law of sitting regents were not ineligible for membership of the councils, and could be brought in to the *vroedschap* by an influential regent family. In this way marriage alliances with non-regent families could help to strengthen a regent's position in a way that a similar connection with another regent could not (a son-in-law, say, from another regent family might well be kept out of the council by a member of his own family). Suitable marriage partners for the sons and daughters of regent families might be found in the upper bourgeoisie of their own town, or in the regent groups of other towns. An impressionistic reading of the evidence might suggest that liaisons between the regent groups of the various voting towns of Holland became more common in the course of the century,[7] and that this was in part a reflection of the degree to which the regent elite in the province as a whole was an increasingly coherent social group, but in the present state of our knowledge this must remain speculative.

An argument against considering the regents of Holland as a single, more or less homogeneous, social group is that the differences between the oligarchies of the various towns was and remained considerable. In many ways a regent of Amsterdam was very different in wealth, life-style and world-view from his counterpart in one of the smaller towns such as Edam or Den Briel. Much the same can be said more generally regarding the regent groups of the larger towns of the province – Leiden, Haarlem, Rotterdam and perhaps Delft, Dordrecht and Gouda too – as opposed to those of the rest. (The Hague to a considerable extent stood apart from the other towns, being profoundly affected by the permanent presence of provincial and generality institutions and their staff and it was, in any case, technically only a village.) The greater wealth and more varied economies of the larger towns produced a regent elite that lived on a distinctly grander scale than the somewhat provincial regents of the lesser centres, but such differences were possibly less important by the end of the century than their common dependence on the proceeds from investments in public loans and on regular dividends from their shares in the VOC. By this time the regents of Holland, and probably of the maritime region as a whole, were heavily dependent on investments in public and semi-public funds and increasingly shared a common life-style and culture. The greater wealth and more cosmopolitan outlook of some should not blind us to the growing homogeneity of the group as a whole.

Outside Holland, and particularly in the land provinces, the urban regents were a more traditional group and were in social and political terms distinctly less independent of noble influence. They are also rather less easy to pin down. There was a different pattern of town government in Gelderland and Overijssel – the so-called 'east-Netherlands' model – from that which was common in the west, and one of its distinguishing characteristics was the lack of a *vroedschap*, i.e. a council with members sitting for life. In this system, magistrates only held office for a fixed period, usually a year, and so the extent of the ruling group is less easy to demarcate with any accuracy.[8] More important, however, was the fact that the towns of the land provinces had experienced severe economic difficulties throughout the Eighty Years War and even in the post-war period could at best only regain their pre-Revolt position. They had not experienced the explosive growth in wealth and population of the towns of the maritime region, and the bourgeoisie were less emancipated from traditional social structures and attitudes. One consequence of this was the continued presence of nobles in the town government long after they had disappeared from the towns of Holland. The regents of these towns were less wealthy, somewhat overshadowed by the social prestige of the nobility of their provinces, but maintained an almost obsessive concern for urban privileges and the rights of their citizens.

The nobility also belonged to the governing stratum, that is to the regent group in the broader sense.[9] Not all nobles were regents: the oligarchic tendencies so characteristic of the Republic were also present in the provincial nobilities and, in addition, catholic nobles were excluded from the ruling elite. Membership of the *ridderschappen* (the noble members of the provincial estates), and thus access to positions of power and profit, in Holland and elsewhere was increasingly restricted, and entry into these provincial elites became progressively more difficult in the course of the century. However, while the nobles had lost much of their political power in Holland, they had an important share in power elsewhere and were probably the dominant element in the politics of Gelderland, Overijssel and the province of Utrecht. The nobles were primarily landowners, though their share of arable land was nowhere particularly high, and they exercised considerable authority in the countryside of the land provinces and Groningen through their monopoly of judicial and police offices, and through the judicial and other rights attached to the manors (*heerlijkheden*) they owned. Even in Holland all important committees and delegations of the States had to include a member of the *ridderschap*, and so in this most regent-dominated province the leading nobles had privileged access to prestigious posts, even if the influence of the nobility as a body was severely limited.[10] In most of the other provinces the nobles had a firmer grip on power at both local and provincial level, and were at least as politically influential as the urban regents, reflecting the more traditional nature of society as well as politics in the land provinces.

The Dutch nobles as a whole were far from being unaffected by the transformation that was taking place in the Republic, and in some ways their position was rather different from traditional aristocracies. In the first place, they may have been primarily landowners but the proportion of agricultural land they held was quite small, and not only in the west of the country. Similarly, ownership of *heerlijkheden* was characteristic of nobles but the rights conferred by this were distinctly limited, the economic benefits uncertain, and the noble monopoly increasingly challenged by purchasers from the towns. There were a number of very rich nobles, but in the main the Dutch nobility were no better off than the regents and many were distinctly less so. A poor regent was a contradiction in terms – wealth was an essential qualification for membership of the regent group – but a poor noble remained a noble. Economically there was a convergence between nobles and regents: not only were regents buying manors and country houses (*buiten*), and in some cases aping the nobles by re-naming themselves after their estates, but the nobility like the regents were becoming dependent on income from public office and investments in public and semi-public funds. By the end of the century the economic base and the life-style of nobles and regents were coming together, yet full social convergence was prevented by subjective factors on both sides. The nobles felt themselves to be different, and this separate status was recognised by the rest of Dutch society, including the regents.[11] Yet throughout the Republic the nobility was dying out: normal demographic attrition and the failure or inability of the government at provincial or generality level to create new nobles meant that already by the second half of the seventeenth century the number of nobles in Holland had fallen drastically; by 1650 there were only twenty-one noble families left in the province and by 1730 the number had fallen to six.[12] The other provinces showed similar falls in noble numbers in the long term, though perhaps the decisive decline came rather later than in Holland. By the early nineteenth century numbers were so low that the new Orange monarchy had to create a new nobility from former regent families, thus bringing about the social convergence between the two divisions of the regent group which had failed to take place a century or more before.

The clear social divide which continued to exist between the regents and the nobility even at the end of the century, but also the suggested convergence in economic and even cultural terms between the two groups, brings into focus the question of the degree and nature of the change which took place in the regent group in the course of the seventeenth century. A view which has achieved a measure of acceptance, though far from universally, is that the regents developed into a sort of urban aristocracy. This process is believed to have come to maturity only in the eighteenth century but to have been already apparent in the later years of the previous century. In this interpretation, the regents developed over the years into a separate social group, marked not just by a monopoly of political power, but also by increasing endogamy together with a life-style and sense of status which cut them off from the rest of the upper bourgeoisie in the towns, even of Holland. The typical regent is seen as a *rentier* who had severed his family's earlier connections with trade, was the owner of a country house – the most imposing of these being those built by Amsterdam regents along the Vecht – and a manor, after which he now named himself. He would perhaps use French in conversation and in his correspondence to signal his cultural and aristocratic pretensions, and would certainly have exhibited that social arrogance matched by complacency which has given the *pruikentijd* – the 'wig period' – such a bad historical press.

Recent research, however, has cast more than a little doubt on this picture of the social position of the regents in the eighteenth century, and perhaps from an unexpected angle. Many of the supposedly distinguishing characteristics of the regent group can now be seen as common to the upper reaches of the bourgeoisie as a whole. Specifically, the better-off families of urban society outside the regent group also tended to retreat from any direct involvement in trade and manufacture and moved towards dependence on investment in the public debt and the VOC. They too bought *buitens* and, if these were on a distinctly less lavish scale than those of the leading Amsterdam regents, then the same could be said of the country retreats of most regents as well.[13] In general, as far as life-style and culture were concerned, it would seem that the gap between the regents and the rest of the upper bourgeoisie was negligible; their political power may well have made the regents arrogant and complacent, but perhaps this was only a special form of the arrogance and complacency which marked the upper reaches of society as a whole.

The character of the regent group was in constant evolution. In the earlier years of the seventeenth century, the regents of the Holland voting towns were mostly still involved in the economic activities which had brought themselves and their families to prominence. Moreover, the booming economies of these towns meant that the wealth of the regents and the competition for regent positions by suitably qualified men were both increasing. In the course of the century, however, the growing burden of work involved in the running of urban and provincial politics, together perhaps with the increasing uncertainty of commercial profits, encouraged regents to become something like professional politicians, and established regent families appear to have become increasingly dependent on investments and the profits, direct and indirect, of office. A university education – usually in law as a preparation for political life – and some version of the Grand Tour became *de rigueur* for the sons of such families. (The education of daughters took more domestic forms, and their travel was usually much more restricted.) Eldest sons would eventually inherit their fathers' places in government, and younger sons would look for profitable administrative positions at town, provincial or even generality level rather than going into business. Some members of regent families even began to appear as officers in the army, in a striking parallelism to the preferred career choices of nobles. However, as a group, even at the end of the seventeenth century the regents remained unmistakably as bourgeois as their origins. There were ambivalences in their social attitudes, but these were inherent in their situation and can also be seen throughout the century. In particular the regents married a fundamental loyalty to the bourgeois virtues with quasi-aristocratic pretensions. They believed that their privileged position was justified not just by personal merit, but by the status and history of their families. Regents, they believed, should come from regent families, and regent families were those which had produced regents in the past. This is not quite the aristocratic conception of blue blood but, in the sense that it implied that the qualities required for government were to a significant extent inherited, it was not far off.

Burgher or bourgeois?

It has been argued above that the regents did not form a separate urban aristocracy but were an integral part of the upper bourgeoisie. However neither this terminology nor the class analysis which it implies are uncontentious; they go to the heart of a long-standing and occasionally acrimonious debate as to the nature of Dutch seventeenth-century society. The nature of middling groups in the Dutch towns – a wide range of people from the better-off craftsmen through to merchants and professionals – has been seen as crucial in this respect. However, given the penetration by market forces of the rural sector – in the maritime region at least – a considerable section of society in the countryside must be brought into the discussion as well: farmers producing for the market, traders, small scale manufacturers, boat and barge operators, and even a smattering of professionals. It is not clear, however, whether these middling groups can be seen as parts of a single class, or whether their nature and interests were too disparate to justify being put under the same heading.

The significance of the dispute over terminology is that it is an indicator of a deeper disagreement. Bourgeois and burgher are terms which imply quite different types of social stratification – a class society or a society of orders.[14] A class is determined by its economic base, in Marx's definition by its relationship to the means of production, and is unified by its sense of common interests – particularly against other classes. The existence or lack of class consciousness has been taken by many historians as the key issue, and it is very largely on these grounds that it has been asserted that classes did not exist in early modern Europe. Instead, European society has been seen as consisting of orders or estates, with clergy, nobles and the third estate (which more or less included everyone not in the first two groups) as the basic categories. These orders were distinguished not by economic position or activities, but by distinct legal positions and status. The underlying assumption of class analysis is that only economic circumstances make social groups different from each other: the control of the means of production differentiates the capitalist from the proletarian. The assumption underlying the society of orders is that people are qualitatively different: to use a more modern terminology, nobles and non-nobles were seen as being genetically different, and clergy were made yet another sort of human being by their calling from God and, in catholic countries, by ordination. The guiding principle of the nobility was honour which was regarded as making nobles the proper leaders of society both in war – the most obvious field for the display of honour – and government. The prime motivation of non-nobles from the peasantry to merchants was, in contrast, the desire for gain; they were quite literally not honourable people and, for the good of society, needed to be guided by those who were.

The middling groups in Dutch seventeenth century society seem on the surface quite clearly to form a class, not an estate or order. Their positions in society were determined by economic circumstances, and they can be stratified satisfactorily according to what they earned and what they owned. There were no significant differences in legal rights between various individuals and groups[15] (though in the towns the distinction between citizens and mere inhabitants could be important), and no sumptuary laws to compel people to dress according to their status. In principle, at least, careers were open to talent though in practice it was not so easy to break through certain social barriers, and some people were clearly more equal than others when it came to a political career. However, such characteristics of Dutch society alone did not make these middling classes a new type of social formation. In the midst of the society of orders, trade and manufactures in the towns had long fostered the development of just such groups governed by just such principles, and nowhere more prominently than in the Netherlands. The roots of a new, capitalist social order can be found in the towns of late medieval Europe, and the middle groups in the Holland towns of the seventeenth century are clearly the lineal descendants of the incipient classes of the earlier period. What is not clear, however, is whether these seventeenth century groups are better seen as *burgerij* or bourgeoisie, as order or class; whether they should be seen as still essentially part of the world of the late medieval Netherlands' town or as the first appearance of a true bourgeoisie in European history. Holland, both town and countryside, must be at the heart of any discussion of this question: if any fundamental change to the social system had taken place in the course of the rapid economic growth of the sixteenth and early seventeenth century it must have taken place here.

One problem with treating the middling groups of the Dutch towns as a bourgeoisie is that they were perhaps too heterogeneous to be meaningfully considered as a single class. Surviving tax records[16] indicate that the proportion of the population with enough money or property to be worth taxing varied from place to place but was possibly around half of the total population in the boom towns of Holland. So the middle ground in urban society can be said to stretch from the skilled craftsman, working for wages – the case of most ship's carpenters, for example – or self-employed as a small-scale producer-shopkeeper, to the textile entrepreneurs of Leiden and Haarlem and the international merchants of Amsterdam and Rotterdam, on the way taking in a large swathe of professionals – doctors, lawyers, ministers – and other specialists such as brokers, notaries, teachers, *schippers* and other providers of transport, and a rich variety of shopkeepers and small to middling traders. All these elements shared to a certain extent in the prosperity which marked the Holland towns through much of the century, but their circumstances and interests were far from homogeneous.

The principles of the society of orders also infiltrated to some extent what might otherwise seem a purely capitalist society, without ever becoming dominant in contemporary consciousness. The internal stratification of the bourgeoisie was affected by legal distinctions which were a hangover from an earlier time but which retained at least some of their force. There was an important distinction between those who were formally citizens (*burgers*) of a town and those who were not. Citizenship conferred some economic privileges, and the full repertoire of urban life was only open to *burgers* – the full scale of relief in sickness and old-age was restricted to citizens, and the civic orphanages were restricted in the first instance to their children. Citizenship could be inherited, bought, or granted as a favour, but only *burgers* were full members of the urban community. Guild members similarly had a monopoly of certain occupations, notably in skilled craft production, and these privileged circles could be difficult for outsiders to break into. The guilds also provided their members with occasions for ritual as well as social support which cushioned them to some extent from the worst aspects of a highly competitive society – while also curbing their individual enterprise. Such distinctions are perhaps easily forgotten but remain nevertheless important survivals from an earlier phase of middle-class development. On the other hand, it is remarkable how smoothly urban society, in Holland especially, absorbed newcomers both from elsewhere in the Republic and from further afield during the years of rapid economic expansion. The defensive aspect of citizenship and guild membership seems to become more important again towards the end of the century when the economy of the maritime region moved into long-term recession.

At the top of urban society were the upper bourgeoisie composed originally of the richer merchants and manufacturers. In the course of the century, many of the families in this section of society began to move away from hands-on activity in trade or production and, like the regent group, became increasingly dependent on income from investments, particularly in loans floated by the States of Holland and the States General, and in the shares of the VOC. They formed a social elite which also included the regents and the leading figures in the administration of province and Generality, together with the judges of the provincial courts. Although the Republic had a notoriously weak central government with a very limited administrative apparatus, this was because much of the weight of government fell elsewhere. In fact, besides the mere handful at the centre, there were a considerable number of lucrative administrative posts at the local and provincial levels. The enormous wealth accumulated by the receiver-general of the Generality, Cornelis de Jonge van Ellemeet[17] at the end of our period, not to mention the less-well-documented but notorious fortune amassed by the grasping and corrupt *griffier* of the States General under Frederik Hendrik, Cornelis Musch, is a spectacular instance but hardly typical. More characteristic are the comfortable incomes available for members of the *Hof van Holland* and *Hoge Raad*, the peak positions for lawyers without political ambitions, and the modest but solid gains to be made in the administration of, say, the Generality Lands. As the gains available from trade and industry became more uncertain, so such posts became more attractive to the upper bourgeoisie as a way of maintaining their often hard-won social position.

The fine houses on the frontage of the newly constructed semicircles of canals round the old centre of Amsterdam were built for members of this urban elite, and they also, like the regents, built or bought country houses so that they could escape the inconveniences of the towns in the summer months. These *buitens* were mostly of rather modest dimensions, but so were those of most of the regents. Their sons went to Leiden, or one of the other universities founded in the Republic after the Revolt, to study law, and it was common for them to undertake an educational journey to France, Germany and Italy, sometimes even taking in England. Daughters would be educated at home to be literate in their own language and probably French also, and to learn ladylike accomplishments as well as the more practical skills of household management under the tutelage of their mothers.

Below this upper level of the middle class was a sector of traders and manufacturers. Towards the bottom of this group, but still economically solid and socially respectable, were the craftsmen who sold the products of their workshops themselves. In effect they were small businessmen, employing apprentices and even other time-served artisans, and operating from a house that was at the same time home, workshop, and retail outlet. In roughly the same stratum of society, though covering quite a wide range of circumstances, were the ubiquitous bakers, innkeepers, and a wide variety of shopkeepers. Members of all these sub-groups could, at their most successful, begin to merge imperceptibly into the category of more substantial traders and entrepreneurs. This latter category, too, covered a considerable range of social conditions but its members were not tied directly to producing the goods they traded in and, by definition they were better off than the stratum of relatively modest craftsmen/shopkeepers. They were prosperous and socially ambitious enough to send their children to good schools – in the case of their sons perhaps even to Latin School – though a training in foreign languages, mathematics and book-keeping was probably considered more appropriate to their condition in life and their expectations.

Professionals of one sort or another were an increasingly important section of the Dutch bourgeoisie. They included members of the established professions, doctors and lawyers, with university degrees and a relatively high social status, as well as groups with a rather more uncertain standing in society, such as teachers and protestant ministers. The prestige of doctors came in part from their academic training but also from the fact that, unlike surgeons, they did not work with their hands. Physical work was considered to be demeaning throughout Europe at this time and, in this respect, the Republic was still to a large extent in thrall to inherited social and cultural attitudes. However, this century also saw the confirmation of the rise of the surgeon from the relatively lowly status of the barber-surgeon trained by apprenticeship, like any other artisan, to the status of recognised professional. Although surgeons continued to be reliant on manual skills as was the case with other craftsmen, and although their work involved contact with blood, pus and other matter which was still to some extent regarded as unclean, they were nevertheless able to overcome these disadvantages and negotiate a significant rise in perceived social status. From the artisan who did much of his work in ale-houses and had a reputation for the all-too-frequent violent use of the tools of his trade – knives and razors – the surgeon was by the late seventeenth century becoming a recognised medical professional with authority over others employed in this field, such as midwives. Apothecaries, too, were beginning to grow in social esteem and rise above the level of simple shopkeeper through the provision of quasi-medical services, and perhaps also because their trade in expensive tropical herbs and spices gave them a certain cachet as well as profit. At the beginning of the century, the shortage in the newly established Reformed Church of suitably trained candidates for the ministry meant that many parishes and churches had to be served at best by *Duitse clerken*, lacking a university education. The aim of a wholly graduate ministry[18] had probably been achieved by the middle of the century, but the status of ministers continued to be somewhat ambivalent. Their salaries varied widely between town and countryside and between town and town, but were high enough in the bigger towns to put them firmly among the middle classes. On the other hand, it continued to be a common criticism of the reformed clergy that they were recruited from the lower classes, but this is misleading. It is true that many towns established bursaries so that aspirants for the ministry from less well off families could study theology at the *Staten College* at Leiden, and this offered some possibility of modest social mobility, but it turns out that many of the recipients were ministers' sons, and a high proportion of ministers in the later part of the century came from clerical families. It was highly unusual for someone from the lower classes to become a minister.[19]

In the educational sphere similarly, while university professors and their counterparts in the illustrious schools at the top enjoyed high status (if not always commensurate salaries), and the pay of teachers in the Latin schools was adequate to maintain a middle-class style of life, at the lower level of schooling neither the professional standards nor the remuneration of teachers appears to have been impressive. On the other hand, levels of literacy were high in the towns of the Republic, at least by the standards of the rest of contemporary Europe, so on the whole teachers even at this low level seem to have been doing their job adequately even if the rewards financially and in terms of social esteem were uncertain.

Another part of the service sector that included a substantial middle class element was transport and shipping. The owners and operators (*schippers*) of cargo and passenger barges and sailing boats, using the canals and rivers which reached most parts of the country at least in the maritime region, formed an important element of the middling classes, given the enormous demand for their services in an economy which depended on the efficient movement of a large variety of goods from one place to another. Also the *stuurlieden* (coxwains) of the herring fleet and of whalers together with officers in the merchant fleet formed a significant middle class element, especially in the more important ports of province and country.

All in all, the very nature of the developed economy of the Republic generated a large and various middle class, but it may also be true that the economic downturn of the later years of the seventeenth century affected middling groups with especial severity. In particular, while the older and more firmly established bourgeois families may have been able to adjust to the lower profit margins and increasing uncertainty of trade by shifting their economic weight onto more secure investments, the broad swathe of traders, shopkeepers and service providers who had flourished in the years of prosperity found it more difficult to adjust to the changing economic circumstances, and this section of society shrank significantly in the course of the long depression. The bourgeoisie as a whole may not have constituted as high a proportion of urban society in the later eighteenth as it did in the middle of the seventeenth century when Dutch prosperity was at its peak, and it may well have been rather different in its composition as well.

The cultural developments in the Republic during the seventeenth century are commonly seen as reflecting, to some extent at least, the transformation which had taken place in Dutch society during the century or more of rapid economic growth.[20] This new, or at least profoundly modified, culture has been seen as reflecting the perspectives and needs of the middling groups in society, typified by the burghers of the Holland towns, and forming a sharp contrast with the aristocratic culture which still dominated Europe as a whole.[21] Against this line of argument, it has to be acknowledged that in some areas, such as humanist learning or perhaps in literature more generally, the Dutch remained firmly in the European mainstream, so the question still remains as to what extent the bourgeoisie of the Dutch towns created their own distinctive culture in the course of this century.

The combination of widespread literacy and a modicum of education for the middle classes together with the possession of at least some disposable income by perhaps as much as 40–50 per cent of the population – and not only in the towns, but also in the more developed areas of the countryside – provided the raw materials for a number of distinctive cultural developments, if not for a wholly new culture. Of most obvious importance is the rise of a market for cheap paintings and prints which played a major part in stimulating the development of the distinctive Dutch School in art. The rooms of Dutch houses were decorated with large numbers of pictures, varying in most cases from the cheap to the cheap and nasty. The wealthier bourgeoisie could afford the luxury of skilfully produced oil-paintings, and these would often be in accordance with conventional artistic taste (using standard themes and iconography). Just below this level, however, were those who could afford to pay more than the minimum for a painting but whose taste was for genre, landscape, seascape, etc. without the obtrusive iconographic trappings of conventional art – their interest in other words was in the overt subject of the painting, not in more or less esoteric symbolism. It can be said that such people lacked the education to appreciate more sophisticated art, but it is perhaps more significant that they antici-pated the realist tastes of the bourgeoisie of a later period. Here was a large new market for modestly priced paintings of a size suitable for hanging in an ordinary burgher home and largely free of the cultural constraints which severely limited what were conventionally considered to be acceptable subjects for art and their treatment.

The high levels of literacy in the Republic meant that there was a large potential reading public, and this was exploited by a particularly dynamic printing and publishing industry through the production of a flood of pamphlets and cheap printed literature. Political developments, theological controversies and sensational events were accompanied from the time of the Revolt onwards by an effectively unstoppable spate of published commentaries ranging from pamphlets of almost book length to flysheets of a few pages. As they were meant to persuade, inform or astound, not to be read as literature, the language they employed was usually more demotic and certainly more direct than the Latin periods which shaped the self-consciously literary prose of the period (not to mention the legalistically obscure and appallingly clumsy language of official documents). The more conversational – and readable – Dutch of the eighteenth century has its roots in these publications for a popular audience. Books, however, appear to have remained something like a luxury item; inventories suggest that Dutch middle-class homes con-tained many pictures but few books. Editions of most books were not large and, while in the middle of the following century the historian Jan Wagenaar's multi-volumed *Vaderlandsche geschiedenis* (History of the Fatherland), despite the substantial price, had sales high enough to make the author financially secure,[22] perhaps surprisingly such a market had apparently not yet developed in the seventeenth century.

The growth in size and the rise in prosperity of the bourgeoisie in the Republic stimulated the development of a material culture of a peculiarly modern sort. Up to this point personal property and house-hold goods had been relatively immune to the vagaries of fashion. The material contents of houses were very limited in number and range, what people owned was intended to last, even clothes were inherited where possible, and only at the highest level of society was consumer behaviour of a modern sort evident. This situation began to change in the course of the seventeenth century in both town and countryside in the maritime region of the Republic.[23] Homes began to contain both a greater number and a wider variety of material goods, as people in the middling groups of society came to have significantly more disposable income which they were prepared to spend on themselves and their domestic surroundings. By the last years of the century trends in consumer behaviour begin to be observable, though as yet only in certain restricted areas such as the popularity of Delft blue and porcelain in general which began to replace other types of pottery at this time. During the seventeenth century there appear to have been notable changes in demand for various types of painting, but the qualitative as opposed to the quantitative demand for art is as yet little researched. The total demand for paintings seems to have fallen as other modes of interior decoration became popular, but this probably only became significant in the eighteenth century.

Despite the unmistakable signs of the emergence of a distinctive middle class culture in this period, there remained a certain ambivalence in burgher perceptions and attitudes. Any straightforward assertion of bourgeois values was undermined by persistent status anxieties and eventually by the retreat of the upper bourgeoisie into *rentier* security. The apparently self-confident statements of the virtues of hard work and the pursuit of profit which form one undeniable aspect of contemporary reality must be balanced, not by the christian guilt at material success emphasised by one study,[24] but by an underlying uncertainty in the face of a hostile value system which expressed the experience and interests of the nobility and was still dominant in the rest of Europe – and far from dead in the Republic itself. The humanist educational system which was the accepted standard throughout Europe at this time was founded on the study of the literature of the Ancient Greek and Roman world as interpreted by the Renaissance, and the values it promoted can be seen as fundamentally alien to the capitalist spirit. Commercial profit and material success in general were seen as ignoble activities and taking interest on loans was interpreted essentially as exploitation of the weak. It is hardly surprising, then, that those who had been exposed to this value system from their childhood came to have at least some doubts regarding the virtues of a commercial society. It was generally accepted, and not just by sitting regents, that certain families were more suited to a share in political authority than others, and that one important qualification for political office was the quasi-aristocratic one of family tradition. In other areas too the urge to freeze family status rather than open it up to free competition was evident: guilds favoured the sons of guildsmen, and in general the relatively privileged clung to their inherited positions and status, while the rest found social mobility more elusive than was entirely consonant with the ethos of a capitalist society.

The readiness shown by the upper bourgeoisie to retreat from active involvement with trade and to become rentiers was in part a rational response to the more difficult economic circumstance of the later decades of the seventeenth century. Nevertheless, it is hard to avoid the suspicion that the attractions of a quasi-aristocratic life-style also played a significant part. However, this retreat was far less extreme or complete than, for example, that of the contemporary English merchants who transformed themselves into landed gentry. The Dutch upper bourgeoisie remained essentially an urban class; they moved to the countryside in the summer months for health reasons as well as for pleasure, but remained firmly based in the towns. Also land was never more than a minor element of the overall wealth of such families, and even those who bought heerlijkheden seem to have done so for other reasons than the economic returns they offered, which were meagre.

There would seem to be little reason to deny that the middling classes in Dutch society in the maritime region constituted a bourgeoisie, but one that lacked a fully developed class consciousness. In objective, material terms this was clearly a class; but subjectively it was caught between two rival value systems and this led to a profound ambivalence. Yet in this very uncertainty, the Dutch middle classes of the seventeenth century only display a trait that was perhaps characteristic of the bourgeoisie of a later age as well.

Outside the maritime region, the burghers seem to have remained much more traditional in attitudes and life-style, but even in the far-from-booming towns of the land provinces there were signs of change. The popular movements which broke out against the entrenched oligarchies in these towns after the death of Willem III, and again in the middle of the eighteenth century, were inspired on the surface by backward looking appeals to largely mythical ancient rights and customs. However, proto-democratic elements were also present and it was from such roots that the Patriot movement eventually sprang. It is significant that, initially at least, this democratic movement was stronger in the small and supposedly backward towns of Overijssel than it was in what were by that time the economically stagnant towns of Holland.

Socio-demographic contrasts and conditions

The Republic was not a homogeneous society: the contrasts between the two main regions – maritime and land provinces – have already become a major theme of this study, and the social and demographic experiences of different groups within Dutch society also display notable contrasts, which should surprise no one. Although there can be disagreement about whether this was a class society or composed rather of orders, there can be no disputing that material conditions of life were very different for the various social groups and at different social levels.

On the whole the demography of the Republic followed what had become by the early modern period the standard West European pattern, marked by a generally late age of marriage for both men and women, together with a negligible proportion of children born outside marriage. These two factors taken together were perhaps the most important elements in determining that overall fertility levels would be relatively low. Taken together with the prevailing high level of mortality, this restricted fertility meant that even small changes in demographic behaviour or circumstances could turn population growth into decline. Dutch society may have broken with the past in many ways in the Golden Century, but the people of the Republic were emphatically still largely without effective defences against the multiple natural causes of illness and death which encompassed them. At least one of the four horsemen of the Apocalypse still rode – a trifle incongruously perhaps – through the well-ordered streets of the Dutch towns.

The persistently high level of mortality was a fundamental demographic fact of the period. The deaths from epidemic diseases were most spectacular and the recurrent visitations of the plague the most terrifying evidence of the general vulnerability of the population. However, the toll taken by the plague in its various forms has perhaps been exaggerated: estimates for the towns of Holland in the seventeenth century suggest that mortality from a plague epidemic was often less than 10 per cent of the total population, though it could exceed 20 per cent.[25] While not the disaster of the plague myth, these are serious enough demographic blows, and they came often: between the beginning of the century and 1666 the plague was noted in Amsterdam in twenty-three separate years, in Leiden fifteen, and in Rotterdam nineteen, but Haarlem was visited by the plague in only five years in this period and The Hague only in seven. Although plague in its bubonic and related forms disappeared from the Republic after the last epidemics in the 1660s, there was – to say the least – no significant fall in mortality in the last three decades of the century. In the absence of plague, mortality was maintained at a high level by smallpox and a host of other infectious diseases. Less spectacular than the great epidemics of the time, but a considerably more significant demographic force was the quotidian toll of infant and child mortality. Infant mortality – defined as death within the first year of life – was most important: perhaps 20–25 per cent of all children died before their first birthday, and the most dangerous period was the first days and weeks after birth. The rest of childhood was less perilous but still dangerous, with possibly another quarter of all children dying before they reached maturity. Reliable figures on age-specific mortality are rare for the seventeenth century in the Republic, but there can be little doubt that these crude estimates are of the right order of magnitude. (The evidence from Maasland, a village in south Holland, shows infant mortality running at over 25 per cent in 1730–59 and only around half of those born there reaching the age of 25 over the eighteenth century as a whole,[26] and it seems unlikely that the situation in the previous century would have been significantly different.) For those who did reach adulthood life became rather less threatening, though medicine could offer little or no effective help against the diseases which proliferated, and death could and frequently did strike at any age. Ageing was more rapid, too: for women, the menopause seems to have come soon after forty, and for both men and women only the most hardy passed sixty. Indeed, in sharp contrast to the present day, the old did not constitute a serious social-welfare problem – there were too few infirm old people.[27]

While mortality was high, fertility was sharply limited by a late average age of marriage for both men and women at all levels of society. Again this phenomenon is part of a general West European pattern and is linked to the circumstance, more social than demographic, that newly married couples were normally expected to set up as separate economic units in separate households. So men waited until they were economically independent and capable of supporting a family before marrying, while women too needed to work for a number of years after puberty to put together a dowry and also to learn the skills they would be expected to bring to a marriage. Marriages were primarily economic partnerships for most of the population, and most men could not afford to have to carry a young and inexperienced wife any more than most women would want to carry the burden of a feckless or incompetent husband. In these circumstances, the age of marriage in the Republic ranged from early to middle twenties for women and mid to late twenties for men, and seems to have varied according to economic circumstances. A buoyant economy allowed for greater opportunities and thus earlier marriages, while in a stagnant or depressed economy couples had to wait significantly longer to find suitable economic niches. Such late marriages, especially for women, cut down the fertility level considerably, and this was exacerbated by child-rearing practices which further limited conceptions. It was common practice, in the absence of other suitable foods for babies and very young children, to continue breast-feeding until about the age of two. While there is no evidence for the widespread use of artificial means of contraception, except for coitus interruptus, prolonged breast-feeding had the unintended effect of inhibiting conception and lengthening the intervals between births, and along with late age at marriage for women contributed to a level of fertility far lower than was theoretically possible.

In the first half of the century, fertility was generally modest but sufficient to produce a small but steady natural increase in population (i.e. apart from the effects of immigration); from sometime in the third quarter of the century, however, a slightly higher marriage age and perhaps lower marriage frequency brought down the natural rate of increase crucially and signalled the end of a very long period of demographic growth and the switch to long term stagnation or even decline.[28] Although demographic developments are not necessarily simply dependent variables of economic conditions, the two do seem to be very closely correlated in the Dutch case, particularly, but not only,

189

in the maritime region which was most dependent on the market and thus on the vagaries of commercial capitalism. Age at marriage seems to have been particularly sensitive to economic fluctuations, and worsening economic conditions and prospects also led to a rise in the number of people never marrying at all. However, possibly the most important single factor in explaining the long term evolution of the Dutch population is immigration. Because of the limitations on the fertility of the Dutch population which have been outlined, the rapid population growth of the early seventeenth century cannot be explained by natural increase alone. In particular the spectacular expansion of the towns of Holland, which had difficulty maintaining their populations by means of natural fertility let alone supporting any rapid growth, had to be fed by immigration, in the first instance from the surrounding countryside but soon from other provinces and finally from outside the Republic.[29] Admittedly, little is known about the demography of these towns in this early period, and it may well be that the surplus of deaths over births which has been observed for later periods is misleading for these economically more dynamic years, but the actual rates of growth achieved were only possible through large scale immigration. Although many of these immigrants were religious refugees in the late sixteenth century and even later, it was the booming economy of the Republic which was the greatest attraction for foreigners. In the later seventeenth century the stream of newcomers to the Republic slowed down as the economy moved towards recession. Immigration continued but its nature changed: less young men were attracted to the Republic and the proportion of young women among the immigrants, particularly coming as domestic servants, rose and so contributed to the surplus of women and falling nuptiality observable in such towns as Amsterdam.[30] This steady stream of newcomers could help to moderate the demographic effects of economic decline, but could not reverse the trend.

Outside the maritime region the population curve may have been different, but the general demographic conditions were very much the same, characterised by a late age of marriage – together with an illegitimacy rate so low as to be statistically insignificant – and persistently high infant and child mortality. Even in the areas of developing rural industries such as Twente in Overijssel, where the development of what has been called proto-industrialisation might lead us to expect a rather different demographic regime, late marriage with its consequent relatively low fertility remained predominant.[31] The land provinces in general differed in one respect from the maritime region as here emigration, to Holland in particular, rather than immigration was a significant demographic factor. That migration between the land provinces and Holland took place on a considerable scale can be stated with reasonable confidence but the extent and rhythms of these movements of people are unclear. Emigration from Deventer to Amsterdam seems to have been strongest in the earlier years of the century, for example, and to have weakened when military operations ceased to be an immediate threat.[32] On the other hand the stream of young women moving from the land provinces to Holland, at least temporarily, as domestic servants seems to have continued throughout the century. Most, probably, would have intended to return home to marry and settle down after earning enough for a decent dowry, but the pitfalls as much as the opportunities in the towns of Holland ensured that many never did. However, while the second half of the century saw the population growth of the maritime region reach its zenith and come to a halt, and even begin to decline in many areas, for the east and south it was just in this period that a slow but steady rise set in. Demographically speaking at least, the balance was beginning to swing away from the maritime region and towards the land provinces.

The fluctuations in internal migration are yet another reminder that the nature and rhythms of social change varied not only from region to region, but from province to province. Moreover, the provinces themselves were far from homogeneous in their economic and social experiences. Within the maritime region Zeeland, after an initial surge in the last decades of the sixteenth century when it benefited from the blockade of the Schelde and from a first wave of immigration from the South, quickly began to fall behind in comparison to Holland. The boom period for the Northern Quarter of Holland lasted rather longer, but its leading trading towns, Hoorn and Enkhuizen, were clearly past their peak by the 1630s. There was little if any further population growth after this point and in this case the correlation between demographic and economic trends seems to have been close. The countryside of North Holland too seems to have hit the buffers in demographic terms by the middle of the seventeenth century and, again, this was a more or less accurate indication of the onset of serious economic problems. Nevertheless, the major divide in social circumstances remained that between the maritime region and the land provinces. In the second half of the seventeenth century, when the former was first reaching its peak of prosperity and then beginning to show unmistakable signs of economic malaise, the rest of the country was only just beginning a slow and hesitant recovery from the difficulties which it had gone through during the war with Spain. So although the third quarter of the century was in many ways the peak of the Republic's prosperity, the land provinces had never shared in the secular boom of the maritime region and for some, perhaps even for most, areas of the latter the days of greatest success were already evidently a thing of the past. Only the leading towns of Holland, and to a lesser extent the countryside of South Holland could enjoy the economic zenith of the Republic to the full.

An image of solid burgher prosperity continues to typify perceptions of the Golden Age, and in many ways quite rightly so, but there was a less favoured aspect of Dutch society even in the booming maritime provinces. Below the level of the independent artisan, who was at least running his own business however small, came a large group of skilled and semi-skilled workers, and beneath them an even wider range of wage labourers in agriculture, transport and manufactures. In the countryside of the maritime region, the transformation which had taken place in the agricultural sector had produced not only a class of capitalist farmers but necessarily also a body of agricultural labourers with little or no land of their own. In the towns, the structural changes in the textile industry were turning artisans into dependent workers, while sailors and fishermen, though undoubtedly possessing considerable skills, had to work for wages that were low even by the standards of the time. Besides these large groups of workers, the booming economy of the first half of the century increased the numbers of jobs available in a wide variety of manufactures, and created a demand for large numbers of porters and dock workers. In both town and countryside transport, particularly by boat and barge on rivers, canals and lakes, provided employment for many, and in the period up to about the 1660s large-scale drainage schemes and canal construction must have required the labour of a small host of navvies.

One of the largest groups of wage-earners, the soldiers of the Dutch army, have received relatively little attention as a social group from other than military historians, perhaps because they were to an extent physically removed from the rest of Dutch society in war time – and the Republic was more often at war than at peace in the seventeenth century. Also the high proportion of foreigners in the army –

perhaps as high as 60 per cent at times – has led to it being seen as an alien element to a significant extent in – or rather not in – Dutch society. Yet the field army was not equally active all year round, campaigns being rare in the winter months, and many soldiers were needed as permanent garrisons of strategically important towns and fortresses. The effect that the army had on Dutch society was very uneven: the presence of troops was an important aspect both of the demographic and of the economic life of the garrison towns of the eastern provinces and the Generality lands, but hardly noticeable in Holland. The large numbers of foreigners in the army should perhaps be regarded as part of the broader flow of immigrants into the country during this period, and many of them eventually settled in the Republic.

There have been attempts to discover a distinct working-class culture in the early modern period,[33] but the subject has proved elusive. Certain groups of workers seem to have developed their own sub-cultures based on group solidarity together with at least a touch of a concern for honour and purity inherited from an earlier time. Textile workers, at first the fullers then the shearers, showed themselves capable of common action in the protection of their own interests. Sailors and especially fishermen did have a sense of a common and separate identity but the dispersed nature of employment for seamen made common action difficult, and for fishermen a combination of the shared ownership of boats and vertical lines of profit-sharing perhaps blurred class lines. Regular pay together with military discipline and loyalties meant that industrial action was rare in the Dutch army – in sharp contrast to the Spanish.[34] Servants, too, despite their very large numbers, were kept apart by their mode of employment, and their bargaining power was undermined by their origins and gender, as many of them were immigrants and a high proportion female. The evidence is limited but it would seem that the labouring classes as a whole shared to a great extent the values of the dominant culture, though modified by group – and possibly regional – variations.

What all these groups of workers – women as well as men, for among the poorest paid were female workers in the textile industry – did have in common was their relative poverty and the precarious nature of their livelihood. The broad spread of wealth through the middling ranges of society in town and countryside was both characteristic and new in Dutch society in this period, yet poverty remained and a majority of the population – even in the most prosperous towns of Holland – probably felt its keen pinch at some stage in their lives. Again the nature of the problem varied from region to region, and place to place, but the poor were everywhere and few could be free of the fear that illness, accident or misfortune might pull them down into poverty. As far as the towns are concerned, despite the large size of the middling groups there, 50 per cent or more on average of the population were not subject to direct taxation because they had too little property and their incomes were too low. This was the area of society where individuals and families were most vulnerable, and which were hit hardest by any economic downturn. This problem was particularly acute in the textile towns of Leiden and Haarlem where a cyclical depression in the demand for wool and linen cloth could throw thousands of families into temporary but severe want. However, it seems that a large proportion of those too poor to pay taxes were able at least to make ends meet for most of the time, feeding and clothing themselves and their families adequately, by contemporary standards at least. It has been calculated that the wages of an unskilled worker were not sufficient to support a family and that at this level of society both wives and children needed to work in order to maintain an adequate income for the family as a whole.[35] On the other hand the same author can also claim that no-one died of starvation in the Republic anymore,[36] which is a bold claim and probably not literally true, but it does suggest the extent to which Dutch society had already diverged in a very important way from the contemporary European norm. In a century when famines were still frequently bringing death, directly and indirectly, on a massive scale in most parts of Europe the Dutch, with their grip on the Baltic grain trade, their advanced agriculture, and – perhaps most importantly – their efficient internal transport system, may have experienced high grain prices but not true dearth. Famine was almost a thing of the past after the serious shortages of the 1590s.

Certain groups were recognised officially as needing and deserving help; these were chiefly those suffering from what might be called life-cycle poverty rather than total and permanent destitution. There was institutional aid for widows with children, for orphans, for the sick, and for the aged and infirm. Although infant and child mortality was the biggest killer, nevertheless death in young adulthood and early middle age was frequent enough to make parentless children a major concern of the civil authorites. One or more municipal orphanages were a standard institution in Dutch towns at this time, though the best provision was often restricted to the children of citizens, and the Reformed Church and other religious organisations also founded orphanages to provide appropriate care for orphans from their own communities. The significance contemporaries attached to the problem of orphans and the importance of the duty owed to them is shown by the fact that one of the most important branches of local government was the *weeskamer* which had responsibility for the supervision of interests and property of underage orphans. The *weesmeesters* with ultimate responsibility for the activities of the *weeskamer* were usually prominent regents, though the *weeshuismeesters* who supervised the running of the orphanages were more likely to be prominent and respectable citizens but outside the regent group.

Widows with dependent children were likewise seen as a group which needed and deserved help. They were likely to be a particular problem in the seaports where sailors made up a high proportion of the workforce, as these were subject to the perils of life at sea on top of the normal dangers of an early death which they shared with the rest of the population. Aid came in various forms but was more usually in kind than in cash and from a variety of municipal and religious instances. There were special provisions for the old, too, with municipal homes for old men and women (separate) and the foundation of *hofjes*, supervised dwellings grouped round a courtyard, was a favourite object of private charity. The number of places available even in a combination of official and private provision remained low, but this reflects the limited nature of the problem rather than suggesting that there were a large number of old people left out in the cold in the Dutch towns. Not many people reached old age and, even for those who did, it was inability to work not age in itself that was seen as the problem. People did not retire but worked until they were no longer able to do so. (This was true at all levels of society even where work was not a financial necessity.)

Quite a high proportion of the population might find themselves in receipt of municipal aid or relief from private charitable sources at one time or another. Most people would run into difficulties at some time in their lives – through widowhood, injury, illness – and economic downturns could throw large numbers into temporary un- or underemployment. The poor relief system which operated in both towns and countryside was designed to alleviate, but not solve such problems. Official relief was often at least partly channelled through the Reformed Church, whose deacons were responsible for charitable works within their community. Those who were not members of the official church could find it more difficult to obtain help, and in any case other major religious groups had powerful incentives to look after their own. For the catholics helping their own poor was an important way of holding the community together and perhaps guarding it against pressures to convert to a confession which could offer more in material terms. In general, the town governments of Holland seem to have been only too pleased to see the catholics take the burden of their poor off an always overstretched municipal poor relief system. Neither official nor private instances saw it as their job to make long term and full provision, the help they offered was intended to be supplementary. The primary resource of the poor, the ill, the widowed and the old was expected to be their family, friends and neighbours, with official and private charity filling in the gaps. Anyone without family or an equivalent social support network was very vulnerable in this society.

Despite the overall prosperity and relatively wide spread of wealth in Dutch towns, the price and availability of bread continued to be a major concern. On the whole, control of the international grain market secured the Dutch population against severe bread shortages, but price and quality remained sensitive issues. Town governments stockpiled grain for use in emergencies and interfered in the market to control quality.[37] Town populations were volatile at best, but bread riots or even serious disturbances were comparatively rare in seventeenth century Holland.[38] For much of the Dutch population, certainly in the towns, the margins of existence were narrow, and so any change in the price of very basic items like bread could have serious knock-on effects. On the other hand, it must be stressed that the food supply was maintained, and that the Republic in the main avoided the famines and dearths which affected almost all of the rest of Europe with depressing frequency.

The rich were rich and the poor poor in the Republic as elsewhere, but the contrasts were perhaps less sharp, and the middle ground certainly larger, than elsewhere in Europe at the time. The economic profile of the population, in the countryside as well as in the towns, was significantly different from that of more traditional societies. The maritime region, of course, had advanced much further in this direction than the land provinces, but it would also probably be true to say that the latter only appear backward in contrast to the highly developed west of the country. In degree of urbanisation, penetration of the economy by market forces, and expanding middle class even Overijssel and North Brabant were quite advanced by the standards of contemporary Europe. So though regional contrasts were significant, they should not obscure the extent to which the society of the Republic as a whole constituted a new phenomenon in European history.

The birth of a secular society

It is perhaps less fashionable than it once was to search for the origins of the modern secular society in the aftermath of the Reformation, and particularly in the Dutch Republic and England in the seventeenth century. It has become difficult to ignore the extent to which the religious divisions of the sixteenth century led to an intensification of strife and, particularly, a renewed stress on the political and social importance of religious unity to the developing states of the time. As a consequence, confessionalisation rather than toleration has come to be regarded as the hallmark of the post Reformation period,[39] with both catholic and protestant Europe attempting to enforce their respective faiths and to impose what was regarded as a true christian morality on the population at large with an altogether new rigour. Moreover, the demand for religious homogeneity and purity is now seen as coming at least as much from below as being imposed from above by intolerant governments. To take perhaps the most notorious example, the Revocation of the Edict of Nantes was not just the work of a bigoted king – though it was certainly that – but was also the response to a widespread and organised public demand. From this perspective, religious toleration and pluralism are likely to be hard to find in the seventeenth century. The historiographical pendulum has, perhaps, swung too far in this respect, for one possible response to religious differences was limited toleration on pragmatic grounds rather than increased repression. This was the outcome in England after the revolution of 1688: at the end of a century scarred by severe civil conflict fuelled to a large extent by religious rifts, relative stability was sought and in the end found through a measure of toleration of protestant dissenters. The role of William (Willem) III and his Dutch advisers in bringing about this relatively benign outcome should not be underestimated, not least because the Dutch Republic had taken this road a century earlier.

As in so many other respects, the Dutch were different in their response to the religious conflicts and problems of the seventeenth century. The pluralism and toleration of Dutch society should certainly not be exaggerated: there was evidently still an urgently felt need for an official, privileged church; complete freedom for catholics was as yet not only politically impossible, but almost if not quite unthinkable; and, above all, any moves towards secularisation had to remain within a fundamentally christian framework. Moreover, failure or refusal to persecute did not mean that dissenting views were seen as legitimate: the belief that there was only one religious truth and only one path to God was still almost universal in the Republic as elsewhere in the Europe of the time. Nevertheless, even if the established myth of Dutch toleration needs at least some modification[40], not least because of the implicit inequality between the tolerated and those doing the tolerating, protestants who were not members of the Reformed Church, catholics and Jews enjoyed significantly greater freedom in the Republic than their counterparts did in the rest of Europe.

The fundamental point in which the Republic differed from the standard contemporary pattern was that, although it was the official confession, there was no legal compulsion to become a member of the Reformed Church. In a religiously divided Europe, membership of a political community and membership of that community's church were expected to be coterminous; religious dissent was regarded as the equivalent of political disloyalty and thus tantamount to treason. In the Dutch case, the official church remained to a significant extent a private organisation with control over its own membership, and there was an inherent, underlying tension between its desire to embrace as large a proportion of the population as possible and its instinct to maintain very high standards of doctrine and conduct for its members. As the Republic emerged from the turmoil of the Revolt in the last years of the sixteenth century only a rather small proportion of the population were members of the Church, and it was probably well into the seventeenth century before even a simple majority were full members.[41] The Reformed Church became the official church of the new Dutch state and was allowed to take over for its own use the buildings of the old church. As time went by its membership increased and reached something like two thirds of the total population by the second half of the century. Formally all holders of political office at every level from town regent to member of the States General and from town secretary to *raadpensionaris*[42] were expected to be members of the

Church, and this was in fact increasingly the case. However, membership of the Reformed Church was not coterminous with membership of the community, and could not be so as long as the former retained the right to exclude from membership those it regarded as unsuitable. Before the Revolt the Reformed Church had endured many years of persecution, and this time 'under the cross' left it with a sense of being a gathered church of believers whose commitment to the faith and readiness to make sacrifices for it was very high, and this inevitably clashed with the desire to embrace the greater part of the population whose commitment was necessarily going to be less absolute. The practical question was whether the Reformed Church was to remain a community of saints or become a church for the community as a whole: in the end it perhaps fell between the two stools by embracing most but not all of the population in most areas of the Republic,[43] and in the process losing something of the rigour of its congregational discipline.

The Reformed Church had had an independent existence before the Revolt and the official introduction of protestant worship, and was never fully under political control. Similarly there was powerful resistance within the regent group to imposing a religious monopoly, particularly if this would involve the coercion of consciences. This was at least in part an ideological position: it was almost a commonplace of an influential strand of Dutch humanist thought from Erasmus to Coornhert and beyond that only persuasion not force was an appropriate tool in religious matters, and this conviction or argument was a significant part of the climate of opinion in which the regents were operating in the difficult and confusing decades just after the Revolt. More important, perhaps, were practical considerations: in the midst of a war and with membership of the Reformed Church notoriously low, any attempt to impose Reformed uniformity on the whole of the population would have been to court disaster. Most contemporary governments would nevertheless have made the attempt: that the Dutch authorities chose not to do so is an indication of their fundamentally secular priorities. Internal peace and order were implicitly preferred to religious purity and homogeneity. In consequence, almost from the beginning of the Republican period there was in effect full freedom of conscience for both protestant dissenters and catholics, though such rights were never clearly guaranteed by law.

The situation of the catholics was always more difficult: they enjoyed freedom of conscience, but were not allowed to worship in public and they were outsiders in their own land. The position was, or became, more favourable in practice than it appeared in theory; as the century wore on the catholics were increasingly able to practise their faith despite the legal prohibitions. By the second half of the century at least, catholics in most areas were able to worship in 'hidden' churches (*schuilkerken*), though there can have been no real secrecy involved either in town or in countryside. It must have been obvious to all but the most innocent what was going on, but as long as a respectable pretence at clandestinity was maintained and a certain discretion observed the catholics were left to worship undisturbed – that is as long as they paid their dues to the local police authority, the *schout* or *baljuw*. The existence of restrictive laws meant that catholic worship could be made more difficult by unscrupulous, greedy or merely bigoted officials at a local level, with no effective legal recourse, but in the long term the priority accorded to civil peace encouraged a distinctly lax enforcement of anti-catholic legislation. It was also at the least convenient for the local authorities that the catholics be allowed to develop their own independent organisations, especially for poor relief.

There was no real attempt on the part of the Dutch authorities to prevent the creation of a new structure for the Catholic Church in the Republic – as a mission territory under a vicar general based in Köln – a task which was more or less completed by the middle of the century.[44] Particularly in those areas where catholics were relatively numerous, it was in the interests of the local authorities to allow them to set up their own social welfare network. It eventually became usual for catholics to organise a separate poor relief system, to run their own orphanages, and in general to look after their own. The peculiar needs generated by the difficult situation of the old church produced a distinctly new social phenomenon, the *klopje*. The new generation of mission priests who took up their tasks in the early decades of the century in the main lacked any sort of organisational infrastructure to help them with their multifarious tasks. There being no place in the Republic for regular orders of monks or nuns, there arose a hybrid order of 'holy virgins' who dedicated themselves to the service of the church but without taking a nun's vows and who, most importantly, worked in the community rather than remaining hidden away in a closed order. Sometimes living alone, sometimes in small communities, the *klopjes* became an indispensable part of the running of the catholic mission in the Republic, although the catholic hierarchy was never really comfortable with them. The idea of an active calling in the world for female religious was more than somewhat challenging to conventional thinking within the Catholic Church, and in any case the peculiar circumstances of the Holland Mission gave the *klopjes* rather more freedom of action and distinctly more influence than the Church felt on the whole to be proper for the laity and particularly for laywomen.[45] In general the relations between clergy and laity had to be renegotiated under the rigours of the situation facing the Church in the Republic: the number of secular and regular clergy in the Mission could never remotely approach the pre-Revolt level and the Church was heavily dependent on the organisational efforts of the laity, and consequently the latter had a far more influential role in church affairs than anywhere else, except perhaps in the rather similar situation of the English Mission.[46]

Although catholics were never subject to persecution for their beliefs, and their situation improved in practice in the course of the seventeenth century, they nevertheless remained at best second-class citizens and at worst excluded by the very fact of their religion from membership of the Dutch nation. In the years immediately after the Revolt, there were still large numbers of regents who were more or less openly catholic, but in the new century this changed and, particularly after the crisis of 1618, all political offices were reserved for members of the Reformed Church. Town governments in Holland became exclusively reformed in theory – and mostly in practice also – after this time, though some irregularities may have occurred from time to time in the countryside. Similarly, catholics were progressively excluded from formal membership of the *ridderschappen* or politically active nobilities of the various provinces. The same exclusion applied to protestant dissenters, but it was still possible for these to feel part of the emergent Dutch nation. Catholics, however, were inevitably side-lined by the protestant, though not necessarily reformed, nature of the national identity which was being forged in the course of the seventeenth and eighteenth centuries. How this affected catholics in the Republic in general is unclear, but it seems likely that in the overwhelmingly catholic areas of the south – States Brabant and Limburg – political loyalty to the Dutch state was tenuous to say the least.

Protestant dissenters – i.e. those who were not members of the Reformed Church – were in a considerably more favourable position. In effect, baptists, lutherans and, eventually, remonstrants enjoyed freedom of worship as well as conscience, though this freedom was never placed on an entirely unambiguous legal basis. Again, members of these religious groups were in principle and largely in practice excluded from taking a full part in political life as they, like catholics, were barred from participation in government at local, provincial or Generality level. They were, however, much easier to fit comfortably into the nascent idea of a Dutch identity than the catholics were. There was a sense that, despite doctrinal and ecclesiological differences, all protestants were essentially on the same side. In contrast, at the beginning of the century it was still conventional among protestants to regard catholics as being in the camp of Anti-Christ, and even at its end the most enlightened protestants continued to see the Catholic Church as essentially an evil institution. Protestant ecumenism made considerable advances in the course of the century, finding its most radical – though not most typical – expression in the collegiant movement in all its diversity. There is some evidence that, in the countryside of Holland at least, mennonites were able and, even more surprisingly perhaps, willing to take a modest part in local government. Protestant dissenters do not seem to have been subject to the same degree of social exclusion that the catholics had to face, and there is little or no trace of the alienation from the political authorities and even from Dutch society as a whole that seems to have shaped popular attitudes in, say, North Brabant.

This remained, of course, an age of fierce religious disputes and the degree of common feeling among the various protestant groups should not be exaggerated. The law was invoked and used against religious views and beliefs which were considered beyond the Pale by conventional opinion. A catch-all term for what was regarded as intolerable was 'socinian', which was used as much as a term of abuse as to describe a precise theological position. What was objected to in particular was the rationalism which was felt to be so corrosive of central christian beliefs. Socinian scepticism regarding the doctrine of the trinity was a fundamental problem for conventional opinion as it was regarded as inevitably implying a denial of the divinity of Christ, which in turn was interpreted as a form of atheism. As true religion was believed to be the sole basis of morality, it followed that atheism could only undermine the moral foundations of society. In consequence, the public expression of atheistic ideas was regarded as being subversive of good order as well as being incompatible with a christian society. Even in this case, however, people could not be prosecuted for holding such beliefs; it was their public expression in speech or print that was banned.

The one occasion when religious disputes threatened to plunge the country into civil war was a special case, as it was a dispute *within* the Reformed Church. The conflict within the Church in the first decades of the century which resulted in the condemnation and expulsion of the remonstrants at the synod of Dordt (i.e. Dordrecht) went to the heart of the nature of the Church as well as to its proper doctrine, and the condemned party was regarded by the orthodox as aiming at the corruption of both. Toleration was not the issue: once the remonstrants had accepted their expulsion from the Reformed Church there were no insurmountable obstacles to them setting themselves up as a separate church – though it has to be admitted that there was at first furious and very vocal opposition to this from the reformed. The new Remonstrant Church found a thoroughly respectable place in Dutch society within a couple of decades of the crisis, and in social and cultural terms its members were much closer to the centre of Dutch life than the baptists.

The way that the Jews who settled in their country – mostly, though not exclusively, in Amsterdam – were treated can be taken as a touchstone of the degree to which Dutch society had begun to diverge from the European norm. Elsewhere in Europe, Jews were either not tolerated at all or subject to more or less severe official restrictions, often backed up by popular violence. Spain, emulated by Portugal, had forcibly converted its Jews at the end of the fifteenth century but the *conversos* remained under suspicion and many fled the country. In eastern Europe, long established Jewish communities came under increasing pressure during the early modern period, marked by a particularly vicious series of pogroms around the middle of the seventeenth century, driving successive waves of refugees west. The first Jewish community in Amsterdam was part of the Iberian diaspora, and this was joined by eastern European refugees later in the century. In the Republic these Jews were able to worship freely, but without ever being given any clear legal right to do so. Despite the uncertainty of their situation they were allowed to build synagogues for the two communities, and there was not even any attempt to make these buildings inconspicuous in the eyes of the christian community. In this their position was more favourable than that of the catholics for whom public worship was unambiguously forbidden by law, but rather less secure than that of the protestant dissenters.

In Amsterdam the relationship between the town government and

the Jewish community was marked from the beginning by a characteristic ambivalence; the regents were prepared to allow considerable
freedom to the Jews in their town, but wished to avoid giving too many
hostages to fortune by an overly lenient public attitude. Consequently,
most important issues seem to have been resolved behind closed doors,
with regular meetings between representatives of the community and
the town government but with little or nothing on paper and nothing
at all announced.[47] The Jews were not forced into a ghetto: they did
tend to settle more densely in a limited number of areas within the
town, but this appears to have been by choice and from convenience.
There were some economic restrictions on Jews, notably their exclusion
from the craft guilds, and an underlying fear that they might in some
way contaminate the christian community explains some other legal
restrictions – such as on the employment of christian maidservants. In
the main, however, it is the extent to which they were accepted into
Dutch society that is more striking in the context of the times. The
favourable reception given to the Iberian Jews in the early years of the
century can in part be explained by their wealth and trade connections,
and also by their situation as fellow victims of Spanish persecution.
The Ashkenazi who came from eastern European later in the century,
however, were mostly poor and distinctly less well connected, but they
had the advantage of finding a situation where favourable terms had
already been negotiated by their better placed brethren. These circumstances allowed the Jews to set up their own educational system,
develop or re-establish their cultural traditions, and make Amsterdam
the most important meeting point between Jewish and christian
thinkers in the seventeenth century. The Jewish community in the
Republic proved capable of producing both the great mediator between
the two traditions, Manasseh ben Israel, and a philosopher who united
both in condemning him, Spinoza. It is not surprising that the latter
felt able to declare that:

> we have the rare happiness of living in a republic, where everyone's
> judgement is free and unshackled, where each may worship God as his
> conscience dictates, and where freedom is esteemed before all things
> dear and precious.[48]

It is true that Spinoza had to be circumspect, particularly with regard
to what he published during his lifetime, but this was not because he
was a Jew but because his ideas were indeed thoroughly subversive of

the conventional religious beliefs of the time, Jewish as much as christian. Religious polemicists in the seventeenth century were all too ready to accuse their opponents of atheism but in Spinoza's case, although he vehemently denied the charge, they had considerable justification as his definition of God was bizarre by any standards.

Freedom of expression was thus far from absolute, and its limits were determined by political as well as religious considerations. That the civil authorities in the Republic were concerned to try to restrict comment in print on political matters is hardly surprising – such matters were regarded as being the business of government alone.[49] Their lack of success is more remarkable: floods of pamphlets and fly-sheets accompanied the major political events of the century,[50] and such sporadic and often inconclusive prosecutions as took place were wholly inadequate to stop them. What perhaps needs to be made clear is that there were distinct limits as to what could be expressed openly in religious matters: there were inevitable restrictions on freedom of speech and publishing in a society which regarded itself as fundamentally christian, and further restrictions came as a result of the official position and influence of the Reformed Church.

The notorious case of Adriaen Koerbagh, who was convicted of blasphemy in 1668 and died in the Amsterdam *rasphuis*, shows how dangerous it could be to upset the sensibilities of the official church. Self-censorship, of course, has left less evidence, but it appears that the limits of what would be tolerated, though far from clear in law, were well understood in practice, and those who challenged these conventions usually took the precaution not only of not using their own name but also of disguising both the publisher and the place of publication. The large number of printing presses which existed especially in Holland made it difficult for the authorities to track offenders down. However, atheism was seen even by the most liberal of thinkers as a threat to the moral basis of society and, similarly, there was as yet little room for a relativism which would accept the validity of religions other than christianity. Even within christianity an inherent protestant bias meant that catholic apologetics in general and attacks on protestantism in particular were frowned upon. On the other hand, the degree to which the Reformed Church could silence its protestant rivals was never clear in principle and varied widely in practice over time and place. The civil authorities at grass roots level had a great deal of lee-way as to how they interpreted their duties in this respect, and neither provincial nor central government could do much about it. At all times, however, the civil authorities had to give considerable weight to the views and prejudices of the Reformed Church. In the course of the century it became by far the largest single denomination, and in the towns of Holland, where otherwise the most liberal policy might have been expected, the Church came to embrace over three quarters of the population.[51] The reformed ministers were an educated and vocal group with considerable popular influence; their views as to what was acceptable had to be taken seriously.

Yet there were limits: the perennial complaints of the reformed about the activities of the catholics were answered by edict after edict confirming the restrictions on them, but there was usually no tightening up of enforcement in practice. The decencies were being observed, that was all. In the end, the local authorities would do what they judged would best serve the peace and order of their communities; they might make concessions to the prejudices of the reformed when it seemed expedient to do so, but their priorities were essentially secular. In the regents' scheme of values, good order and prosperity came before confessional unity or the religious purity of the community, and in this respect they differed sharply from their counterparts in the rest of seventeenth century Europe.

Another way in which the secularisation of Dutch society manifested itself was in the loosening or even ending of the ties between certain social institutions and religion. The process can be seen both in official or formal bodies and in less formal social practices which were losing their religious significance or connotations, and becoming focused on more secular purposes such as conviviality or mutual help. One obvious and important example is poor relief, though here the involvement of religious institutions remained generally strong. Local authorities took over responsibility for the provision of aid to those in material need even if they chose often to act in part through the deacons of the Reformed Church. The latter, of course, lacked the financial and capital resources of the old church, and so their ability to act depended on how much its collections brought in, and on subsidies from the civil authorities. The motives behind poor relief were more broadly humanitarian – though understood in the light of christian teachings – and expedient than purely religious. The prime aim was to help to maintain the stability of the community rather than helping to save the souls of those who gave to the poor – or of the recipients of relief. There was, however, a countervailing force in the tendency of dissenters and catholics to look after their own poor, both to preserve them from the temptation to convert to calvinism and as an expression of communal solidarity within these groups.

Similarly, the care of orphans was a particularly pressing problem in an age where the early death of adults was common, and the secularisation of mainstream support was counterbalanced by the foundation of separate institutions by religious minorities. The orphanages in the towns of Holland came under the control of the town governments in the course of the Revolt, if they had not already been before. They could be restricted to children of citizens or accept all orphans, but in either case they were municipal institutions with primarily secular functions.[52] They were run independently of the Reformed Church, but as municipal institutions they would naturally be associated with the official church and the orphans would be brought up in its teachings and attend its services. In reaction to this linkage between municipal care and reformed orthodoxy, catholics and protestant dissenters sought to found institutions to take care of their own orphans. However, in Friesland at least, the confessionalisation of poor-relief seems to have been a response to the difficulties stemming from economic stagnation and decline and was not characteristic of the years of growth and prosperity.[53]

Thus in the midst of a general process of secularisation there was a tendency towards the independent provision of welfare and other services by separate religious communities. It has been suggested that these developments were part of a broader movement after about the middle of the seventeenth century which to a significant extent anticipated the *verzuiling* or pillarisation of Dutch society in the late nineteenth and early twentieth centuries.[54] This greatly exaggerates the degree of separation between the various religious groups: even if there was some movement in this direction, the separate 'pillars' were clearly not as distinct in the seventeenth century as they were to be later. However, the protestant and even specifically reformed character of public life in the Republic made it an alien environment for catholics and to some extent for protestant dissenters also. Secularisation would in the end create a religiously neutral public space, but only after the fall of the Republic.

The craft guilds had had an important religious dimension before the Revolt, with religious processions, private chapels and endowments, but these disappeared under the new situation in the Republic. The guilds retained their economic role of organising and regulating their crafts (under the firm control of the town governments), and they remained important in reinforcing group solidarity through social activities, but now without the religious dimension. The civic militia, too, changed in the course of the Eighty Years War from semi-private *schutters'* guilds, with strong religious overtones, to *schutterijen*, municipally organised militias with strong convivial elements but without the religious implications which had informed much of such activity in the past.

In so far as Dutch society remained firmly christian in character and its politics restricted to members of the Reformed Church, it seems hard to make a case for any significant progress towards secularisation during this century. Catholics, who were not only excluded from politics but also alienated by the markedly protestant character of the emergent Dutch national identity, would certainly have known that they were not living in a religiously neutral society. Yet there are unmistakable signs that the link between religion and political community had already been decisively weakened. Despite the privileged position of the Reformed Church, this was a religiously pluralist society and one, moreover, in which there was surprisingly little inter-denominational conflict. Despite the general protestant distrust of the Catholic Church, and despite the fact that the Republic was at war with major catholic powers for much of this period, there were apparently no anti-catholic riots during the seventeenth century. Indeed, the most serious religiously motivated violence came as a result of the remonstrant–contraremonstrant split within the Reformed Church, not of clashes between denominations.

The regents as a group put secular goals such as order and prosperity ahead of religious purity, and more and more areas of social life became religiously neutral, at least as far as protestants were concerned. There were formal and informal restrictions on what could be published, but this still left the Republic as by far the most open society in Europe with regard to freedom of the press. Protestant dissenters suffered no social disabilities, and catholics too were equal under the law. Although both minorities were barred from politics, this was not a disability which affected them alone: given the oligarchic nature of the Dutch political system, the vast majority of the members of the Reformed Church similarly had no chance of sharing in the exercise of political power. It is true that an atavistic need for a common religion as a force for unity and as a necessary component of national identity persisted into the eighteenth century; but it is also true that the existence in practice of a number of different churches and sects in the Republic was already working to make this relationship obsolete. In this respect as in so many others, the Republic had to a considerable extent, though not entirely, broken with the social pattern of the past. A secularised society was beginning to take shape by the end of the century, but the catholics in particular had to suffer from the persistence of older attitudes and perceptions. Indeed, until well after the end of the Republic and when secularisation had in other respects made spectacular progress, the catholics were still to a significant extent outsiders in their own society, particularly in relation to the degree to which Dutch national identity remained decidedly protestant.

How different was Dutch society?

Travellers' accounts and the remarks of other contemporaries give the impression that the Republic was seen as in many respects a curiosity in seventeenth century Europe. Such comments usually, but by no means always, suggest that such Dutch deviations from the European norm were a bad thing. In contrast, already by the later eighteenth century the peculiar virtues of the Republic in the Golden Age were being used by Dutch commentators as a way of highlighting the moral deficiencies that were seen as being one of the main causes of the economic decline of the Dutch state. In modern historical writings the consensus until recently has been both that the Dutch had been different and that this was on the whole a very good thing.[55] The complacency which was all too often evident in such judgements has perhaps inevitably provoked something of a backlash, and a new orthodoxy is emerging which stresses the similarities between Dutch experience, even in the seventeenth century, and that of the rest of Europe, and plays down the significance of such differences as undeniably existed. This historiographical fashion is a valuable corrective in so far as it throws light on important but neglected aspects of Dutch seventeenth century history and is a useful reminder that, whatever its peculiar characteristics, the Dutch state was an integral part of Europe. However, it is far from the whole truth, and perhaps suffers from allowing the trees to obscure the wood.

There can be little serious doubt that Dutch society was different from that of the rest of Europe; the question is rather whether the differences that existed were sufficient to suggest that this was a distinct type of social system. The Republic was a small country, both in area and population, and through the nature of its economy was in constant and intense contact with the rest of Europe. To a large extent this meant that the Dutch were necessarily part of wider European social patterns, and that perhaps Dutch seventeenth century society should rather be seen as an anticipation of more general European developments or as a peculiar modulation on a common European theme. A related question is whether this was the first modern or capitalist society, or whether it is better understood as a development of the urban society of the later Middle Ages in the Netherlands. If, as has been argued, this was the first modern economy,[56] must it not also have produced the first modern society? On the other hand, perhaps Dutch capitalism at this time should be seen as an extension of the late medieval urban economy of the region as much as the first example of a peculiarly modern form of capitalism. There is also a further qualification to be made: what was different about the Dutch was to be found primarily in the maritime region and in its most obvious form in Holland, while the rest of the country was distinctly more in line with conditions in the rest of north-western Europe.

The best period in which to explore such issues is the two or three decades after the middle of the century when the results of a century and a half of overall growth intensified by sixty or so years of boom can be observed. Before this brief period of fruition, Dutch society was still changing rapidly, and after it the long-term economic trend turned decisively downward and society began to adjust to the effects of stagnation and recession rather than growth. At this time the maritime region reached the peak of its process of urbanisation with something over 60 per cent of the population of Holland living in the towns, and the economic distinction between town and countryside had largely disappeared. Both sectors were now more or less equally integrated into the market economy, and the social stratification of the rural areas had become very similar to that of the towns. The overall population of the region had reached its peak and stabilised (though the details of demographic developments can only be estimated) by these years, with only a handful of the largest towns of Holland continuing to show significant growth.[57] The situation of the land provinces was significantly different, as they had largely missed out on the boom years, and were only now able to resume the modest degree of economic growth and social change which had characterised the region in the early sixteenth century. Nevertheless even here the proportion of the population living in towns was well above what was normal for even the more developed parts of the rest of Europe, and the power of the Holland economy had sucked them into the market economy to a degree hardly less complete than was the case in the maritime region. Whether the land provinces, States Brabant and the other Generality Lands benefited from this development, or whether they should be seen as quasi-colonies of Holland, is another matter entirely.

The sort of social stratification typical of the late medieval town had now spread to the whole of Dutch society, at least in the maritime region. What was most remarkable was the rise of the bourgeoisie in both town and countryside. This is obvious in the towns with the growth in size and wealth of the middling section of society, but it is also true of the Holland countryside. The rural bourgeoisie consisted not only of the group of large-scale farmers producing for the market, but also of those involved in the flourishing craft and, especially, transport sector. Indeed, it could be argued that the influence of a bourgeoisie of this sort was greater in the rural areas of the maritime region than in the towns. Whereas in the towns all political power was in the hands of the regents and the upper bourgeoisie could rival the social influence of the *smalle gemeente*, the villages were run by men of much more modest means who, in Holland at least, to a large extent had eclipsed the local nobility in political as well as social and economic terms.

The decline and near fall of the nobility in the maritime region of the Republic was one of the aspects of Dutch society which marked it off most clearly from a Europe which was still almost universally dominated by its nobles. In Holland, the economy was run and the tone in society was set by the bourgeoisie, while the nobility fell drastically in numbers as well as being marginalised economically and politically. In Friesland too the old nobility would appear to have lost out to a new oligarchy of largely urban origin.[58] It is true that the social prestige of the nobility survived almost intact even in the heart of the new society in Holland, but this represents an ambivalence which was to be expected when the rest of Europe was still under the spell of a noble culture and ideology. Even after most of Europe had moved into the era of industrial capitalism, the social preeminence of the nobility proved remarkably persistent, so it is hardly surprising if the effects of a millennium or more of cultural brain-washing were not wiped out in a mere century and a half. In addition, the decline of the nobility was largely confined to the maritime region, at least in political terms. The social influence of the nobles in this region also seems to have remained high, though there is reason to believe that their economic position may have weakened significantly, as their demographic situation certainly did.[59] Overall, the nature of the break with traditional society is exemplified in the incomplete and ambivalent bourgeois triumph over the nobility.

The aspect of Dutch life that perhaps impressed contemporaries as most distinctive was the extent of religious toleration, and it is significant that this was far more condemned than praised. For most of Europe, there could be only one truth and so any deviation from the public church and its teachings was by definition not just wrong but an affront to Christ, and any community which was prepared to tolerate such blasphemy in its midst might expect, and would certainly deserve, divine retribution. Such conventional beliefs were also held by the Reformed Church, but it was unable to translate them into public policy. Although the regents were members of the public church and shared its beliefs and prejudices, their essentially secular priorities, together with the principled distaste for religious persecution of any sort which was a powerful strand in the cultural tradition of the Netherlands, ensured that protestant dissenters would have almost total freedom of worship and even catholics freedom of conscience – and increasingly of practice too, if exercised with discretion.

The openness of Dutch society was limited by the almost universal assumption of its fundamentally christian character, which meant that atheism and other radical questioning of received ideas and beliefs were in principle unacceptable, though in practice it was only their too public expression which was likely to cause trouble. However, the social weight of conventional thinking was more powerful than is often suggested, and those professing quite minor variations on orthodoxy could find themselves in difficulties. Throughout the second half of the century the Reformed Church did its best to suppress cartesian rationalism, not only in theology but also more generally in the universities, and was able to win at least formal support from the States of Holland at first. Even in the last decades of the century, Balthasar

Bekker, too, was condemned and suspended from his position as minister in Amsterdam because of his questioning of conventional beliefs and attitudes towards the question of witchcraft. The effects of the struggle of the Reformed Church against what it regarded as the spiritual corruption of the age – its battle against rationalism and the first shafts of the Enlightenment – reached beyond the church itself. Cartesians in the Dutch universities had to exercise considerable caution in what they taught and wrote, and the new learned periodicals which sprang up in the Republic in the later part of the century were not entirely free to print what they liked in the sensitive areas of theology and philosophy.

Nevertheless, this Dutch version of the christian society was compatible with a remarkably high degree of religious toleration. The reasons for this singular development are complex, but a vital contribution was made by the generation of a set of essentially secular priorities for the state. Traditionally, the prime purpose of the political community and the justification of the powers held by its governors was the protection and preservation of the true religion. Although all holders of political office in the Republic were required to be members of the Reformed Church, the Dutch state moved significantly closer to a new conception of the purpose of the state. The preservation of independence, the maintenance of public order and the promotion of common prosperity became the primary guidelines for political action, and these were not only essential secular common aims, they normally took precedence over spiritual and religious concerns. The Republic was a christian country but its central aims as a state ignored considerations of religious purity, and this may have contributed to its contemporary reputation for hypocrisy.

By the end of the century, there was the clear beginning of the development of a public space which was religiously neutral, at least between varieties of protestantism. Here the catholics, too, could find a considerable measure of common ground with their protestant fellow-countrymen. While remaining profoundly christian, Dutch society had moved a considerable way on the road to the privatisation of religion and the creation of a set of common political purposes no longer dependent on religious justifications which are among the prime characteristics of the modern secular state.

Most, if not all, of the rest of Europe was clearly still in an earlier stage of social development than the Dutch, but the latter were by no means as clear of the trammels of the past as is sometimes suggested. The heart of the new society that was developing in the Republic lay in the province of Holland and, to a less pronounced extent, in the maritime region as a whole. The land provinces had broken less decisively with the past, though in comparison with much of contemporary Europe even they showed unmistakable signs of having moved into the capitalist era. To some extent the society of the future could already be seen in the Republic by the second half of the seventeenth century, but this is only part of the picture. Traditional forms and perceptions were still present in ways which are often difficult to pin down and even more difficult to evaluate, but Dutch social life cannot be fully understood without a proper appreciation of the force of these survivals. On the other hand, the pattern offered by the Dutch at this time contrasts significantly with the bourgeois society depicted by historians of the nineteenth century. Yet while it is true that Dutch society in the seventeenth century was in many ways not as modern as it seems, the same could be said of nineteenth century Europe – both were to a significant extent still in the *ancien régime*.

Nevertheless, the unease – even distaste – which Dutch society inspired in many foreign contemporaries is a significant indication of the degree to which it was seen as fundamentally different at the time.

Notes

1   R. Willemsen, *Enkhuizen tijdens de Republiek* (Hilversum, 1988), 91–2.; C.M. Lesger, *Hoorn als stedelijke knooppunt. Stedensystemen tijdens de late middeleeuwen en vroegmoderne tijd* (Hilversum, 1990),141–3.

2   A.M. van der Woude, *Het Noorderkwartier* (Wageningen, 1972),1, 184–5; Piet Boon, *Bouwers van de zee: zeevarende van het Westfriese platteland, c.1680–1720* (The Hague, 1996), 23–4, suggesting that in West-Friesland (part of North Holland) at least the demographic decline may well have set in rather earlier.

3   No stadhouder was appointed by Holland, followed by most of the other provinces, after the death of Willem II in 1650 but Willem Frederick, of the cadet branch of the family, remained stadhouder in Friesland and took over the post in Groningen.

4   General treatment of the regents in the seventeenth century include most recently, J. de Jong, *Een deftig bestaan. Het dagelijks leven van regenten in de 17e en 18e eeuw* (Utrecht and Antwerp, 1987), and J.L. Price, 'De regent', in *Gestalten van de Gouden Eeuw*, ed. H.M. Beliën, A.Th. van Deursen and G.J. van Setten (Amsterdam, 1995), 25–62.

5   See D.J. Roorda, *Partij en factie* (Groningen, 1961).

6   See, for example, the drift away from active involvement in trade of the merchant families studied in Luuc Kooijmans, *Vriendschap en de kunst van het overleven in de zeventiende en achttiende eeuw* (Amsterdam, 1997).

7   E.g. C. Schmidt, *Om de eer van de familie. Het geslacht Teding van Berkhout 1500–1950* (Amsterdam, 1986). This family had branches in a number of Holland towns by the second half of the seventeenth century.

8   A recent study of a town government of this sort is J.C. Streng, *'Stemme in staat'. De bestuurlijke elite in de stadrepubliek Zwolle 1579–1795* (Hilversum, 1997), esp. 95–119.

9   For an introduction to the topic, see J.L. Price, 'The Dutch Nobility in the Seventeenth and Eighteenth Centuries', *The European Nobilities in the Seventeenth and Eighteenth Centuries*, vol.1, ed. H.M. Scott (London, 1995), 82–113.

10 For a different, and perhaps more nuanced, view, see H. van Nierop, *The Nobility of Holland. From knights to regents, 1500–1650* (Cambridge, 1993), 203–7.

11 Van Nierop, *Nobility of Holland*, 214–19.

12 Van Nierop, *Nobility of Holland*, 51.

13 See J.J. de Jong, *Met goed fatsoen. De elite in een Hollandse stad, Gouda 1700–80* (Dieren, 1985); L. Kooijmans, *Onder regenten. De elite in een Hollandse stad, Hoorn 1700–1780* (Dieren, 1985); M. Prak, *Gezeten burgers. De elite in een Hollandse stad, Leiden 1700–1780* (Dieren, 1985).

14 For a helpful introduction to the discussion, see Peter Burke, 'The language of orders in early modern Europe', in *Social Orders and Social Classes in Europe since 1500*, ed. M.L. Bush (London, 1992), 1–12.

15 Except, of course, that women were treated differently by the law than men. Children, too, were inferior to adults in legal rights.

16 Most obviously the records of the taxes on wealth (200th penny etc.) which were imposed frequently but irregularly, but also the registers for the *Familiegeld* of 1674 which was in the event never levied.

17 See B.E. de Muinck, *Een regentenhuishouding omstreeks 1700. Gegevens uit de privé-boekhouding van mr. Cornelis de Jonge van Ellemeet, Ontvanger-Generaal der Verenigde Nederlanden (1646–1721)* (The Hague, 1965).

18 However, candidates for the ministry read theology but did not necessarily take a degree. They were admitted to the ministry after being examined on their knowledge and orthodoxy by a Church commission.

19 A rare exception is the subject of Willem Frijhoff, *Wegen van Evert Willemsz. Een Hollands weeskind op zoek naar zichzelf 1607–1647* (Nijmegen, 1995).

20 E.g. J.L. Price, *Culture and Society in the Dutch Republic during the Seventeenth Century* (London, 1974).

21 For the classic account of the distinctive nature of Dutch seventeenth century culture, see Johan Huizinga, *Dutch Civilisation in the Seventeenth Century* (London, 1968), but note that this was originally written in the 1930s.

22 L.H.M. Wessels, *Bron, waarheid en de verandering der tijden. Jan Wagenaar (1709–1773), een historiografische studie* (The Hague, 1997), 85–6.

23   See, for example, Jan de Vries, 'Between purchasing power and the world of goods: understanding the household economy in early modern Europe', John Brewer and Roy Porter (ed.), *Consumption and the World of Goods* (London, 1993), 85–133.

24   As suggested by Simon Schama, *The Embarrassment of Riches* (New York, 1987).

25   Leo Noordegraaf and Gerrit Valk, *De gave gods. De pest in Holland vanaf de late middeleeuwen* (Bergen, NH, 1988), 52–9.

26   D.J. Noordam, *Leven in Maasland* (Hilversum, 1986), 180–8.

27   A.Th. van Deursen, 'De oude dag in een Hollands dorp', in *In gemeenschap met de tijd* (Amsterdam, 1997), 25–36.

28   Jan de Vries and Ad van der Woude, *The First Modern Economy* (Cambridge, 1997), 77–8.

29   De Vries and Van der Woude, *The First Modern Economy*, 73–4.

30   De Vries and Van der Woude, *The First Modern Economy*, 75–6.

31   C. Trompetter, *Agriculture, Proto-Industry and Mennonite Entrepreneurship. A History of the Textile Industries in Twente 1600–1815* (Amsterdam, 1997), 97–8.

32   Paul Holthuis, *Frontierstad bij het scheiden van de markt. Deventer: militair, demografisch, economisch; 1578–1648* (Houten/Deventer, 1993), 118–20.

33   Rudolf Dekker, 'Labour conflicts and working-class culture in early modern Holland', *International Review of Social History*, 35 (1990), 377–420.

34   Parker, Geoffrey, 'Mutiny and Discontent in the Spanish Army of Flanders, 1572–1607', in *Spain and the Netherlands 1559–1659* (London, 1979), 106–21.

35   A.Th. van Deursen, *Plain Lives in a Golden Age* (Cambridge, 1991), 7–8.

36   Van Deursen, *Plain Lives*, 59.

37   Renée Kistemaker, 'Amsterdam's Municipal Control of Food Supplies', *Rome–Amsterdam. Two Growing Cities in Seventeenth-Century Europe*, ed. Peter van Kessel and Elisja Schulte (Amsterdam, 1997), 221–34.

38   R. Dekker, *Holland in Beroering. Oproeren in de 17de en 18de eeuw* (Baarn, 1982), 121–2.

39   See, for example, R. Po-Chia Hsia, *Social Discipline in the Reformation. Central Europe 1550–1750* (London, 1989); Heinz Schilling, 'Confessionalization in the Empire: Religious and Societal Change in Germany between 1555 and 1620', in *Religion, Political Culture and the Emergence of Early Modern Society* (Leiden, 1992).

40   The notion of Dutch toleration is attacked with almost indecent enthusiasm in M. Gijswijt-Hofstra (ed.), *Een schijn van verdraagzaamheid: afwijking en tolerantie in Nederland van de zestiende eeuw tot heden* (Hilversum, 1989).

41   The situation is complicated by the existence of 'amateurs' (*liefhebbers*) who attended services regularly but were not formal members. It is possible to count members, but not *liefhebbers* .

42   The *raadpensionaris* or grand pensionary, formally the legal adviser to the States of Holland, was in practice the head of the government of the province, and only rivalled by the princes of Orange for leadership in the Republic as a whole.

43   With the notable exception of States Brabant which remained or became almost homogeneously catholic.

44   Some areas in the south of the country were outside the Holland Mission, remaining part of existing bishoprics with their headquarters in the Spanish Netherlands.

45   Marit Monteiro, *Geestelijke maagden. Leven tussen klooster en wereld in Noord-Nederland gedurende de zeventiende eeuw* (Hilversum, 1996); E. Schulte van Kessel, *Geest en vlees in godsdienst en wetenschap* (The Hague, 1980), chaps ii, iii.

46   Cf. the analysis of the rôle of the laity in the Catholic Church in England before emancipation and the return of the hierarchy in John Bossy, *The English Catholic Community, 1570–1850* (London, 1975).

47   R.G. Fuks-Mansveld, *De Sefardim in Amsterdam tot 1795* (Hilversum, 1989), 10.

48   Spinoza, *The Chief Works of*, vol. 1, transl. and ed. by R.H.M. Elwes (New York, 1951), 6.

49   S. Groenveld, 'The Mecca of Authors? States Assemblies and Censorship in the Seventeenth-Century Dutch Republic', in *Too Mighty to be Free: censorship and the press in Britain and the Netherlands*, ed. A.C. Duke and C.A. Tamse (Zutphen, 1987), 63–86.

50   Craig E. Harline, *Pamphlets, Printing and Political Culture in the Early Dutch Republic* (Dordrecht, 1987).

51   The concentration of catholics in the Generality Lands and in some regions of the countryside boosted their numbers in the Republic as a whole.

52   See, for example, Anne E.C. McCants, *Civic Charity in a Golden Age. Orphan Care in Early Modern Amsterdam* (Urbana/Chicago,1997), a study of the *burgerweeshuis* for the orphans of citizens.

53   Joke Spaans, *Armenzorg in Friesland 1500–1800* (Hilversum/Leeuwarden, 1997), 228–9.

54   S. Groenveld, *Huisgenoten des geloofs* (Hilversum, 1995).

55   However, a recent re-reading of Paul Zumthor's *Daily Life in Rembrandt's Holland* (London, 1962), which was first published in French in 1959, reveals a surprising lack of sympathy with the subject.

56   De Vries and Van der Woude, *The First Modern Economy.*

57   Though Dordrecht appears to have a late resurgence at the very end of the century, see Hubert Nusteling, 'De bevolking: van raadsels naar oplossingen', in *Geschiedenis van Dordrecht, 1572–1813*, ed. Willem Frijhoff, Hubert Nusteling, Marijke Spies (Hilversum, 1998), 72–108.

58   J.A. Faber, *Friesland*, 1, 349–61.

59   Price, 'The Dutch Nobility', 91–2.

5

Survival in a Hostile World

THE TREATY of Münster with Spain in 1648 marked the close of a distinct phase in the history of the Dutch Republic. Up to this point the fundamental foreign policy aims of the Dutch state had been clear and largely uncontroversial: to survive as an independent state and to gain recognition from the other countries of Europe, and the Spanish monarchy in particular, of this status. There had been room for disagreement about how best to achieve these ends and over the precise terms that would be acceptable from the Spanish, but not about the objectives themselves. One of the reasons for Oldenbarnevelt's fall had been the growing conviction among his opponents that he could no longer be trusted to pursue these ultimate goals. Similarly, support for Frederik Hendrik's more aggressive foreign policy initiatives waned in the States of Holland when suspicions arose that he was tending to give more weight to the dynastic interests of his own house than to these common aims. In general, however, the establishment of a fully independent Dutch state was an objective which could unite practically the whole country.[1] After the final settlement with Spain, however, it became much less clear what the main lines and objectives of Dutch foreign policy should be – apart, of course, from the defence of what had been won in the long struggle with Spain. The situation that the new Dutch state had to face in Europe as it emerged from the conflict was distinctly less clear-cut than it had been in the earlier years of the century but, possibly, no less dangerous.

The settlement at the end of the Eighty Years War gave the Dutch almost everything they wanted, including not only full recognition of Dutch independence but also the continuation of their blockade of the Schelde – and thus of Antwerp's maritime trade – and what amounted to a free hand in the East Indies. (As Portugal, now in full revolt against Spain, was the chief victim of the successes of the VOC, perhaps this was less considerable a concession as far as the Spanish were concerned than it would have been a decade earlier.) Subsequently, despite a certain amount of friction over the precise demarcation of their competing jurisdictions in the Overmaas region near Maastricht,[2] Dutch relations with Spain became surprisingly amicable, and the Spanish became a problem because of their weakness rather than because they posed any direct or deliberate threat to the interests of the Republic. By the 1660s, it was becoming clear that Spain's position in the southern Netherlands was vulnerable in the face of French expansionism, and this was dramatically demonstrated by the ineffective resistance offered to the French invasion of 1667. From this point onwards, until the reversal of alliances at the beginning of the war of the Spanish Succession, Habsburg Spain was one of the more reliable members of the Dutch system of alliances, and preserving the Spanish Netherlands from being absorbed by France became one of the central aims of the foreign policy of the Republic.

The Dutch had broken their obligations to France (according to the treaty of 1635) by making a separate peace in 1648, leaving the French to fight on alone against Spain. In retrospect this can be seen to have brought to an end more than half a century of co-operation, though with some interruptions, between the Republic and France in the common cause of opposing what both countries perceived as the Habsburg threat. The situation in Europe appeared very different to both powers after 1648, and these divergent interests combined with French resentment at what they regarded as Dutch ingratitude to drive the two countries apart. Until the end of the 1650s the civil disturbances within France known as the Fronde together with the continuation of their war with Spain disguised the full extent of French military potential, but already the slogan *Gallia amicus non vicinus* – i.e. France as a friend but not as a neighbour – could be taken as typifying the ambivalent Dutch attitude to the French. French ambitions in the southern Netherlands were the immediate focus of Dutch apprehensions, and within a few years from the beginning of the personal rule of Louis XIV, the threat posed to the Republic by an aggressive France became a major concern of Dutch foreign policy and remained so until after the end of the century.

The end of the Thirty Years War left a large part of northern and most of central Europe exhausted, and it took two or three decades before the economic and social damage caused by the war was fully repaired. The war had only partly clarified the political and military balance in the region, and this uncertainty added considerably to the instability and vulnerability of the Holy Roman Empire in particular to outside intervention. However, one thing was clear: for a fleeting moment in the 1620s it had appeared possible that the Habsburgs might be able to reverse the trend of centuries and turn the Empire into an effective monarchy with a strong central government, but the settlement of 1648 finally and definitively ended their hopes of a resurgence of Imperial power. While it would be a mistake to ignore the considerable influence the emperors continued to wield within the Holy Roman Empire, nevertheless the centre of Austrian Habsburg power from now on was to be their Bohemian and Austrian lands where they were constructing the foundations of what was to be effectively a new state. It was to be some decades after 1648, however, before it became clear what the nature and strength of the new Austrian Habsburg state was. Although Sweden had emerged from the war as a nominal victor with a much bigger territorial stake in the Empire, in retrospect it seems that its brief period as a great power in Europe was already over, though the weakness of its potential rivals in northern Germany and the Baltic littoral disguised the underlying vulnerability of the Swedish Baltic empire for a considerable time. Within the Holy Roman Empire proper nearly all the constituent territories had suffered badly during the war but Brandenburg, despite its unwieldy addition of territories in the Rhineland and East Prussia to its north German heartland, was beginning to emerge as the most powerful state by a considerable margin. In contrast, the war seems to have caused Saxony's definitive decline to the second rank.

As far as the Dutch Republic was concerned there were definite advantages in this new situation, though even these turned out to have their downsides. If the final defeat of Habsburg ambitions in the Holy Roman Empire removed the threat of a powerful and catholic-dominated state on its eastern border, then the shift of the strategic weight of the Austrian Habsburg power to central Europe made it at the same time considerably less valuable as a potential ally against France. Similarly, while Brandenburg was generally a friendly power, not least because of religious sympathies and the personal predilections of the elector Friedrich Wilhelm, it was also uneasily sandwiched between Swedish Pomerania and the Habsburg lands and thus more than a little constrained in its freedom of action. It seemed that in northern Europe there was no serious threat to Dutch independence and interests but, by the same token perhaps, they could expect to find little help from the region if it came to a confrontation with France.

The problem of England

The one power in northern Europe which could have been a reliable ally for the Dutch proved to be nothing of the sort. England was, potentially at least, one of the leading protestant powers in Europe, and might have been expected to share Dutch concern regarding French expansion, on both political and religious grounds. Yet the Dutch and the English fought three wars against each other in this period – all the result of English aggression – and it was only the revolution of 1688 which turned England into a firm ally against France. So how to handle England remained a central problem for the Dutch until the last decade of the century. On the one hand, an alliance with England seemed to offer the solution to the basic dilemma of Dutch foreign policy but, on the other, the English steadfastly refused to play the role the Dutch thought proper for them. As the Dutch saw it, the English too had a vital interest in checking the hegemonic ambitions of France, but this view was not shared by the courts of Charles II and James II. De Witt, after the apparent success of the Triple Alliance between England, the Republic and Sweden in 1668, was unable to solve this problem, and Willem III did little better while he limited himself to diplomatic means in the face of what both Dutch leaders regarded as English perversity. In the end, military intervention was the catalyst which helped to bring to power in England men whose perception of the situation in Europe was much more in line with that of the Dutch.

The three Anglo-Dutch wars were damaging to Dutch trade and fishing in particular and to the economy in general but were by themselves no threat to the survival of the Dutch state – even in the third war, it was the French army not the English navy that threatened to destroy the Republic. It is commonly said that these were trade wars[3] but, while it would be foolish to disregard the degree to which economic rivalry could sour relations between the two countries from time to time, this is at best an inadequate explanation of these conflicts and in respect of the third war simply wrong. It would be truer, though still oversimplistic, to say that they were the acts of fragile English regimes seeking to strengthen their internal political positions through what they hoped would be popular – and successful – wars.

The Dutch economic success of the first half of the century had inspired envy and resentment in England. As far as trade was concerned, wherever the English went, both inside and outside Europe, it seemed that the Dutch had got there first. Particular bitterness was caused by the ease with which the VOC outstripped the English East India Company in the race to control the trade in Indonesian spices and other desirable Asian goods. English frustration took symbolic form in complaints about the so-called Amboina massacre of 1623, an unpleasant but minor incident which was trotted out as a stick with which to beat the Dutch for over sixty years. The Dutch domination of the North Sea herring fisheries was another constant source of friction, with the Dutch refusing to accept the English claim that their sovereignty stretched over the fishing grounds. Dutch control over the finishing and distribution to the rest of Europe of English woollen cloths similarly gave rise to the feeling that English economic weakness was being exploited by the Dutch. The failure of the Cockayne project (1614), partly as a result of a Dutch ban on the import of finished cloths from England, gave a particular focus to such resentments, and formed another recurrent item in the litany of English complaints. This is the conventional picture provided by English texts: English trade, manufactures and colonial expansion were blocked at every point by the Dutch, and thus the only way in which England could achieve its place in the sun was by defeating the Dutch in one way or another.

It is important, however, to note that this is a very partial view of Anglo-Dutch economic relations in the seventeenth century. Although the English economy played only a very minor part in the Dutch trading system, the powerful Dutch economy was of vital importance to England. The other side of the coin of supposed exploitation was the multitude of economic services which the Dutch provided for the relatively underdeveloped English economy. The cloth industry is a prime example of this dependency. The Merchant Adventurers had long been dependent on a staple on the European mainland, and had no independent trading network for the distribution and sale of their cloths in Europe. For much of the seventeenth century it was the Dutch who provided these services for what was still probably England's most important export trade. More generally, it seems that English trade to the continent, in the first half of the century at least, was very largely carried in Dutch ships and organised by Dutch merchants. The Dutch economy provided England with goods and services it could not (yet) provide for itself, and the disruption to the English economy during the first two Anglo-Dutch wars was considerable. Historians so far seem to have had ears for those who complained about the Dutch rather than those who benefited from close and symbiotic relations with their booming economic system. The Dutch also provided the English with a model for emulation: for many contemporary English economic reformers and theorists the Dutch system was a model of good practice, and learning from their success seemed the best way to tackle the economic problems faced by their own country.[4]

In the attention given to the friction between the Republic and England over the latter's attempts to implement the Navigation Act (1651),[5] it is easily overlooked that the First Anglo-Dutch War (1652–4) was preceded by English attempts to forge a union between the two protestant powers, and was ended by a remarkably mild peace-treaty in which the chief Dutch concessions were political not economic. In retrospect the war seems something of a mistake stemming from confusion of purpose in an English government which as yet lacked any firm governing hand. There were interest groups who believed they would benefit from a war with the Dutch,[6] and there was an apparent groundswell of hostility to the Dutch which could be exploited, but these were only contributory factors. It was rather an inchoate mixture of disappointed religious enthusiasm and the political insecurity of the new regime which sparked off a conflict which Cromwell brought to an end as soon as he was strong enough to do so.

The second of the wars (1665–7), too, appears to have been the act of an as yet insecure regime looking for a cheap victory to enhance its popularity rather than trying to pursue the long (or even short) term interests of the country. A group centred on the king's brother, James, and the Royal Africa Company were urging the economic benefits to be gained from war with the Dutch, though their motivation was perhaps not as straightforwardly economic as was once thought.[7] The English ambassador in the Republic, Downing, also enthusiastically supported an aggressive stance, not because he thought that a war with the Dutch would be in the interests of England but because he was mistakenly convinced that De Witt would back down and make significant concessions. It is true that popular anti-Dutch feeling could still be whipped up, but it cannot be said that the war was in any sense a response to the pressing logic of economic necessity. The third war was, of course, the consequence of the decision of Charles II and a small group of advisers to ally with France at the treaty of Dover (1670). Charles's motives are, and are likely to remain, obscure but pursuit of the fundamental interests, economic or otherwise, of his country were clearly not among them.

It is easy to sympathise with the frustrations of De Witt and later Willem III as successive English governments stubbornly refused to recognise what the Dutch statesmen saw as England's true interests. Indeed, in contrast to the view, held perhaps more by later historians than by contemporaries, that the Dutch Republic was a serious threat to England's future greatness, many on both sides of the North Sea believed that the common interests of the two countries far outweighed mere economic rivalry. On the English side this viewpoint surfaced intermittently in the 1640s and achieved a brief but vivid prominence in the early 1650s with the plan for some sort of a union between the two protestant and republican powers, but this proposal was understandably rebuffed by the more pragmatic Dutch. The alliance of 1668 was witness to the belief of both De Witt and the chief English negotiator, Sir William Temple, that halting French expansion in the Southern Netherlands was a vital interest of both the Republic and England. For the next twenty years this theme of a common, protestant interest in opposing the ambitions of Louis XIV ran as a counter-point to the actual foreign policy of Charles II and James II. After De Witt's fall, Willem III became the personification of this perception of the European situation, and the powerful opposition which grew up in England in these years seized gratefully on this as one of their principal themes.

While the government of Charles II attempted to exploit anti-Dutch sentiment to justify its wars with the Republic, during the third war this tactic seems to have lost much of its effectiveness, not least because France was rapidly becoming the new bugbear. From this point on, the English opposition took what was perceived to be the threat to the survival of protestantism, both at home and in Europe more generally, as their defining idea, and made an alliance with the Dutch to deal with this problem one of the central planks of their criticism of the court. Through the Popish Plot and the Exclusion Crisis, the policies of Charles and James were depicted as favouring France in Europe and absolutism and, whether consciously or not, intolerant catholicism at home. Increasingly a Dutch alliance seemed vital as much for the preservation of the ancient constitution and the protestant church as for dealing with more distant continental concerns. (English insularity has deep roots.) The climax came in 1688 with Willem's invasion to preserve the constitution, the Church of England – and, most importantly from the prince's point of view, to bring England into the European conflict on the side of the Republic. From the Dutch point of view, it worked; in the course of the new king's reign, the Republic and England were firmly united as the heart of a European coalition against France, and this alliance continued even after his death.

France: the great dilemma

The seemingly inexorable rise of France in the second half of the seventeenth century presented the Republic with a problem to which there was no satisfactory solution. The Dutch dilemma was, in brief, that taking the lead in opposition to French expansion proved in the end to be too great a financial strain on the state and also inflicted serious damage on an economy that was already beginning to falter, while staying neutral seemed to involve too great a risk, not just to Dutch interests but to the very survival of the Republic. From the 1660s onwards the question of how to deal with France was the central issue of Dutch foreign policy, and after the trauma of 1672 there was a marked tendency to view every French move with the utmost suspicion. There were voices urging a more friendly policy towards France, but time after time the force of their arguments was undermined by French actions which betrayed the, perhaps naïve, trust of such Francophile groups. Ultimately, the most convincing advocate of anti-French policies was the French government itself.

The extent of French military power had already begun to be apparent in the last years of the Thirty Years War, but it was only after the end of the Fronde and the beginning of Louis XIV's personal rule that it became clear how far the balance of power in Europe had been upset by the greatly increased power of France. The immediate problem, however, was not so much French strength as the weakness of Spain. Despite being on the losing side in the Thirty Years War, the image of Spanish power lingered on for some years, Spain held its own in the continued war with France during the 1650s, and it was only its inability to provide any adequate defence of the Southern Netherlands against the French in 1668 which revealed the extent of its decline. An additional complication was that from the very moment of his accession in 1665, the fragile health of Carlos II together with his inability to produce an heir meant that a dispute over the succession to the Spanish

Habsburg lands could have broken out at any time. Unexpectedly, Carlos survived year after year and the outbreak of war over the Spanish succession did not in the event come until after the end of the century. Nevertheless the vulnerability of the Spanish Netherlands became a major concern of the Dutch, and its preservation as a necessary buffer between the Republic and France became a fundamental aim of Dutch foreign policy.

The problem with regard to the Southern Netherlands was not just the fear that it could be conquered by the French, but that France might gain the region rather more legitimately through a deal with the other claimants to the Spanish succession. In either case, the Republic's buffer would have gone. De Witt tried to deal with the problem by an amicable agreement with France, hoping that legitimate French concern could be met by neutralising the region. Such hopes were dashed by the French invasion in 1667 to back up Louis's spurious claims to a share in the succession after the death of Philip IV. This forced De Witt into the Triple Alliance to limit French gains in the region, though a French agreement with the Austrian Habsburgs over the partition of the Spanish empire – Carlos II, it must be remembered, was expected to die at any moment – may have done more to stay Louis XIV's hand. From the French point of view this was a further sign of Dutch ingratitude to add to their abandonment of France at the Peace of Westphalia and – along with resentment at Dutch economic strength – explains Louis's decision to attack the Republic.

The cost of the war of 1672–8, together with the perceived damage to the Dutch economy which it caused, gave new encouragement to those who believed that some form of agreement with France was both desirable and attainable. The States of Holland, under the determined leadership of Amsterdam, pushed through the peace of 1678 against the wishes and better judgement of Willem III, and a similar alignment of forces tied the prince's hands in the following years, particularly over the French invasion of Luxemburg in 1684. The groups favouring peace with France, or at least a less exposed position for the Republic, feared that the more consistent anti-French policy was sacrificing the fundamental interests of the country to short-term considerations. In their view the military and political strength of the Republic rested on its economic success, and unremitting war with France would inevitably damage trade and thus undermine the very basis of Dutch greatness. Looking back from the perspective of the collapse of Dutch power almost immediately after the end of the War of Spanish Succession, who can say that they were entirely wrong?

Yet the invasion of 1672 was a traumatic event and its memory was a powerful support for Willem and those who thought like him. The Republic seemed to have come close to total defeat in the summer of that year, in which case the Anglo-French plans envisaged significant loss of territory for the Republic, leaving the prince of Orange ruling over a weak rump which would inevitably have been dependent on France.[8] So from this point onwards, the magnitude of the threat from France seemed indisputable and any miscalculation in this respect threatened to lead to a repeat of the mortal danger of the *rampjaar* (the year of disaster, i.e. 1672). Willem thus had many supporters in his crusade against France and they were inspired as much by conviction as by loyalty to the prince. However, the difficulty of finding reliable allies among the European powers and the high costs and indecisiveness of the later years of the war of 1672–8 raised questions as to the wisdom of the prince's unbending hostility to France. Until more effective help could be found, it was perhaps better not to take too exposed a position against France. Was it necessary to oppose every small advance by the French, especially considering the high risks involved?

Willem III has been seen as a defender of protestantism and even as a champion of European 'liberty',[9] in contrast, he was projected by his domestic enemies as being fired by ambition both for himself and his house. However, his prime concern from the moment in 1672 when he was called on to deliver his country from the French peril was to protect and further the interests of the Republic – as he understood them. His persistent attempts to build up anti-French coalitions, his opposition to the peace made at Nijmegen, and his risky intervention in England in 1688 can all best be explained by his conviction that the France of Louis XIV was an ever present threat not just to the interests of the Republic but its very existence as an independent force in European politics. He was a loyal member of the Reformed Church and shared a general concern for the future of protestantism, but it was not religion which caused him to oppose French expansion or to invade England. He was undoubtedly ambitious, with a strong sense of what was due to him and his house, and this could lead him into mistakes – his mishandling of the offer of the title of duke of Gelderland is a case in point[10] – but such ambition, again, does not explain the fundamental direction of his foreign policy. He had a claim to the English throne both through his wife and on his own account, but he would not have pushed this claim home if it had not been in the interests of the Republic for him to do so. The preservation of English liberties and the protection of protestantism were invaluable as propaganda points to gain support for his cause in that country, but his primary aim was to bring England into the European conflict on the Dutch side against France, and in this he succeeded. The Enterprise of England could not have taken place without support from the States of Holland and, crucially, Amsterdam and this would not have been forthcoming had it not been seen as in the interests of the Republic as a whole and not just of the prince.

So in the last decade of the century, as a result of armed intervention and revolution, England finally made more or less common cause with the Dutch against France. A combination of this alliance and further evidence – not least the reintroduction of prohibitive tariffs on Dutch goods – of the very real threat French policy represented to Dutch interests served to unify political opinion in the Republic. Amsterdam's support for Willem over the expedition to England showed that the formerly pro-French forces in the Republic had finally swung round to accepting the hard necessity of curbing the power of France. Neutrality which would allow the Dutch to pursue their economic interests in peace no longer appeared to be an option. Even after Willem's death in 1702 the Dutch continued on this course. Under the leadership of Anthonie Heinsius as *raadpensionaris* the Republic, together with England and the rising power of Austria, was at the heart of the coalition which fought France to a standstill in the Spanish Succession War. However, the English abandonment of the alliance forced the Dutch to make peace with the French at the treaty of Utrecht in 1713 on what were, from their point of view, not entirely satisfactory terms. In the following years it rapidly became apparent that the long conflict had overtaxed, perhaps quite literally, the resources of the Republic, and it was never again able to play the part of a major power in Europe.

The consolidation of regent rule

The second half of the century began with an attack on regent power by Willem II which re-opened the ideological divide between republicans and orangists. Then for over two decades came the dominance of the republican True Freedom (*Ware Vrijheid*) under Johan de Witt. After the collapse of this republican regime as a result of the French invasion in 1672, Willem III took over the leadership of the Republic for the rest of the century. Although the events of 1650 and 1672 were dramatic and caused modifications to the way in which the political system worked, neither crisis led to any fundamental change in the system itself. The political dominance of the regent oligarchy remained effectively intact, despite the oscillations between the dominance of True Freedom and government by a stadhouder. This is most obviously the case for Holland, the key province politically, but even in the land provinces, where Willem III came to exercise a degree of influence which became notorious, the stadhouder had to achieve his ends by manipulating the existing oligarchic system rather than replacing it.

An aspect of the Dutch political system that has received less attention than perhaps it deserves is the continuous change and development in the way that the central government worked in practice. In theory, of course, there was only one proper way of running the Republic and this was the one justified by precedent, custom, and conformity to the ancient liberties of the provinces that composed the Republic – though republicans and orangists disagreed over precisely what that was. Expediency or efficiency had nothing to do with the matter. In practice, Oldenbarnevelt had set up a workable system of government for the Republic in the 1590s, in which the lead was taken by Holland and himself as its chief minister. Maurits's successful coup in 1618 inaugurated a new way of governing the Republic, with the leadership and unprecedented influence going to the Orange stadhouders, Maurits and his successor Frederik Hendrik. This process of change continued in the second half of the century: De Witt's regime looked back to the system under Oldenbarnevelt for inspiration and legitimation but was not just a matter of turning back the clock constitutionally, and Willem III picked up where Frederik Hendrik (rather than Willem II) had left off but had to work in significantly different ways. The stadhouderless system was to an important extent a reaction against the excesses of Willem II, and the restored stadhoudership of Willem III also had to deal with the mistrust inspired by his father's actions. The autocratic manner, however, in which Willem exercised his authority for three decades led to an accumulation of resentment among the regents throughout the Republic; so it is hardly surprising that after the prince's death without a direct heir in 1702 a second stadhouderless period was inaugurated which was to last for most of the first half of the eighteenth century.

Yet, important as such changes were to decision making in the Republic, particularly in regard to foreign policy, there is an important sense in which they were only superficial perturbations of a system which remained essentially unchanged at a more fundamental level. In the towns, in the countryside, and to a large extent at the level of provincial government as well, the regents continued to dominate, and any change that took place seems to have been in the direction of a greater consolidation of oligarchic control, rather than any challenge to the structure of regent power. Whether it was a stadhouder or a *raadpensionaris* of Holland who headed the government of the country, he had to work with and through this republican system. The States General and its dependent Generality organs drew their power and authority from the constituent provinces of the Republic; in theory, and to a large extent in practice also, the central government was the servant of the provinces and not their master. In turn, the provinces themselves were controlled from below by their constituent elements, chiefly the privileged towns and the nobles (though in Friesland there was at least a remnant of a political role for rural free-holders). Moreover, some provinces had very little effective unity: Groningen (*Stad en Lande*) was permanently riven by differences between the town Groningen and the surrounding countryside (*Ommelanden*); Overijssel was not only divided into three quarters, but in addition the three leading towns laid claim to a high degree of autonomy; and Gelderland, too, had separate representative bodies for its three quarters and only a flimsy adminis-tration for the province as a whole. Even in Holland, perhaps the most highly integrated province, the States were governed by the towns and not the other way about. Such a system could be very unwieldy and was enormously difficult to coerce; regents were capable of a sheer bloody-mindedness approaching the heroic in defence of what they saw as local interests. The Republic could only be run by working with the grain of regent power, not against it.

For Johan de Witt, working with the existing political structure was not only a practical necessity but was at the ideological core of the True Freedom. He was a member of a leading regent family of Dordrecht, and as *raadpensionaris* of Holland his political influence depended on his ability to persuade and manipulate the regents of his province. In turn, his leadership in the Republic came primarily from his position as representative of Holland's interests, and the decentralised nature of the political system also allowed him to make the most of Holland's fiscal strength and relative unity of purpose. De Witt was a regent, and his two decades of leadership of the Republic showed the oligarchy in complete and unchallenged control of the country for perhaps the first time. In a longer perspective the message of his long period of political dominance is distinctly more ambiguous: on the one hand, the republican system ran the country successfully even during two bruising wars with England yet, on the other, the regime collapsed rapidly and even ignominiously under the strain of the initial defeats in the war with France in the summer of 1672. There were thus two incompatible lessons to be learnt from the experience of the first stadhouderless period: the Republic did not need a prince of Orange as stadhouder to be governed successfully – and yet there were circumstances when such leadership appeared indispensable.

The princes of Orange stood outside the oligarchy to some degree, but they were most successful when they acted as *primus inter pares* rather than as quasi-sovereigns. It is important to remember that they were technically only officers in the service of the Republic as far as their most important positions were concerned. They were appointed as captains general of the army by the States General, and as stadhouders by the respective provincial States.[11] Their accumulation of posts together with the charisma which attached to their house gave them enormous potential influence, especially through their powers of patronage which enabled them to build up powerful provincial clienteles. However, such patronage systems were a method of manipulating the system that was not so very different from that employed by De Witt; both were ways of working with and through the oligarchy not against it.

Willem II's actions in 1650 showed just how important it was to work within the system and not to try to subvert it. He first used his influence in the land provinces to force through a decision on the military budget against the opposition of Holland, then he arrested six leading politicians from Holland and sent troops against the heart of the opposition to his policy, Amsterdam.[12] The march on Amsterdam failed, and with it the attempted coup. The prince made some face-saving gains: his leading opponents among the Amsterdam regents were induced to resign their offices, and the States of Holland proved ready to compromise over the size of the military budget. Willem had not won: the policy of Holland remained in essence the same and Amsterdam, under new leadership, was as opposed to the prince's policies as ever.[13] He died before the end of the year and so it is impossible to say what would have happened had he lived, but it seems clear that he would have had either to learn to work with the system or try to break Holland's resistance by military force – no wonder, therefore, that there was rejoicing in some quarters at his death. Twenty two years later, Willem III swept into power as a consequence of the manifest failure of De Witt's regime both diplomatically and, more important, militarily, and the *wetsverzettingen* in Holland and Zeeland in the summer of 1672 provided him with well-disposed regents in the urban oligarchies. Nevertheless, despite the apparent strength of his position, he still could only succeed with the co-operation of provincial and local notables, and the Holland regents soon proved to be distinctly less malleable than the prince might have expected. He was forced to make peace with France in 1678, was prevented from re-opening the war in 1684, and needed support from Holland to launch the Enterprise of England in 1688. In the last case, the co-operation of three of the four burgemeesters of Amsterdam appears to have been vital. Although Willem increased his power in the land provinces considerably, after they had been freed from French occupation, through the introduction of the *regeringsreglementen* (governing regulations), he still could not lead the Republic effectively without the consent of Holland. He might lose patience with the regents, who were inclined to put provincial or even local interests before what Willem saw as the needs of the Republic, but he had to bully, manipulate or persuade them into consent if he wanted to achieve anything.

The consolidation of oligarchical power was in part at least a consequence of the changing social context of the late seventeenth century. The untrammelled oligarchic rule of the first stadhouderless period coincided with the brief period of relative social and economic stability between the rapid growth of the first half of the century and the beginnings of decline in its last quarter. Willem III's period in power similarly fitted more or less neatly into the years when the earlier confidence in continuing economic growth had disappeared, and stagnation coupled with fear of decline were becoming characteristic of the Dutch experience. In retrospect it seems entirely appropriate that De Witt should have presided over the period when the Republic was at the peak of its economic strength and international standing, and it seems hardly less appropriate that Willem III should have taken over leadership of the Dutch state when its situation was beginning to weaken economically and the political and military position to become more threatening.

The ending of the period of rapid economic and social change around the mid-century allowed the existing oligarchy to consolidate its position. In general, the changing economic environment was more favourable to those who were already rich than to those who were trying to make their fortunes. In the first half of the century the buoyant economy, certainly in the maritime region, had encouraged rapid social mobility and produced a stream of new families wealthy enough to make a plausible claim on a place in the political elite. After about 1650, opportunities were harder to come by, most of the economic niches were already taken, and social mobility became more problematic. Later, as slower growth turned into stagnation and even decline in some sectors, social structures tended to ossify. It became markedly more difficult to move from the middling classes into the social elite, and thus to become eligible for membership of the regent group.

It can be argued that the increasingly hostile economic environment encouraged a defensive attitude of mind which showed itself in social attitudes as well as in economic behaviour. In practical terms, existing regent families had considerable advantages over outsiders: the profits of office together, perhaps, with privileged access to some public investments were increasingly important in enabling regent families to maintain their social position. Whereas in the past involvement in trade and manufactures had offered very attractive economic opportunities, now safe investments in the public debt of Holland or the Republic, or in the shares of the VOC seemed more attractive – in particular because collectively the regents could protect their investments through their control of the political system. Indeed, it came to appear that the whole system of public finance was principally designed to secure the financial interests of the political elite. The social elite too could use their accumulated capital, often built up over generations, to protect their position in society, and this defensive approach to life could have marked effects on family strategy. The preservation of a family's wealth could involve restricting marriage opportunities for younger sons and daughters, incidentally and unintentionally increasing the possibility of families disappearing through demographic failure. That there was still some movement into the regent group in the eighteenth century seems in part at least to have been because a number of regent families did indeed die out and needed to be replaced.[14] In the main, however, established regent families had the social and economic resources to maintain their position within the oligarchy; they became increasingly a cautious and conservative group socially as well as financially. The same economic atmosphere which encouraged the regents to change from entrepreneurs to *rentiers* made it more difficult for outsiders to achieve the sort of economic success which might make them eligible for entry into the oligarchy. Moreover, the profits and perquisites of office available to the regents, and carefully shared out between them, could be a vital part of their financial strategy and cause them to cling on to office even more grimly than before.

Despite their rather different economic circumstances, a parallel process of consolidation of the political elites has been observed in the land provinces also. The various nobilities of these provinces showed a marked tendency to close up in the course of the seventeenth century, even though overall numbers were falling. The quasi-nobility of the Ommelanden of Groningen which had been fairly open up to this point, had closed itself to newcomers by about the middle of the century. Similarly in Utrecht, Gelderland and Overijssel access to the *ridderschappen*, the noble members of the States of these provinces, and other positions of power and profit was progressively restricted. Demographic attrition hit these closed groups as well, but with no new nobles being created in the period of the Republic their absolute numbers could and did fall drastically. For those who were left, however, the pickings were richer.[15] In Friesland what remained of freeholder influence on government was being undermined by a combination of nobles and town regents, creating in the process an oligarchy that was as distinctive as most Fries political institutions but just as effective in monopolising political power as elsewhere. Friesland and Groningen had shared in the post-Revolt boom to a considerable extent, and here the formation of a more closed oligarchy more or less neatly coincides with the end of the years of prolonged economic growth. In contrast, the land provinces had shared only marginally, if at all, in the economic miracle of the maritime region, and here the oligarchic process seems linked to a permanent shortage of resources rather than a marked change in economic circumstances peculiar to the second half of the century. On the other hand, by the same token there is less evidence of actual economic decline, and it may well be no coincidence that in the following century the first explicit attacks on oligarchy as a system came in Gelderland and Overijssel where the rural economy was experiencing something of an upturn rather than Holland. Under the spell of past greatness, the latter had become conservative rather than innovative and this had profound social as well as economic effects.

From prosperity to economic difficulties

The years between the Treaty of Münster and the outbreak of the war with France in 1672 can be seen as the height of the Republic's achievements in terms of power and influence in Europe and the wider world as well as economic success. The first stadhouderless period can also be seen as the time when the Republic was most clearly a republic, and so in a sense was most purely itself. From this perspective, the return of a prince of Orange to power in the Republic can be put alongside the wars with France and the faltering economy as signs that the days of Dutch greatness were numbered.

It would be misleading, however, to exaggerate the degree of change which had taken place by the end of the century. There is an underlying continuity in this period which can too easily be disguised by changes of regime and accidents of international relations. In foreign policy, for example, for all their obvious differences there were fundamental similarities between the policies of De Witt and Willem III, and these stemmed from what seem to have been essentially similar perceptions of the Republic's place in Europe. Both identified France as the major problem facing the Republic, and both regarded England as potentially the most useful ally in dealing with this threat. De Witt came to power in the early 1650s when neither the extent of Spanish decline nor the power of France were as clear as they were to become, but by the 1660s how to deal with France, especially in regard to the Spanish Netherlands, had become his central preoccupation in foreign policy. De Witt's attempts to reach an amicable arrangement which would balance Dutch interests and French ambitions were unsuccessful and he turned to an alliance with England to limit French gains in the Spanish Netherlands. In the short term this policy appeared to be a success but in the end it was wrecked by Charles II's change of allegiance. Willem III also faced the frustrating experience of trying to make the English fulfil their treaty obligations and keep them out of the pocket of Louis XIV. In contrast to De Witt, the prince came to power in a situation which was all too bleakly unambiguous, and this experience determined the shape of his policy for the rest of his life. Where his perception of the situation facing the Republic differed from De Witt's was that the experience of 1672 had convinced him that the French king could not safely be appeased but had to be checked by force.

Once Willem had decided that a mutually beneficial agreement with France was not possible, then only the second of De Witt's strategies was left, i.e. to construct an alliance against France looking particularly to England. Again he was operating in a significantly different atmosphere than his predecessor, as the French near-success of 1672 had not only alarmed the Dutch themselves but had made the Austrians, Spain and some of the German princes distinctly more apprehensive about French ambitions. In parallel to De Witt's dilemma after 1668, however, he also had to deal with the persistent refusal of English governments under both Charles II and James II to recognise that France constituted any threat to English interests. One very important difference in the situation of the two Dutch leaders was that Willem's membership of the English royal family, and later his marriage to the princess Mary, gave him opportunities of influencing English politics simply not available to a *raadpensionaris*. Most spectacularly, he was able to intervene militarily in England without it looking too much like a foreign invasion, and cover his seizure of the throne with a claim to legitimacy. Princes could do some things in the seventeenth century which ordinary Dutch citizens could not, but otherwise the general lines of foreign policy show remarkable continuity between the *raadpensionaris* and the prince of Orange; the difference was one of style and circumstances rather than substance.

The foreign policy dilemmas of the last decades of the century coincided with the loss of *élan* in the Dutch economy, and this might well suggest a link between the two. Indeed, one of the standard explanations of Dutch decline, economically as well as politically, has been that the strain of the long years of war with France between 1672 and the end of the War of Spanish Succession in the next century finally outstripped the Republic's resources. Certainly the cost of the military and naval effort eventually crippled the fiscal system of Holland and thus of the Republic as a whole,[16] and it has also been argued that the high taxes needed to pay for the wars fatally undermined the competitiveness of Dutch manufactures.[17] However, it would be too simplistic to suggest that the military struggle with France caused Dutch economic decline. It would be truer to say that the difficulties the Dutch had not only in meeting the costs of war but also in coping with the economic problems it brought with it were symptoms of the underlying weaknesses of the Dutch economy that were beginning to emerge.

War had always been an important part of the life of the Republic: it was born in an armed Revolt, independence was achieved through war and had to be defended by armed force.[18] The Dutch economic miracle had taken place despite the Revolt and the Eighty Years War, and so war alone cannot be taken as a satisfactory explanation of Dutch decline. The experience of war in the earlier seventeenth century had offered alluring economic opportunities to the Dutch, most notably in the East Indies, but it had also made access to Spanish markets and trade to Spain's colonies difficult though probably not impossible. Similarly, although the Republic was not formally involved in the Thirty Years War, Dutch trade with the Baltic region was disrupted by military activities during the conflict, not to mention the abortive plans of the Spanish to attack Dutch trade in this area directly. So it would be misleading to suggest that the Dutch economy thrived because of war, as it might well have done even better in a more peaceful environment, even taking into account the problems this would have set for their extra-European trade and colonial expansion. The costs of war in the earlier part of the seventeenth century had certainly not been small. It required a large-scale military effort to hold the Spanish Army of Flanders in check, and by the 1630s the Republic was maintaining an army of around 75,000 men. The naval threat from Spain was, perhaps, not so immediate, but considerable expenditure was still needed to protect Dutch trade and fisheries from the depredations of the Dunkirk privateers, as well as provide protection against Spanish naval expeditions such as that of 1639. The financial demands of the war against Spain brought with them the inevitable short term fiscal difficulties, and Holland in particular emerged from the war with a considerable burden of debt.[19] Yet, although the economic effects of war for the Dutch in the first half of the century are far from easy to calculate, it nevertheless seems clear that neither public finances nor the economy in general can be said to have been severely damaged by the experience.

The wars with France from 1672 onwards, in contrast, seem to have been more difficult for the Republic to cope with almost from the start. Economically, a central problem was the importance of the French market for Dutch trade and manufactures. Exports to France had already been severely hit by the punitive tariffs imposed in 1667, inspired by Colbert, and after the Republic's territory had been freed from French troops their abolition became a major war aim for the States of Holland. For all their eagerness to bring the war to an end, the regents of Holland insisted that moderation of these tariffs was an essential precondition of peace with France, though it is interesting to note that what the Dutch saw as a national interest was seen by the French as a sectional one. The disruption of the Dutch trading system caused by the war with France (1672–8) also opened up opportunities to rivals: after England made peace with the Republic in 1674, its trade with the Baltic increased markedly, and largely at Dutch expense, as long as the latter were still embroiled with France. The Dutch were able to reassert themselves in this region after 1678, but the awareness of the existence of rivals capable of stepping into their shoes increased the Dutch sense of economic vulnerability.

War also became appreciably more expensive in the last decades of the century: the enormous numbers of troops that Louis XIV's France was able to put in the field were the spur to a phase of considerable growth in the size of European armies,[20] and the Republic was soon having to support an army that was around a third greater than had been necessary during the earlier peak in the size of their armed forces in the 1630s. The cost of maintaining an adequate naval force had risen considerably as well. In the first half of the century, overall costs could be kept down by hiring merchant ships, which could be transformed into warships without too much difficulty when the need arose. However, the Dutch defeats in the First Anglo-Dutch War had demonstrated unequivocally that converted merchantmen were hopelessly outclassed by the new specialist warships. From this point on only specially designed and constructed ships-of-the-line could hold their own in battles at sea, and this new type of ship was not only expensive to build but also cost a great deal to maintain in a seaworthy condition.[21] In consequence, war was more expensive for the Dutch both on land and at sea than it had been earlier in the century. Fiscally, too, the Republic seems to have been already overstretched by the time of the war of 1672–8. To pay for the war, normal taxes were increased and supplemented by a sufficient number of taxes on property and wealth to make the rich as well as the middling classes squeal. The weight of excise duties was heavy and fell disproportionately on the poorer sections of society, but the 200th Penny and similar impositions could only hit those with wealth to tax. That the better-off sections of society perceived this as an almost intolerable burden may not just have been the common response of the wealthy to anything approaching an equitable taxation system, but might well be an indication that these social groups were feeling markedly less secure economically than they had been before the Dutch economy began to falter.

Rather than invoking the wars with France as the cause of, or at least a major factor in, Dutch economic decline, it might be better to see the economic problems which it was experiencing as the reason the Republic found the military effort occasioned by this conflict so difficult to sustain. Had trade still been as buoyant and manufactures as competitive as in the earlier years of the century then the financial demands of the French wars would have been considerably easier to bear. From the 1590s onwards, the Dutch effort in the Eighty Years War had been made possible by the economic boom; there were, of course, some occasional setbacks but these could not counteract the strong long-term growth in almost all sectors of the economy which continued until around the mid-century. In contrast, the first French war came at a time when the overall economy was growing much more slowly, if at all, and when complaints from merchants about the falling profitability of trade suggest that the mood of confident expansion had already turned into a rather more diffident ambition to hold on to what had been gained. The costs of war had also been rising in the first half of the seventeenth century but they had been borne by an economy that grew at what was probably an even faster rate; from 1672 onwards the renewed increase in the financial demands of war could no longer be matched by a similar scale of economic growth. Thus the French wars were a relatively greater drain on the overall economy of the Republic than the Eighty Years War had been, at least after the economic take-off of the 1590s. The problems which the Dutch economy was experiencing in these years made it more difficult for the Dutch state to bear the burden of the long years of war with France but the war did not cause these problems, although they were exacerbated by the disturbances to Dutch trade which did stem from the conflict.

The Dutch Republic was able to play the role of a major power in

Europe throughout the second half of the century, but it emerged from the Spanish Succession War in a seriously weakened state and it eventually became clear that it had become at best a second rank power. There are puzzling aspects about both the fact and the speed of this decline: on the face of it the Dutch state was still wealthy enough to be a significant force in Europe – certainly considerably more wealthy than Prussia which nevertheless proved able to rise to the rank of a major power in the course of the eighteenth century – and the rapidity of its fall from major power status seems to require an equally dramatic explanation. There seems little doubt about the proximate cause: the States General and the States of Holland were left with a crippling burden of debt, and Holland at least – always the key factor in the finances of the Republic – was never able to pull itself out of the fiscal hole that it had dug for itself in the wars against France. However, there were also political and social reasons why what was still a relatively wealthy country could not deal effectively with its burden of debt. In the eighteenth century, the regents and their allies in the upper middle classes invested an increasing proportion of their capital in public loans, and they became more and more dependent on these provincial and generality debts as a safe haven for their funds and as a provider of a steady revenue for themselves and their families. The financial survival strategies of regent families required the existence of a large public debt in which they could invest, particularly as their control over the political system meant that they could ensure that both investments and interest payments remained safe. In addition, the economic uncertainty of the late seventeenth century was turning into unequivocal decline, and this made the fiscal problems worse not least because it encouraged the upper bourgeoisie to continue their move out of trade and manufactures and into safer investments such as loans to the States of Holland or the States General.

There is, however, another way of looking at it. Only the mortal threat to the very survival of the Republic which France seemed to represent during the reign of Louis XIV forced the Dutch to take a leading part in the warfare of the period. This was a role they had never wanted: their ideal was to be allowed to pursue their economic ends in peace, and in this sense they had never aspired to the position of a major power. The dangerous situation in Europe in the later seventeenth century had compelled them to fight against their will and perhaps above their weight. After the end of the Spanish Succession

War, Europe was a much safer place for the Dutch: France was relatively weaker, and England was not only much more powerful but was now committed to keeping the French out of the Low Countries. Under these new conditions, the Dutch could perhaps happily retire from the ring.

Notes

1   Although it was less self-evident what the boundaries of the Republic should be. In particular, at least a substantial minority must have hoped to include more of the southern Netherlands – if not all of it – in the new state.

2   J.A.K. Haas, *De verdeling van de landen van Overmaas 1644–1662* (Assen, 1978).

3   The classic expression of this view is Charles Wilson, *Profit and Power: a Study of England and the Dutch Wars* (London, 1957), though it should be noted that he excludes the third war from his analysis.

4   Joyce Oldham Appleby, *Economic Thought and Ideology in Seventeenth-Century England* (Princeton, 1978), chap. 4.

5   Intended to encourage English shipping by requiring that foreign goods could only be imported in English ships or those of the country of origin – thus specifically not by the Dutch.

6   J.E. Farnell, 'The Navigation Act of 1651, the First Dutch War, and the London Merchant Community', *Economic History Review*, 2nd series, 16 (1963), 439–54.

7   Steven C.A. Pincus, 'Popery, Trade and Universal Monarchy: the ideological context of the outbreak of the Second Anglo-Dutch War', *English Historical Review*, vol.cvii, no. 422 (Jan. 1992), 1–29.

8   The English hoped to make important gains but, realistically, the French would have been the real winners.

9   S.B. Baxter, *William III and the Defence of European Liberty, 1650–1702* (London, 1966).

10   A curious incident: his supporters engineered the offer in 1675, but Willem had to turn it down because of its manifest unpopularity.

11   Although the term is loosely used to indicate the leading position of successive princes of Orange, there was no position of stadhouder for the Republic as a whole, only separate stadhouders for each province.

12   H.H. Rowen, 'The Revolution that Wasn't: the Coup d'Etat of 1650 in Holland', *European Studies Review*, 4 (1974), 99–117.

13   Note, however, that many, if not most, historians dealing with this episode have seen it as a victory for Willem.

14   See J.J. de Jong, *Met goed fatsoen. De elite in een Hollandse stad, Gouda 1700–80* (Dieren, 1985), 167–9; M. Prak, *Gezeten burgers. De elite in een Hollandse stad, Leiden 1700–1780* (Dieren, 1985), 191; L. Kooijmans, *Onder regenten. De elite in een Hollandse stad, Hoorn 1700–1780* (Dieren, 1985), 120–1.

15   J.L. Price, 'The Dutch Nobility in the Seventeenth and Eighteenth Centuries', *The European Nobilities in the Seventeenth and Eighteenth Centuries*, vol.1, ed. H.M. Scott (London, 1995), 82–113.

16   J. Aalbers, 'Holland's financial problems (1713–1733) and the wars against Louis XIV', *Britain and the Netherlands*, 6 (1977), 79–93; R. Liesker, 'Tot zinkens toe bezwaard. De schuldenlast van het Zuiderkwartier van Holland 1672–1794', in *Bestuurders en geleerden*, ed. S. Groenveld, M.E.H.N. Mout and I. Schöffer (Amsterdam/Dieren, 1985), 151–60.

17   Charles Wilson, 'Taxation and the Decline of Empires, an unfashionable theme', in *Economic History and the Historians* (London, 1969).

18   J.L. Price, 'A State Dedicated to War? The Dutch Republic in the Seventeenth Century', *The Medieval Military Revolution*, ed. Andrew Ayton and J.L. Price (London, 1995), 183–200.

19   These wars were fought on the credit of Holland rather than the States General.

20   Jeremy Black, *A Military Revolution? Military Change and European Society 1550–1800* (Basingstoke, 1991), 6–7, 29–30.

21   J.R Bruijn, *The Dutch Navy in the 17th and 18th centuries* (Columbia, SC, 1993), 73–4.

6

Intimations of Mortality

D UTCH ECONOMIC supremacy proved to be short lived: the period of almost uninterrupted overall growth seems to have come to an end around 1650, and within two decades the first signs of decline had become unmistakable – at least in retrospect. Although the Republic remained the leading trading and financial power in Europe until well into the eighteenth century, not only was this position already coming under threat in the last third of the previous century but at the same time the Dutch economy as a whole was beginning to display serious structural weaknesses. The economic environment in which the Dutch had to operate began to change in ways that they did not fully understand – and could have done little about in any case – and the social and economic structures which had evolved and matured in the century and a half of expansion proved to be much less suited to the challenges of this new era. However, the extent to which the Dutch were already in economic difficulties before the end of the seventeenth century should not be exaggerated: with the advantage of hindsight the omens are tolerably clear, but the Republic was still the most powerful economic force in Europe. Wars with England and France interrupted their trade and disrupted the markets for their manufactures, but these could still be interpreted by contemporaries as temporary setbacks rather than systemic problems. At the end of the century, it still seemed that only peace was needed to restore the Dutch economy to full vigour. In the event peace did not come until too late, and the days of unproblematic economic success never returned.

Although population growth is not an unerring indication of economic health – in more recent times, particularly, effective contraceptive techniques have meant that poverty is no longer the main cause of demographic stagnation or decline – this was generally the case in early modern Europe, and so the levelling off of the Dutch population in the second half of the seventeenth century is an important indicator of a fundamental change in the economic situation. Although the larger towns of Holland may have continued to expand until the 1670s, growth had already ceased elsewhere in the maritime region by the mid-century at the latest, though the land provinces may have seen a modest demographic recovery after the end of the Eighty Years War. The total population of the Republic showed no significant further growth in the later seventeenth century.

Further evidence is supplied by the long-term trends in agricultural prices and rents, which began a century of depression around 1670, if not earlier. Partly this was a result of general European conditions, with a combination of a stagnant population and perhaps some overall rise in supply at this time bringing down the general price-level for agricultural products. Unfortunately for the Dutch rural economy as a whole, the consequent fall in profits coincided with a period of very high domestic taxes necessitated by the wars against France. Caught between these two trends of falling prices and rising taxes, farmers found their profit margins squeezed and this brought down rents, which in turn affected the wider Dutch economy. A prosperous and dynamic agriculture had been a vital part of the Dutch economic miracle, and the continued vigour of this sector was crucial to the health of what was a highly integrated economic system.

The Dutch trading system, too, encountered problems in this period, but it was and is difficult to disentangle the short-term disruptive effects of the wars with England and then France from any underlying trends. The Anglo-Dutch wars inflicted considerable damage on the Dutch merchant fleet and temporarily disrupted the pattern of Dutch trade, particularly in Europe, but the long-term effects were negligible.[1] On the other hand, the hot and cold wars with France were serious problems because of the importance of the French market for Dutch trade and manufactures. Yet it was still possible to believe that only peace was needed to restore the prosperity of the Dutch trading system. It was equally difficult for contemporaries to assess the health of Dutch colonial trade. In particular, the highly successful VOC was experiencing problems serious enough to inspire an official but eventually inconclusive enquiry into its finances and economic organisation in the 1680s.[2] The problem for the company lay not just with an almost impenetrable accounting system, which made it nearly impossible to calculate overall profitability, but also in a combination of rising costs in Asia and increased competition on the

European market, both of which were difficult if not impossible to control. The VOC continued to expand its territorial base, notably in Sri Lanka and Java, and appeared in many ways stronger than ever, but infrastructural costs were rising and, while the Dutch maintained their strong position with regard to the trade in eastern spices, new products over which the company could never establish the same sort of control were becoming increasingly important in the trade between Asia and Europe.

The economic environment in which the Dutch economy had to operate began to change significantly in the second half of the seventeenth century, though here again the short-term disruptions caused by wars the Dutch could not avoid obscured the degree to which a distinctly new economic order was already beginning to emerge in Europe by the end of the century. Not necessarily the most important, but certainly the most obvious way in which the situation in Europe turned against the Dutch was the rise of protectionist policies in other countries, in part as a result of the triumph of mercantilist thinking. Successive Navigation Acts in England (1651 and 1661), aimed at undermining the Dutch carrying trade, and France's prohibitive tariffs on Dutch imports brought in by Colbert in 1667, were only the most prominent examples of a more general tendency throughout Europe. Increasingly, states were attempting to stimulate their own economies through erecting tariff barriers particularly to shelter their domestic manufactures. The central importance of the French market for the Dutch trading system meant that the French impositions were especially damaging, but tariff walls were rising throughout Europe, making this market a significantly more hostile place that it had been in the earlier years of the century. It was not just a matter of alterations in government policies or mercantilist theories; such protectionist measures would have been impossible to sustain if other countries had not been able to produce for themselves the goods and services the Dutch had formerly provided.

The balance of economic power in Europe was swinging against the Dutch: in the last decades of the seventeenth century England was finally beginning to shake off its subordination to the Dutch economy, and France was starting to use its greater domestic resources to develop both its manufactures and its trade. However, it was not just that England and, later, France were beginning successfully to challenge 'Dutch Primacy' in trade in Europe and the world, but that the nature of the European economy was changing in such a way as to undermine the very basis of Dutch commercial supremacy. To a considerable extent the Dutch staple market, acting as economic middle-man for an imperfectly integrated European market system, had been at the root of Dutch economic success, and it was this that was rapidly becoming an anachronism in late seventeenth century Europe. The European economy as a whole no longer needed the intermediary services provided by the Dutch in quite the way it did in the earlier years of the century; the staple function was one important aspect of the Dutch economic miracle that could never be resuscitated, though the Dutch wasted a great deal of effort in the following century attempting to do so.

Regional and local variations

During the long period of growth and expansion, the Dutch economy had shown marked regional differences, not to say contrasts, and in the period of economic uncertainty which followed there were similar disparities in the experiences of different parts of the Republic. The major contrast is again provided by the maritime region and the land provinces, though this time not always in favour of the former. However, local variations within the two broad regions were perhaps even greater in this period than they had been before. In particular some formerly prosperous towns and areas of the maritime region were already in difficulties as early as the middle years of the century, and were in unambiguous decline by its last quarter.

In the later seventeenth century, the two main economic regions of the Republic continued to have quite distinct histories. The land provinces had suffered more directly from the adverse economic consequences of the Eighty Years War, and were able to enjoy a phase of mild economic recovery in the second half of the century. While they cannot be said to have escaped entirely the economic problems that were beginning to beset the maritime region, their less developed economies proved distinctly less vulnerable to the changes which were affecting the economic climate of the Republic as a whole. Indeed, the process of decline would in the long run do something to redress the balance between the two regions, as the depression bit deeper in the maritime provinces and modest growth proved possible in the formerly less prosperous land provinces.

However, the land provinces could not, of course, escape entirely unscathed from the economic difficulties facing the Republic in the later seventeenth century. In particular, the depressed level of prices for agricultural products was a serious problem for a region in which a much higher proportion of the population lived and worked on the land than was the case in the maritime provinces. Similarly, although the tax burden in the land provinces was less spectacularly high than it was in Holland, it may well have weighed even more heavily in real terms on these poorer areas. Caught between low prices and high and rising taxes, farmers big and small felt the pinch by the end of the century. On the other hand, while small-holding peasants had practically ceased to exist in Holland, they continued to be numerous in the east and south and thus provided a pool of cheap labour which began to attract manufactures to some areas. Whereas in Holland the workers in the textile industry had to be paid at least something like a living wage as this was usually their sole employment, manufacturers could find a much cheaper source of labour in areas where commercial farming had not yet squeezed out the smallholding peasant.[3] In Twente and North Brabant textile entrepreneurs could put work out to spinners and weavers who were not wholly dependent on their wages to survive, as they also had their own small plots of land as well as the possibility of other agricultural earnings. In consequence, textile manufacture began to migrate to these areas before the end of the seventeenth century, though this development only took off in the following century.[4]

In the long term, it was the maritime region which suffered most acutely from the accelerating economic problems which afflicted the Republic from the last third of the century onwards. The highly specialised agriculture of this region, geared to production for the market, proved necessarily vulnerable to a fall in the general price-level and to discriminatory tariffs in France and elsewhere. A high proportion of the very large urban population, especially in Holland, was dependent directly or indirectly on employment in fishing, commerce and a variety of manufactures, and all these sectors were beginning to experience serious difficulties by the last years of the century. Structural problems were starting to emerge in the economy as a whole and the effects on employment in the towns was particularly serious and in some cases, notably Leiden and Haarlem which were heavily dependent on the textile industry, all but catastrophic in the long run. While the overall impact was less severe than in these textile centres, not only did the towns cease to grow but the proportion of the total population living in towns actually began to fall by the eighteenth century.

The maritime region was not homogeneous, however, and some towns and areas were affected both more severely and earlier than others. Even in Holland there were marked local differences: notably, the towns of North Holland seem to have begun to experience economic difficulties at least by the mid-century, and from this point on only a handful of the largest towns of Holland showed much resilience. Similarly, the long period of economic growth seems to have come to an end in the countryside of the north of Holland earlier than elsewhere and before the slump in agricultural prices hit the rural economy in the south of the province. The prosperity of the countryside in North Holland had been based on a fruitful combination of advanced farming and involvement in fishing, trade and manufactures – after all the main centre of shipbuilding in the Republic was the *Zaanstreek* – but this complex interlocking system was disrupted and finally destroyed as a result of increasing difficulties in all these areas. This unfortunate combination of factors meant that both towns and countryside in this area anticipated the more general economic problems of the country by some decades. Here, however, it also initiated a process which would eventually lead to a profound change in the social and economic structure of the area. By the end of the seventeenth century the North Holland countryside was already well on the way to the retreat from the dynamic mixed economy of earlier years to an almost exclusive reliance on farming which was apparent by the end of the eighteenth century.[5]

What the maritime region as a whole had in common, however, was the vulnerability of an economy that was not just heavily dependent on trade, but even more so on the mutually beneficial interaction of the various economic sectors. In the years of growth a highly commercialised agriculture interacted with booming trade and fishing to stimulate activities in the manufacturing and service sectors. The depression in agriculture, setbacks to the herring fishery and the end of mercantile expansion set this positive feedback mechanism into reverse, as problems in one area inevitably had consequences in the others. Although there were differences in the timing and intensity of the recession, no part of the region was wholly unaffected. Even those large towns – Amsterdam, Rotterdam, The Hague – which in many ways proved most resilient faced problems from about the 1670s which prevented their further growth – or so the population figures would suggest.

The end of the demographic boom

The general growth in the population of the northern Low Countries which had gone on for at least a century and a half by 1650 slowed down and then stopped in the later seventeenth century. In some areas growth may already have turned into decline before the beginning of the eighteenth century, in others it certainly did. Although there is still a lot that is uncertain about the demographic history of the Republic, it seems reasonably clear that the total population of the country continued to rise until about the 1670s then stagnation set in. However, although there may well have been local falls there seems to have been little or no overall decline before the eighteenth century.

In Holland the general picture masks important local variations to some extent. The continued growth in the total population of the province after the mid century seems to have been almost entirely concentrated in a handful of the largest towns: in this period there was little, if any, increase either in the smaller towns or in the countryside as a whole. The demographic history of Amsterdam in this period remains problematic, but recent estimates suggest – with a degree of plausibility at least – that while the rapid increase of the town's population came to an end around the crisis year of 1672 slower growth continued until about 1740.[6] It was of course by far the largest town in the Republic: on these figures its population reached just over 200,000 by 1670, and continued to expand to a peak of around 240,000 in 1740.[7] Rotterdam too continued to grow until the 1670s, reaching a peak of about 45,000, but after this point stagnation and even some decline set in until the middle of the following century. The Hague was to some extent a special case: as the centre of government for both Holland and the Republic as a whole its population was not mainly determined by straightforward economic factors, and it grew after the mid century to reach about 20,000 in the 1670s and there was some further growth even after this point. Leiden had around 65,000 inhabitants in the 1670s and it is possible that it was also still growing up to this time, but subsequently there was no question of further growth but rather of the beginning of what was to be a spectacular demographic decline by the late eighteenth century.

Apart from these few larger towns, the population had ceased to grow after the middle of the century in both the towns and the countryside of Holland. The period of steady growth seems to have ended earlier, perhaps well before the middle of the century, in the north of Holland. The fragmentary evidence suggests that the population of both town and countryside in North Holland might not simply have stagnated but have actually started to decline in the second half of the century. This area appears to have been particularly hard hit by the changing economic circumstances of the later seventeenth century, but it was not alone. The population of Friesland, too, had ceased to grow by about 1650 and may even have fallen somewhat by the end of the century.[8] Demographic growth had come to an end in most towns and probably all the countryside in the maritime region by the middle years of the century, and only the continued expansion of the biggest towns enabled the population of the region to grow for another decade or so. A notable local exception to this rather gloomy picture is the *Zaanstreek*, which benefited from the decline of ship-building and allied manufactures in the towns of the province. The large village of Graft seems to have grown little after the census of 1622, but to have held its own until 1680 at least.[9] Of course, the demographic resilience of the handful of large towns was to a considerable extent the result of immigration, and some at least of this would have come from the surrounding country areas, suggesting that some surplus was still being produced there. However, it is also possible that it was immigrants from the land provinces and from outside the Republic which enabled Amsterdam in particular to continue to grow in the later years of the century.

The overall picture for the land provinces was rather different, though not much more buoyant overall. By the middle of the seventeenth century the region as a whole had perhaps only recovered the population level it had reached before the disruptions of the Revolt and the Eighty Years War and, in contrast to the maritime provinces, growth continued into the eighteenth century and may even have accelerated. Overijssel showed quite rapid expansion in the late seventeenth and early eighteenth century, particularly but not only in Twente, while the population of Drenthe and the Veluwe (a region of Gelderland) grew rather less spectacularly but still made an impressive contrast to the situation in the west and north.[10] In the south the demographic recovery after the Eighty Years War appears to have been hindered by the recurrence of military operations in the region, particularly in the early years of the Spanish Succession War. The towns in the east and south showed little demographic vitality but in the main avoided the absolute fall in numbers which affected many of the small towns of Holland. On the other hand the faster rate of growth in the countryside meant that the proportion of the population living in towns in these areas fell after 1650.

Whether it was an increase in mortality or a decrease in fertility – or a combination of both – which led to the stagnation and decline of the population in the maritime region is not entirely clear. On the one hand, after the last great outbreak in the 1660s, plague disappeared from the Netherlands, but this does not seem to have brought overall mortality rates down. Smallpox and other epidemic diseases proved just as effective a curb on population though in less dramatic ways. There is also some evidence to suggest that the rising levels of poverty in the towns increased vulnerability to disease. In general, however, there is little to suggest that mortality rates, which were in any case already high, increased significantly in the later seventeenth century. It seems more likely that the worsening economic circumstances of the period led to a rise in the mean age of marriage and a fall in nuptiality, and so to an overall decline in fertility. In addition, immigration, both into the maritime region from the east and south and from outside the Republic, had played an important part in the expansion of the towns of Holland. It is possible – though far from certain – that deaths had always exceeded births in these boom towns, which meant that a stream of immigrants was needed just to maintain population levels never mind sustain the very rapid growth of the early seventeenth century. The less rosy economic circumstances of the later years of the century made the towns and the Republic in general considerably less attractive to economic migrants than they had been in the boom years, though without some continued immigration the population of this region might have fallen even faster than it did.[11] The modest growth in the east and south can similarly be linked to economic conditions, and thus have been primarily a result of higher fertility through a lower average age of marriage, for women in particular.

A new vulnerability

These demographic developments seem to have been very largely the result of the changing economic circumstances of the late seventeenth century. Although not unequivocally in decline – at least not yet –

nearly all areas of the Dutch economy were beginning to show actual or potential weaknesses. In such a highly integrated system where the market had penetrated more thoroughly than it had anywhere else in contemporary Europe, problems in one area inevitably had repercussions in the rest of the economy. When the economy was expanding in the sixteenth and early seventeenth centuries, advances in one sector had stimulated growth in others, but now difficulties in one area began to create or exacerbate problems elsewhere. The very modernity of the economy which was the result of the long period of economic growth made it vulnerable in ways which were to become characteristic of developed capitalism. If this was the first modern economy, it was about to experience a less enviable characteristic of capitalist development and suffer the penalties of the pioneer.

Just as the rapid modernisation of the agricultural sector in the maritime provinces had been of fundamental importance to the development of the Dutch economy as a whole in the sixteenth and early seventeenth centuries, so the onset of what turned out to be almost a century of depressed agricultural prices and, consequently, rents played a major part in undermining the health of the economy as a whole. The fall in the attractiveness of investment in the rural sector had already been signalled by the decline in drainage and reclamation schemes which became apparent before the middle of the century. A great part of the total of land reclaimed in the early modern period was drained between the Revolt and the 1640s, and a number of drainage schemes which were seriously mooted after this period in fact came to nothing in the changed atmosphere of the second half of the century. Instead, Holland in particular moved from the attack to defence with regard to the problems of water control, and more is heard of serious flooding not to mention the problems which the *paalworm*[12] was beginning to cause for the sea defences of the province. As indicated above, the root problem for Dutch agriculture was probably the downward movement of international price levels for their produce. This cut down the profitability of Dutch agricultural exports at the same time as it made imported food cheaper, thus undercutting even the home market for Dutch farmers. As farmers in the maritime provinces in particular were primarily specialised producers for the market they were particularly vulnerable to such changes in market conditions.

The overall problem was exacerbated by the heavy tax burden that farmers, along with the country as a whole, had to bear in the period of the French wars. Also it seems that many rural communities in the maritime region were having to pay significantly more to maintain their essential drainage and sea-control systems in these years. Although the farming community throughout the Republic was affected by the combination of rising taxes and falling prices, it seems likely that the highly specialised and commercially orientated agriculture of the maritime region was hardest hit. At the extreme, some farmers were forced to default on their rents, and there are even cases of properties being abandoned because the tenants or owners could no longer afford to pay the taxes due on them. The less specialised agriculture of the eastern provinces may have fared somewhat better, but everywhere times were becoming hard for an agrarian sector which had played so vital a part in economic growth in the past.

The manufacturing sector too was beginning to encounter intractable problems, though the picture here was not as uniformly grey as it was for agriculture. While some of the traditional bedrocks of Dutch manufacturing, notably textiles, were beginning to falter, others were still expanding and many would continue to flourish into the eighteenth century. However, the omens for long-term growth and development were not good. In particular, the sector as a whole was dependent both on outside supply for most of its raw materials and half-finished goods and on foreign markets for its products, and thus was vulnerable to the conditions of international trade in general and to the mercantilist policies of major suppliers and markets in particular. In general, small scale artisan production serving local markets may have experienced short term falls in demand as a result of temporary economic difficulties – such as the effects of the French invasion of 1672 – but could still be supported by what continued to be a relatively prosperous society; manufactures which depended to a crucial extent on foreign markets were another matter, and could decline through factors quite beyond Dutch control.

Typically for pre-industrial economies, the most important export industry in the Republic, in terms both of wealth creation and employment, was textiles. Although most, if not all, towns had a textile industry of sorts, the great centres were Leiden for woollen cloths and Haarlem for linen. The home market alone could not maintain the production levels achieved by these towns, and the French market was of particular importance for both branches of the industry. Thus the disruption to the trade with France that came as a result of wars and prohibitive French tariffs was a major threat to their continuing prosperity. The heavy import duties imposed in 1667 were an early taste of the damage that such tariffs could do to Dutch manufactures and, although they were rescinded at the Treaty of Nijmegen in 1678, their reintroduction in 1687 helped to precipitate renewed war with France. In addition, the second half of the century saw increasingly effective competition from the textile industries of England and Silesia, not to mention the encouragement given to French production by the protective tariffs.

Such problems were exacerbated by the burden of taxation required to finance the Republic's military and naval efforts in the later seventeenth century, which lay as heavily on manufactures as on agriculture. The structure of the Dutch taxation system put an especially heavy reliance on a whole series of *accijns* (excise duties) on consumer goods, forcing up the cost of living and thus wages – at least in towns like Leiden and Haarlem where their workers were in the main totally dependent on these earnings. These higher labour costs forced up the prices of Dutch textiles and thus lowered their competitiveness. Such relatively high wages further encouraged the industry to move to Twente and North Brabant to take advantage of the supply of rural outworkers who were able to work for lower wages because they had other sources of economic support. Paradoxically, the less developed nature of agriculture in these areas provided a cheap workforce for an ailing industry.

However, the picture was far from being totally bleak throughout the manufacturing sector. While some traditional industries, notably textiles, were beginning to encounter serious problems, others – both old and new – held their ground or continued to expand, in some cases until well into the eighteenth century. While shipbuilding withered away in the port towns of Holland, it held up quite well in the villages of the *Zaanstreek*. Though much remains unclear, the peak of prosperity here may well have been reached by the 1670s but unequivocal decline is not evident until the following century.[13] Among industries which continued to expand up to, and even beyond, the end of the seventeenth century were the potteries of Delft and clay-pipe making at Gouda. So the overall situation for Dutch manufactures was not one of unrelieved gloom, and the Dutch could still believe that there was nothing fundamentally wrong; if the financial burden of war could be lifted and French tariffs moderated perhaps all would yet be well.

The financial sector, too, remained strong and Amsterdam remained the most important capital market in Europe until well into the eighteenth century. While the trade and manufactures of the Republic faced increasing problems in the later seventeenth century, the financiers of Amsterdam seem to have assumed an even more important role in the floating of loans and provision of credit on a European scale. However, whereas during the boom years of the Dutch economy the availability of cheap capital had been an important stimulus to investment in trade and manufactures, by the early eighteenth century – and perhaps already in the last decades of the seventeenth – a gap had opened up between the continued prosperity of the financial sector and the general health of the economy. The presence in Amsterdam of some of the most important banking houses brought attractive opportunities for those with money to invest and enabled a tiny elite of financiers to become very wealthy. The prosperity of the financial sector helped to sustain in the rest of Europe the belief that the Republic was still a rich country, but the benefits to the rest of the Dutch economy appear to have been minimal, and the profits available may have seduced capital away from more productive domestic investments.

Fishing and, to a much lesser extent, whaling were of crucial importance to the economy of Holland as a provider of export articles but perhaps most significantly as a direct or indirect employer of a considerable part of the working population. A decline in this area would have a serious impact on employment in the province. The herring fishery was by far the most important sector, though cod and other sea fishing and fishing in the lakes, rivers and the Zuyder Zee provided much needed protein for home consumption, and it seems – like so many other aspects of the Dutch economy – to have already reached its peak by the mid-century. Subsequently, it suffered badly in the course of the Anglo-Dutch wars, either through losses of boats and catches on the fishing grounds or because the fishing fleet was kept in port as the Dutch navy could not adequately protect it from attack, and similar damage was experienced during the wars with France. The herring fishery had suffered comparable losses in earlier wars and survived – indeed flourished – but this time other factors combined with these short-term losses to bring about serious and continuing decline. Competition from other countries together, possibly, with changing patterns of consumption undermined the export markets for Dutch herring, most seriously in the Baltic region. In addition, the average catch per boat had fallen drastically by the middle of the eighteenth century, possibly as a result of over-fishing, but it is not clear whether this was already the case in the later seventeenth century. Whaling was able to overcome the technical problems of the mid-century – the right whale had retreated under the Arctic pack-ice and had to be hunted there – but specially built, stronger-hulled, and thus more expensive, ships were required. It could not, however, even begin to compensate for the fall in employment which resulted from the decline in the much larger herring fishery.

Trade and shipping had been, perhaps, the most spectacular as well as the most visible parts of the great Dutch boom and the continued resilience of this sector helped to disguise from contemporaries, and not least from the Dutch themselves, the underlying weaknesses of the economy. The overall volume of Dutch trade fluctuated considerably in the later seventeenth century, largely under the influence of warfare, but there was no question of any general decline and there may well have been some underlying growth. Indeed, the Dutch retained their position as the leading trading power in Europe until well into the eighteenth century. Yet, while the level of Dutch trade remained high in the later seventeenth century, the relative position of the Dutch was beginning to weaken, as the trade of England especially, but also of France, began to grow more rapidly.[14] Also, it may well be that trading profits were falling in this period; certainly Amsterdam merchants among others were voicing complaints to this effect as early as the 1660s. In so far as the Dutch trading system was based on its entrepôt function, it was a house built on sand; as other countries developed their own, independent trading connections, the need for the mediating role of the Dutch economy was progressively eroded. Understandably, Dutch economic policy until the late eighteenth century took as its first priority the preservation of the entrepôt which was seen as having been the key to the trading success of the past, but it was a hopeless search for a past which could not be retrieved. Already in the last decades of the seventeenth century changing conditions in Europe and, indeed, in the world, meant that clinging to past methods and priorities would in the end prove to be useless and even counterproductive. However, it is doubtful whether there were other policies available which could have done more than cushion what appears to have been an inevitable decline.

Extra-European trade, even to the East Indies, also began to show ominous signs of vulnerability in these years. It had long been clear that the WIC had failed to realise the hopes of its founders; its economic direction was uncertain and its colonising attempts had come to very little. The ambitious Brazilian adventure, far too expensive for a private company, even one as well-supported as the WIC, was already doomed by the mid-century, and final defeat came soon after. New Netherland was ceded to England (in return for Surinam) at the end of the Second Anglo-Dutch War. This left only a few small Caribbean islands and some footholds on the South American mainland. The company went bankrupt in 1674 and was refounded on a much more modest scale, concentrating largely on sugar production and slave-trading. Its contribution to shoring up the faltering Dutch economy could only be minimal.

In contrast, the VOC had been a spectacular success earlier in the century, and its importance for the economy of the Republic as a whole perhaps even increased in the final decades of the seventeenth century. Even here, however, fundamental problems were beginning to appear. Apart from increasing competition in the European market, especially from the English East India Company, the VOC suffered from organisational weaknesses and what were to prove insoluble structural imbalances. Contemporary awareness that underneath the prosperous surface all was not well with the company was shown by the official enquiry into its activities and financial structure set up at the beginning of the 1680s, though this achieved little. There were two major problems facing the VOC in these years: European demand for oriental goods was moving away from spices to commodities over which the Dutch had far less control; and the costs of the conquest of Sri Lanka and the almost inadvertent but inexorable take-over of Java, as well as the maintenance of the company's infrastructure in the East, were putting too great a strain on its finances. However, up to the end of the century it was the slowing down of the company's expansion that caused apprehension; real decline for the VOC was an eighteenth century phenomenon.

A society on the defensive

The changes which took place as a consequence of the growing economic difficulties in these years were in the main subtle and perhaps more qualitative than quantitative. Economic stagnation, with unmistakable decline in some sectors more or less balanced by at least modest growth in others, did not bring about dramatic upheavals, but the general direction in which society was to move in the years of economic depression was foreshadowed in these years. After the relative stability of the third quarter of the seventeenth century, economic insecurities began to create stresses within Dutch society and conservative and defensive attitudes began to predominate at all levels. The economic and social opportunities opened up by the long boom had encouraged individual and collective ambition and optimism; in the less promising circumstances of the last decades of the century people were more inclined to cling on to what they had rather than to take chances to try to improve their positions. A once brash and aggressive society was becoming staid and cautious.

In some places economic decline had already become not just a threat but a reality by the end of the century. By this time the smaller towns of Holland in particular had not only ceased to expand, but were well into what in some cases would prove to be a well-nigh catastrophic decline. Unfortunately, the social consequences of the economic downturn are far from clear, particularly for the last quarter of the century, but the general direction – if not the speed and precise location – of social change is reasonably evident. The members of the upper bourgeoisie could hope to maintain their social position by the careful redeployment of their financial resources. Families at this level could also try to maintain their leading position in society by attempting to prevent the dissipation of family wealth by limiting their fertility. In particular, cautious marriage strategies together with an increased rate of celibacy among younger brothers and sisters were adopted, with the aim of maintaining the wealth and dignity of the family by limiting the number of children produced. On the whole this approach worked quite well in achieving its intended aim, but recent research among urban regents in particular has shown that it was often all too successful and led to the demographic failure of a number of families. A combination of relatively few children and low nuptiality, besides protecting wealth and social status, made families vulnerable to the unpredictable ravages of accident and, especially, disease. A similar pattern of behaviour seems to have been adopted by the nobility throughout the Republic as well, with even more dramatic results. In this case the outcome was a dramatic decline in numbers which was already becoming evident well before the end of the seventeenth century.[15]

There is some evidence that the relative size of the middling groups in society was falling not only in the especially vulnerable small towns of Holland but in the urban sector in general. As the economic decline came earlier and more harshly in the smaller towns, so the impact on this section of society was already evident here before the end of the century, while in the bigger towns it may have manifested itself more as a growing sense of insecurity rather than any unequivocal erosion of the middle ground in urban society. Artisans, artisan–traders, shopkeepers and shopkeeper–traders, together with a whole range of providers of goods and services linked to general economic prosperity, found that there were fewer suitable economic niches available in the later years of the century. The ranks of the middling classes were also eroded by changes in the organisation of some manufactures which pushed skilled occupations down into the ranks of wage labourer. The independent producer–trader was particularly vulnerable in the harsher economic climate of the later seventeenth century, but the increasing importance of the merchant entrepreneur in the organis-ation of a whole range of manufactures was undermining his position in any case. This process had already been evident in the boom years of the textile industry, but the full extent of the social and economic demotion of weavers and other skilled workers revealed itself with increasing harshness as the industry declined. Rising unemployment and wages which were inadequate to support a family led eventually to a marked degree of social disintegration in the great textile towns, with a notable rise both in the number of legal separations by married couples and in the incidence of abandonment of wives and children.[16]

Of course, those below the middle ranks of society were liable to suffer most from any economic problems, through low wages, under-employment and unemployment. They were also hit by the growing inability or unwillingness of the rest of urban society to bear the rising burden of both occasional need and permanent poverty. Again the pattern is most obvious in the smaller towns whose communal re-sources were shrinking in the second half of the century at the same time as welfare demands on them were growing. Up to about the middle of the century, poor relief systems, care of orphans and other welfare provisions in the Dutch towns, in accord with long-standing communal traditions and buoyed up by ever rising prosperity, had in many ways served as examples of good practice for the rest of Europe. Now as the economy ceased to grow, it became more difficult to sustain the system in the declining towns; both long-term and cyclical poverty increased, putting almost intolerable strains on static or declining resources. The larger towns were able to hold back the tide until the following century, but even here structural falls in employment put increasing strain on welfare institutions. In response, provision for the poor became fragmented, with in particular the various religious groups looking after their own, at the expense of municipal provision.

The end of overall growth in the economy and the first intimations of long term decline affected the rural sector in the maritime region as much, if not more, than the towns. The secular downturn of agricultural prices and rents seems to have begun generally in the 1660s or early 1670s but, as with the smaller towns, some areas hit the buffers to growth rather earlier than this and were clearly in serious trouble before the end of the century. The social effects in terms of occupational structure may have been most evident in North Holland, and may also have emerged earlier here than elsewhere, but throughout the maritime region the rural economy which had been one of the prime motors of Dutch economic growth was in difficulties. Worsening conditions further undermined the position of smaller farmers and encouraged the trend to larger average farm sizes in Holland as a whole.

One of the most obvious pointers indicating the severity of the social strains in the countryside is general demographic stagnation and, later, decline. In the case of North Holland, the available evidence suggests that not only had the population ceased to rise well before the mid-century, but that the severe demographic decline which was evident by the later eighteenth century was already well advanced by around 1700. The most plausible explanation of this reversal of the demographic trend lies in fundamental changes to the economy of the area. As was the case with the smaller towns of Holland, there was little economic growth and increasing economic difficulties in the countryside of North Holland after the 1620s or 1630s. The link between these economic and demographic transformations had to be mediated by social and cultural factors: there were other possible reactions to the worsening economic conditions than those which were in the event opted for by the people of the area. Falling fertility through later marriage and possibly higher rates of celibacy seem to have been the cause of this population decline, and this was the result of a series of individual choices, themselves largely explicable in social and cultural terms.

In the Northern Quarter of Holland there was by the end of the eighteenth century a fall in the proportion of the population living in the towns as, although the population of the rural areas declined, it fell even faster in the towns.[17] The timing of this reversal of urbanisation remains obscure, but it seems safe to assume that it was at least under way in the second half of the seventeenth century. In Holland as a whole, however, although the absolute numbers of people living in towns fell considerably after about the 1670s, their proportion of the total population remained stable at around 61 per cent, in contrast to the land provinces which saw some rise in the urban population in the same period and yet a mild decline in the degree of urbanisation because of a slow but steady rise in the rural population of this region.[18] These figures, showing a stable level of urbanisation in Holland, disguise significant changes in the balance between the towns. A handful of large towns – Amsterdam, Rotterdam and The Hague – continued to grow into the late seventeenth century and subsequently, with minor oscillations, held their own while nearly all the rest had more or less ceased to grow earlier in the century and were probably already shrinking before its end. It was not just the smaller towns which suffered: Leiden, which had been the second largest town in the province soon after mid-century, and Haarlem were also among the losers and, while the timing of their decline is unclear in detail, it was clearly well advanced before the middle of the following century.

The experience of the land provinces in the later decades of the seventeenth century was significantly different. Agriculture here was also caught in the scissors movement of falling prices and rising taxes, but this does not seem to have entirely halted the modest recovery of the region's economy after the problems of the first half of the century. It may well be that the last quarter of the seventeenth century saw the end of the long period of relative economic decline of the land provinces and the beginning of a long-term swing of the economic pendulum in their favour. Within the context of overall economic stagnation and decline, the maritime region was hit much harder and the land provinces showed more resilience and began to make up at least some of the deficit which had accumulated during the long boom in the west. If they had been something like its colony during much of the century, the land provinces were now able to benefit at least to some extent from the difficulties Holland was now experiencing.

Again, while it is necessary to avoid simplistic equations between population movements and economic trends, the demography of this region during the later seventeenth and early eighteenth century shows a buoyancy largely lacking in the west. Although the precise timing remains uncertain, the long term direction is clear: the population of the region as a whole rose in the second half of the seventeenth and throughout the eighteenth century. In part this can be seen as a re- covery after the serious economic and social disruptions during the war with Spain, but it was also an indication that the region was beginning to recover at least some of the ground it had lost in the previous century and a half. There were, of course, differences between various parts of the region. Twente seems to have grown more rapidly than most of the rest, and in North Brabant the population rise of the late seventeenth seems to have halted in the first half of the eighteenth – a setback which can be linked in a large measure to the direct effects on the province of the Spanish Succession War. Moreover, the social con- sequences of this population growth do not seem to have been as devastating, for Overijssel at least, as was once thought.

Some years ago it was argued that demographic growth in Overijssel in the course of the late seventeenth and eighteenth cen- turies led to a progressive immiseration of a peasantry forced to eke out a living on smaller and smaller plots of land.[19] In the Twente quarter of the province, at least, it is now clear that this was not the case: although the existence of relatively cheap labour brought an important textile industry here, cultural constraints helped to maintain a con- siderable degree of social stability. Here proto-industrialisation did not lead to the growth in the size of families to maximise their labour potential (as theory predicts it should), rather family structure re- mained relatively unchanged. A continued link with the land, together with ingrained social attitudes and cultural preferences, preserved the demographic *ancien régime* of late age at marriage and consequently modest fertility in Twente until almost the twentieth century.[20] Nevertheless the presence in Twente of a class of small-holding peasants which could provide relatively cheap but skilled labour drew the woollen textiles industry away from Holland, and specifically Leiden, and made possible the start of a successful new manufacturing sector in the area. In turn the putting-out system employed by the merchant entrepreneurs who ran the new industry stimulated the creation of a new social group of weavers and spinners subsisting partly from earnings from the textile industry and partly from their own plots of land together with a variety of rural employments. Similar conditions led to the growth of a textile industry in North Brabant also, with similar social and economic results. Although the full implications of these developments were only to be apparent in the eighteenth century, their beginnings can be traced back to the last decades of the seventeenth. In this case, as in so many others, these years were a crucial turning point with far-reaching consequences for the social structure of both the developing and declining areas.

The economic balance between the two main regions of the Dutch Republic was beginning to change after more than a century of unquestioned superiority for the maritime provinces, and the roots of the turnaround can to a significant extent be traced to the last thirty or so years of the seventeenth century. However, it must be stressed that these were far from being boom or golden years for the economy and society of the land provinces: times were becoming harder here too, but not to the same extent as in the previously more prosperous western part of the country. In Drenthe, with its almost total dependence on agriculture, the depression in prices for agricultural products created severe problems, but farming proved rather more resilient than in Holland. What might have been seen as a less advanced economic structure proved an advantage in these difficult circumstances; mixed farming which combined rye, sheep and pigs predominated, in contrast to the highly-specialised rural economy of Holland, and this allowed a more flexible response to the difficult times of the late seventeenth and early eighteenth century. Not for the last time a highly developed economic system proved vulnerable to fundamental changes in the international economy outside its control, while less developed regions could at least adapt more easily to the changing circumstances.

The beginning of Dutch decline?

At first sight it might seem strange that there is a question mark in the title of this section; the economic problems and structural difficulties discussed so far would seem to be more than just auguries of what was to come. Certainly, in retrospect it seems clear that the weaknesses which were becoming evident in the last quarter of the seventeenth century were the root causes of the economic decline and the consequent social malaise of the following century. However, it would be a mistake to exaggerate the extent to which overall decline had set in by the end of the seventeenth century, especially as the land provinces were moving to a distinctly different rhythm than the maritime region. Moreover, in recent decades historians have embarked on a re-evaluation of the eighteenth century in the Republic and the simple story of overall political, economic, social and cultural decline is in the course of being replaced by a much more nuanced account. This process of reinterpretation began with the suggestion that the economic decline of the eighteenth century was to a considerable extent relative rather than absolute, i.e. that the Dutch lost their leading position in the course of the eighteenth century but that nevertheless in many respects the Republic was little, if at all, worse off than it had been at its peak in the previous century. In some areas and in some sectors of the economy, of course, the decline was both severe and absolute but overall the economy proved to be considerably more resilient than the bleak picture contained in the conventional account.[21] The social problems caused by the collapse of the textile industry in Leiden and Haarlem or, less spectacularly, by the economic difficulties of the smaller Holland trading towns were not necessarily typical of the Republic as a whole. If the later economic decline was neither so severe nor so universal as was once supposed, then the problems of the later seventeenth century should certainly not be exaggerated.

At the end of their Golden Century, the Dutch were still a wealthy society and still a formidable economic force in Europe and the world.[22] Although some sectors of the economy, perhaps most notably the agriculture of the maritime region, were showing unmistakable signs of vulnerability, others were holding their ground and some at least were continuing to grow. If it is tempting to see the expansion of gin and brandy production in Schiedam as a sign – if not a cause – of social dislocation, the same can hardly be said of the continued growth of the pottery industry in Delft or of clay-pipe production in Gouda – at least not in quite the same sense. Dutch trade was experiencing difficulties in maintaining its position and profitability but if there were some signs of slippage it was from a very high peak. As far as fishing was concerned, it was unclear whether the difficulties which were experienced in this period were primarily the result of the disruptions during warfare, to which it was peculiarly and unavoidably susceptible, or an indication of structural problems. With around fifteen years of war between 1672 and the end of the century, it was tempting for the Dutch to believe that most, if not all, of the economic problems they were facing could be solved by lasting peace. With the benefit of hindsight it is clear that there were more deep-seated flaws in the Dutch economic system, and that these might have been exacerbated but certainly not caused by the damaging effects of the wars with France in these years. In the first half of the century, the Dutch economy had been able to grow, indeed boom, despite almost constant involvement in warfare; after the 1660s this was no longer the case.

At the end of the century the social effects of this economic slippage were as yet limited as far as most of the Republic was concerned. However, the developments in some areas – notably the Northern Quarter of Holland – were already indicating what was in store for much of the rest of the country in the eighteenth century. This area had been at the cutting edge of the modernisation of the economy in the sixteenth century and it was now leading the way into what seems in many respects a social regression as much as an economic depression. The complex interaction between agriculture, manufactures, trade and fishing which had lain at the heart of the area's former prosperity was breaking down: the trading towns were in full decline, demographic as much as economic, and the rural population was retreating into agriculture at the expense of other activities. In general these northern parts of Holland were well on the way to becoming the economic and social backwaters they were by the end of the following century. Even here the manufacturing villages of the *Zaanstreek* proved able to keep their heads above water for some considerable time to come, and the picture for the rest of the country was considerably less gloomy. However, there is some evidence to suggest that in the towns of the maritime region at least, the middling groups in society were being eroded by the economic pressures of the time, and that economic privation was beginning to affect the general level of health of the poorer section of the urban population. Social problems were increasing at a time when the resources to alleviate them were shrinking. Again, the full effects of these developments were only to become obvious later, but in many parts of Holland at least the portents were already ominously clear.

Notes

1   Studies of these wars from the English side have tended to exaggerate both the damage done to the Dutch and the advantages gained by the English economy. The latest account, though in most respects admirable, is disappointing from this point of view: J.R. Jones: *The Anglo-Dutch Wars of the Seventeenth Century* (London, 1996).

2   F. Gaastra, *Bewind en beleid bij de VOC 1672–1702* (Zutphen, 1989).

3   J.L. van Zanden, *The Rise and Decline of Holland's Economy* (Manchester, 1993), 35–9.

4   For Twente, see most recently C. Trompetter, *Agriculture, Proto-Industry and Mennonite Entrepreneurship 1600–1815* (Amsterdam, 1997).

5   The declining importance of sea-faring in the economy of one part of North Holland is examined by Piet Boon, *Bouwers van de zee: zeevarenden van het Westfriese platteland, c. 1680–1720* (The Hague, 1996).

6   A convenient summary in English of recent reseach is: Hubert Nusteling, 'The Population of Amsterdam and the Golden Age', in *Rome–Amsterdam. Two Growing Cities in Seventeenth Century Europe*, ed. Peter van Kessel and Elisja Schulte (Amsterdam, 1997), 71–84.

7   H.P.H. Nusteling, *Welvaart en werkgelegenheid in Amsterdam 1540–1860* (Amsterdam/Dieren, 1985), 95–6.

8   J.A. Faber, *Drie eeuwen Friesland. Economische en sociale ontwikkelingen van 1500 tot 1800* (Wageningen, 1972), 1, 57–8; 2, table II.10.

9   A.Th. van Deursen, *Een dorp in de polder. Graft in de zeventiende eeuw* (Amsterdam, 1994), 15–18.

10   De Vries and Van der Woude, *The First Modern Economy* (Cambridge, 1997), 54–5.

11   De Vries and Van der Woude, *The First Modern Economy*, 72–6, for a discussion of the rôle of migration in the population history of the Republic.

12   A crustacean which weakened the sea defences by drilling into the wooden parts of the sea dykes.

13   De Vries and Van der Woude, *The First Modern Economy*, 299–300.

14   The argument that Dutch economic decline was relative rather than absolute was first elaborated in Johan de Vries, *De economische achteruitgang der Republiek in de achttiende eeuw* (Amsterdam, 1959).

15   J.L. Price, 'The Dutch Nobility in the Seventeenth and Eighteenth Centuries', *The European Nobilities in the Seventeenth and Eighteenth Centuries*, vol.1, ed. H.M. Scott (London, 1995), 82–113.

16   Donald Haks, *Huwelijk en gezin in Holland in de 17de en 18de eeuw* (Assen, 1982), 184–93.

17   A.M. van der Woude, *Het Noorderkwartier* (Wageningen, 1972), 1, 109.

18   De Vries and Van der Woude, *The First Modern Economy*, 61 and ff.

19   B.H. Slicher van Bath, *Een samenleving onder spanning: geschiedenis van het platteland in Overijssel* (Assen, 1957), though it should be noted that the author's chief focus was conditions in the nineteenth century.

20   Trompetter, *Agriculture, Proto-Industry and Mennonite Entrepreneurship*, chap. 5. For the continuation of such attitudes in this area into the nineteenth century, see F.M.M. Hendrickx, '*In order not to fall into poverty.' Production and Reproduction in the Transition from Proto-industry to Factory Industry in Borne and Wierden (the Netherlands), 1800–1900* (Amsterdam, 1997).

21   Johan de Vries, *De economische achteruitgang*; see more recently J.L. van Zanden, 'De economie van Holland in de periode 1650–1805: groei of achteruitgang?', *Bijdragen en Mededelingen betreffende de geschiedenis der Nederlanden*, 102, 1987, 562–609; J.C. Riley, 'The Dutch economy after 1650: decline or growth?', *Journal of European Economic History*, 13, 1984, 521–69.

22   Indeed, Israel, *Dutch Primacy*, 381–2, 399–400, sees Dutch 'primacy' in trade at least as extending well into the eighteenth century.

7

Dutch Society in the Golden Century

THE DUTCH still commonly refer to their period of greatness in the seventeenth century as the *Gouden Eeuw* – Golden Century – which, besides containing an allusion to the economic success of the Republic in this period, can also be read as hinting at the myth of a golden age. There is indeed a sense in which the *Gouden Eeuw* has become more a myth than a simple descriptive term for a period of history, and it seems to have taken on something of this mythical character, if not yet the name, almost before it had come to an end. For the Dutch, an idealised image of their seventeenth century experience has existed since the eighteenth century, and to an extent continues to exist, in a dimension quite distinct from normal canons of historical criticism. At a trivial level it takes its place, along with clogs, tulips and windmills, as a marker of what it means to be Dutch, particularly for outsiders; at a deeper level, it has acted as a touchstone by which the Dutch have judged their later history. The burden of the *Gouden Eeuw* has been heavy: the great period of Dutch history – politically, economically, culturally – came at the very beginning of the existence of the Dutch state, and consequently the later history of the Netherlands has been in danger of seeming a permanent anti-climax. Succeeding generations have had to come to terms with the *Gouden Eeuw*, creating and recreating, interpreting and reinterpreting it according to the perceptions, and the needs, of the time. These versions of the past have not always been positive – in the nineteenth century it was usual to deprecate the Republic for the weakness of its central government and its almost total lack of what was felt to be a proper national consciousness, in contrast to the centralised Orange monarchy with its romantic sense of national identity – but what all the various interpretations of the Golden Century have had in common is the assumption that they were reacting to something that had actually existed.

The classic accounts of the Dutch seventeenth century – Busken Huet's *Land of Rembrandt*, Muller's *Our Golden Century* and Huizinga's *Dutch Civilisation*[1] – despite, and perhaps even because, of their considerable merits have helped to make the idea of the golden century a dominant element in the standard version of Dutch history, and have to an extent obscured the fact that the golden century is no more than an interpretation of the past, and like any other interpretation open to revision in the light of new information or a significantly different perspective. Our knowledge and understanding of the Dutch seventeenth century has grown enormously with the expansion of scholarship over the last thirty or forty years, and this necessarily raises the question whether the inherited reading of the Dutch past is still valid or even useful, either as myth or history. Yet, as more and more specialised studies on a wide range of different topics have appeared, some of them hardly dreamt of in earlier concepts of historical writing, it has become considerably more difficult to produce a coherent picture of the period as a whole. Nevertheless, a critical examination of what is still the dominant interpretation offers promising perspectives. If in the end the idea of the *Gouden Eeuw* seems to be getting in the way of a better understanding of the Republic in the seventeenth century then it might have to be discarded especially as, when seen from the perspective of the social history of the period, it can be legitimately doubted whether it ever existed.

The rhythms of social change in the Northern Netherlands during the early modern period closely paralleled the secular trend in the economy and, though they are less easily measured, the same might be said of cultural developments as well. This observation is partly a tautology, as essentially social and economic change are different aspects of the same phenomenon. Culture, too, in its broadest sense can be seen as an aspect of social life and thus necessarily changing with it, though here there is the intriguing possibility that there may be significant lags between changes in society and the cultural adjustments to these developments. In any case it does seem that the period of greatest economic success coincided, not unexpectedly, with the emergence of a distinctive form of society in the Republic, and was accompanied by an equally distinctive culture, not just in terms of the art and literature produced at the time, but also in a more general sense as well. This is not to suggest that all these social and cultural changes were simply the result of economic developments, but rather that the interaction between these various elements produced a distinctive and to a large extent coherent period in Dutch history. If this observation is true, then it offers some support to the concept of a golden century.

On the other hand, it may be doubted at the very least whether the chronological seventeenth century and the *Gouden Eeuw* coincided. The beginning of the Dutch economic boom can be placed before the start of the century. Israel puts the take-off of the trading economy in the 1590s,[2] but this was only possible because of the fundamental economic and social developments that had already taken place in the Northern Netherlands in the century or more before this point. Dominance in the Baltic grain trade, the expansion of the herring fisheries, a high degree of urbanisation, and the diversification of the rural economy, had all been established by the time of the Revolt against Spain. The economic development of the Northern Netherlands was interrupted by the Revolt, but for Holland in particular this disruption was of relatively short duration. Indeed, while independence proved to be an enormous stimulus to the Dutch economy, the Revolt in the northern provinces of the Netherlands only survived because the economy of the key province, Holland, was already strong. If the roots of the golden period must be placed well before 1600, it is similarly becoming increasingly clear that in many ways the period of Dutch greatness was over well before the end of the seventeenth century. This has long been recognised to be the case for art and literature, and now appears true to a large extent for the economy as well. The last thirty years of the century are probably better seen as a period of transition than as an integral part of the *Gouden Eeuw*. Such modifications of the chronology of the golden age at both ends suggest that it should be placed in the period from, at the latest, the 1590s to around 1670, and thus not only excluding a good part of the seventeenth century but also lasting rather less than a hundred years.

Such reconsiderations of the timing of the Dutch period of greatness are interesting but perhaps do little to undermine the concept of a *Gouden Eeuw*. More important in this respect is that the recognition of the fundamental importance of the social and economic changes which took place before the seventeenth century – and to a large extent even before the Revolt – has been joined by a notable revaluation of the eighteenth century to suggest a greater continuity in the history of the Northern Netherlands in the early modern period than the concept of the *Gouden Eeuw* would allow. If the distinctive features of the golden age were to a significant extent the result of developments which took place before the Revolt, and if the eighteenth century decline is to some extent at least a historiographical illusion, then the three centuries from the early sixteenth to the end of the eighteenth century can only be properly understood as a whole. Seeing the sixteenth century as a prologue to the Golden Century and the eighteenth century primarily as its aftermath begins to appear fundamentally unhistorical.

Viewed from the perspective of social history in particular, the early modern period in the northern Netherlands constitutes a single process with its own rhythm of development and change: the emergence of a distinctive type of society, and then the modifications to this society resulting from a less favourable economic environment. The society of the golden century has to be understood in this context, especially as the timing of these consecutive phases could show considerable local and regional variations. Not only did the *Gouden Eeuw* as a common Dutch phenomenon last less than a century, in some areas it ended much earlier than in others, and it might even be questioned whether it extended to the land provinces to any significant extent at all. While the Dutch Republic did experience a period of economic dominance, cultural fertility and distinctive social developments, these elements did not emerge phoenix-like from the flame of Revolt, but were the outcome of a much longer process; nor was the later descent into economic fallibility, related social problems, and cultural conventionality quite as unhappy a resolution to the drama as was once thought. There were down sides to the Dutch society of the *Gouden Eeuw* and the Republic of the eighteenth century, while it may have been less vigorous and original, remained in many ways the most civilised society in Europe and deserves to be understood on its own terms and not as a pale reflection of the golden century.

Laying the foundations for the *Gouden Eeuw*

The society that emerged in the Republic by the middle of the seventeenth century was the product of a process of development and change in the northern Netherlands which can be traced back to the beginning of the sixteenth century if not earlier. Although some of these developments were strongly evident in the land provinces up to the time of the Revolt, nevertheless the process as a whole was clearest in the maritime provinces and most strongly developed in Holland. The high degree of urbanisation which was such a striking characteristic of Dutch seventeenth century society was already well-advanced in this province before the Revolt, with around 50 per cent of its population living in towns, although these towns were distinctly smaller than their seventeenth-century counterparts. Similarly the penetration of the countryside of Holland by market forces was already bringing about economic diversification in the rural sector by the early sixteenth century at the latest. The rest of the maritime region followed the Holland pattern to a less pronounced extent. Even Zeeland, which had in many ways a rather different economic development to that of the rest of the region, shared this precocity. Indeed, it has been argued that at least as far as agriculture was concerned, it had already completed its transformation by the beginning of the seventeenth century, after which no fundamental change took place until well after the end of the Republic.[3] In general the northern provinces of the Netherlands were relatively advanced both economically and socially on the eve of the Revolt; they were already moving strongly into a capitalist phase and had a degree of urbanisation which was radically different from the rest of Europe.

The impact of the Revolt on this relatively advanced society was decisive for seventeenth century developments, but not everywhere in the same way. From the time of the rising in Holland and Zeeland in 1572 there were almost twenty years of disruption which affected all of the area which later became part of the Dutch Republic. Even in these difficult years, however, the worst was over quite quickly for Holland and Zeeland. Up to the Pacification of Ghent in 1576 the war had been fought in these two provinces and, although this agreement did not stave off hostilities for very long, when the conflict broke out again it did so well away from their territory. There were still internal problems for Holland until Haarlem and Amsterdam had been brought over to the rebel side but after this point the province was able to resume the economic advances of the pre-Revolt period. As rebellion transmuted into the long war with Spain, the economy of Holland and the maritime region in general, although far from unaffected by the conflict, was nevertheless able to grow and by the 1590s was already taking off into a trading boom. In contrast, for the rest of the Eighty Years War the land provinces were in the front line. The war consisted in the main of fairly small-scale sieges and manoeuvres rather than pitched battles but it went on for decade after decade – relieved only by the Twelve Years Truce (1609–21). The movement of troops, foraging, and the imposition of contributions severely disrupted the rural economy of the region while the towns, when not actually under siege, suffered from constant interruptions to their trade links as well as from the devastation of their hinterlands. The result was that in the whole arc of provinces from Bergen op Zoom to Groningen the promising economic and social developments of the pre-Revolt period were rudely interrupted and these economic difficulties formed a painful contrast to the rising prosperity of the maritime provinces. In the second half of the century, after the Treaty of Münster, growth could resume in these hard pressed areas, but it could do little more than repair the damage done by the long years of war. The Revolt produced a radical change in the balance, political as well as economic, between the two major regions of the Northern Netherlands and ensured that, while the maritime provinces entered the *Gouden Eeuw*, the land provinces could only look on with envy at the experience of their more fortunate compatriots.

Thus the Revolt – or perhaps more the Eighty Years War which grew out of it – had far-reaching effects for the Republic in the seventeenth century, but the Revolt in turn has to be seen to a large extent as the result of the economic and social developments of the earlier sixteenth century. If the economy of Holland – and this province is the vital element in this respect – had not been as strong as it was then the rising of 1572 might well have still occurred but would almost certainly have failed if it had. The nature of the changes which were taking place, particularly the growth of the towns and the rising importance of the bourgeoisie, were equally significant in making the Revolt possible and eventually successful – at least in the North. The break with Spain swept away the top level of government and thus allowed the regents to establish their predominance in the new state which emerged from the struggle, and the new regime proved much more in sympathy with the needs of the Dutch economy than the Spanish could ever have been. It is an intriguing question whether there could have been a golden century without the Revolt and the break with Spain. Continued persecution of protestants and the subordination of Dutch[4] interests to the geopolitical needs of the Spanish *monarchía* would certainly have hindered the economic growth which was the essential foundation of the *Gouden Eeuw*, but for the rest the complex nature of the phenomenon defies the often trite speculation of what has been called virtual history. What can be said is that the same economic and social forces that brought about the Revolt and to a large extent made its success possible also laid the foundations for the unique character of Dutch society in the seventeenth century.

Decline reassessed

While it has always been clear that the golden century could not have come from nowhere, and so the sixteenth century has enjoyed at least some reflected glory as its prologue, the eighteenth century was until quite recently conventionally depicted in terms of almost unrelieved gloom. However, it was no more plausible that all positive aspects of the *Gouden Eeuw* would wither so rapidly or all at the same rate, than that it could have sprung out of nothing. There has been a necessary reaction against the accepted account of the eighteenth century and this has initiated a process of reassessment which has taken two main directions. One approach, while starting from a seventeenth century perspective, has questioned the extent and timing of the decline. The other has attempted to treat the eighteenth century on its own terms rather than as an etiolated version of the golden century. Although the first type of reinterpretation has produced some important work, the second is arguably of more fundamental importance, as it implicitly refuses to take the *Gouden Eeuw* as the defining element of early-modern Dutch history. To this extent it can be seen as part of an attempt to relieve the history of the Netherlands of the burden of always being compared to the glories of the seventeenth century and inevitably never being able to come up to scratch.

Following the first approach, the sharp economic contrast with the golden century has been blurred in two ways: on the one hand the beginnings of the economic and social malaise, which are still accepted as marking the Republic in the eighteenth century, have been brought well back into the seventeenth century; and on the other the nature and even the reality of the decline has been questioned. It has been pointed out that various sectors of the Dutch economy continued to prosper and that more generally, although there were notable black spots, the Republic remained a relatively wealthy country throughout the eighteenth century. Part of the reason for the prevailing image of decline has been the understandable tendency to focus on Holland which had been the power house of the Dutch economy in the golden century. Holland suffered an economic decline relative to the rest of the country in the eighteenth century, and it was here also that the most glaring examples of economic failure occurred, notably the collapse of the textile industry in Haarlem and Leiden with its devastating social consequences for these towns. Similarly, the rapid descent of both towns and countryside of North Holland to the condition of economic backwaters has understandably received considerable attention. Seen from the perspective of the Republic as a whole, however, both the economic situation and its social consequences appear much less unrelievedly gloomy. The Europe-wide agricultural depression was a difficult time throughout the Republic, but this ended before the middle of the eighteenth century and in any case the Dutch rural economy proved remarkably resilient – certainly in comparison to many of the trading and manufacturing towns of Holland. Also the Dutch lost their economic supremacy in Europe and much of their position as a major economic force in the extra-European world in the course of the eighteenth century, which has made this period less of a cause of patriotic pride in later generations. Nevertheless, it has been plausibly argued that this was more of a relative than an absolute decline, with the Dutch staying more or less where they were while others, and especially Britain, surged ahead.[5] By contemporary standards the Dutch economy was reasonably successful, and was still liable to arouse the envy of foreigners.

Rather than being seen simply as a decline from the achievements of the seventeenth century, the economic problems of the late seventeenth and eighteenth centuries (and later) are better regarded as a necessary, and not entirely unsuccessful, process of transition and adjustment to changing economic circumstances. From this perspective, the growth of the textile industry in Twente is as important as its decline in Holland, and it is the successful adaptation of Dutch agriculture to new circumstances which becomes impressive. In addition, although Dutch commercial policy was obsessed with what proved to be the unrealistic aim of trying to resuscitate the staple market, nevertheless Dutch trade more or less held its own in the eighteenth century. In the towns of Holland, the decline of labour intensive sectors of the economy such as manufactures for export and the herring fishery brought structural unemployment on a large scale, together with marked demographic decline. For other sectors of the economy, other areas of the country, and other classes of society the eighteenth century was considerably less traumatic. The Dutch economy in the eighteenth century is perhaps better understood if it is viewed as fundamentally different from, rather than as an impoverished version of, the spectacularly successful economy of the previous century.

The contrast between the *Gouden Eeuw* and the eighteenth century is further tempered by a keener awareness of the less favourable aspects of the seventeenth century experience in the Republic. Not all areas of the country had an equal share in the economic boom, and rapid social change brought more problems than opportunities for some sections of the population and for many individuals. The economic growth of the maritime region did nothing to abolish poverty in the region, and this was a major and growing problem in the booming towns of Holland. The transition from the ebullient society of the first two thirds of the seventeenth century to what has been pejoratively called the periwig period (*pruikentijd*) was not all loss. Also, one respect in which Dutch seventeenth century society was clearly not modern was in its almost total helplessness in the face of disease. Given that understanding of the causes of diseases and how to treat them was still wholly inadequate, it is quite possible that the increase in the availability of a variety of medical services did more harm than good to the health of the population in general. If the focus is shifted from the economic and social to broader cultural issues the situation becomes even less clear cut. Although the great achievements in painting and literature were over by the late seventeenth century, these years of economic and social uncertainty saw the blossoming of the early Enlightenment in the Republic, and in the eighteenth century the Republic became in many ways the model of the 'enlightened' society. This Dutch Enlightenment, though marred by a certain complacency, was moderate and fundamentally christian in character – and eminently reasonable. Despite – or possibly even because of – its fall from economic leadership and great power status, the Republic can still be seen as one of the most desirable places to live in eighteenth century Europe (though it has to be admitted that the competition was not great).

The *Gouden Eeuw* reconsidered

Not all was golden in the *Gouden Eeuw*, and not all of the seventeenth century was golden. It is now clear that there are problems with the timing of the Dutch economic miracle in at least two respects: at a general level the dating of its beginning and its end have come into question; and, more fundamentally, the rhythm of growth, prosperity and decline seem to have been so different in various parts of the Republic that it is no longer clear that it makes sense to think in terms of the golden century as a coherent period at all. Of course, both the implicit argument and the contents of this book suggest that the concept remains not only viable but even indispensable to a proper understanding of the Dutch seventeenth century. However, this approach can only work if the problems facing this interpretation are recognised. In part, the idea of the *Gouden Eeuw* is a consequence of a Hollandocentric approach to Dutch history in this period; given the economic and political predominance of this province such an approach is justifiable and in a sense unavoidable, but there is another reality to the Dutch experience in these years which needs to be recognised. The land provinces experienced a very different seventeenth century than Holland: for this half of the Republic the golden century is hard to find.

As regards the question of dating, the arguments for putting the end of the golden century much earlier than was once assumed are becoming particularly persuasive. It now seems safe to conclude that the great Dutch economic boom came to an end soon after the middle of the seventeenth century, and that the last twenty five or thirty years of the century marked the transition to, if not unambiguous decline, then at least a considerably more troubled period of Dutch economic history. Some indicators – long-term trends in grain prices, for example – would suggest, indeed, that the long period of economic growth came to an end even earlier, perhaps before the middle of the century. In any event, for some areas even within the generally buoyant maritime region the golden century was notably brief, and growth had turned to stagnation and even decline by the 1630s or 1640s. This appears to have been the case in the smaller towns of Holland and the Northern Quarter in general. The dating is even more problematic in the case of Zeeland, as here the boom appears to have been over almost before it had begun. Both the commerce and agriculture of this province seem to have followed rather different rhythmns from the maritime region as a whole: the period of very rapid economic expansion and change seems to have been largely confined to the last decades of the sixteenth century and to have come to an end soon after, though in this case the growth phase was succeeded by a prolonged period of stability rather than immediate decline. This evidence suggests that though Zeeland was able to share in the golden century to some extent, its history in the late sixteenth and seventeenth century had its own distinctive character and was not just a weaker version of that of Holland.

From an economic and social point of view, the land provinces together with North Brabant can be regarded as missing out on the *Gouden Eeuw* almost entirely. The eastern provinces were far from overshadowed by the maritime region in the half century or more before the Revolt, but the upheavals accompanying the break with Spain brought economic and demographic growth to a halt, and the long years of war which followed involved almost continuous fighting on their territory. Consequently, these provinces continued to suffer losses in population, disturbances to trade, and hard times for manufactures almost up to the end of the Eighty Years War. Only after the middle of the seventeenth century could they begin to experience even modest growth, and this pattern makes their experience of the seventeenth century almost a mirror image of that of the maritime region. North Brabant had been part of what had been the most economically dynamic province in the Habsburg Netherland in the years before the Revolt but subsequent events split it off from the rest of Brabant and the struggle to control this border area led to some of the fiercest and most prolonged fighting of the war with Spain. States Brabant emerged from the conflict not only economically damaged but also as a politically and religiously underprivileged quasi-colony of the Republic. Here too there was a measure of recovery after the Treaty of Münster, but in this instance the economic upturn, unspectacular as it was, was all too soon interrupted by the effects of the long wars with France, the Spanish Succession War being particularly disruptive. In this buffer area, the golden century is even harder to find than in the land provinces generally.

Even within the maritime region there were significant differences in the nature and timing of the boom. Economic growth and the consequent social changes were considerably stronger in Holland than in the rest of the region, and there is a sense in which the golden century took place in Holland alone rather than in the Republic as a whole. Yet even within the leading province there were important differences: North Holland experienced particularly vigorous growth in the late sixteenth and the early decades of the seventeenth century, and Hoorn and especially Enkhuizen were among the most dynamic of the trading towns during this period, but the growth phase ended comparatively early here, and decline may well have set in well before the middle of the century. South Holland was the area where the *Gouden Eeuw* was strongest and lasted longest, but even here there is a certain contrast between the leading towns – Amsterdam, Leiden, Rotterdam, The Hague and, perhaps, Haarlem – which continued to expand economically and demographically into the last third of the century and the other towns of this sub-province which ceased to grow rather earlier. With all these differences the golden century was nevertheless a reality for Holland, and probably for much of the maritime region as well. It was here that the most vigorous and prolonged phase of growth took place, and where the social effects of these economic changes were most marked. This was not a monolithic process, and its timing and intensity varied from place to place, but there were fundamental changes in both urban and rural society throughout the region. Even the land provinces, although standing aside from the transformation that was taking place in the west, could not be unaffected by the momentous changes taking place throughout the maritime region.

Similarly, just as there were marked local and regional differences in the experience of the golden century, so some sections of society were affected more than others and, while the boom offered economic and social opportunities over the whole range of society, there were inevitably losers as well as winners in the abrasive society of this turbulent period. In rural Holland, smallholders were squeezed out by the bigger free-holders and tenant farmers, and this process seems only to have accelerated as the rural economy came under pressure later in the seventeenth century. In the textile industry the position of the independent master-craftsman was weakened through the rise of the merchant–entrepreneur, and skilled workers were steadily forced out of independent business and into wage labour – which meant a loss in status perhaps even more significant than the fall in income involved. There was a notable expansion in the relative size of the middling classes, and this became a society that was much less polarised by extremes of wealth and poverty than most of the rest of Europe at this time.[6] Nevertheless, about half the urban population in Holland at any one time had too little money or property to be worth taxing directly. In periods of particular economic difficulties – resulting, for example, from a downswing in the trade cycle, or the effects of war – the proportion of the population in need of at least some help could rise alarmingly, and even in normal times relief for the poor, widows and orphans was the major social challenge facing contemporary town governments.

There is some evidence, too, that this was not perhaps such a golden age for women whatever their social class. Women were prominent and very visible in social and economic life, especially through the predominant role they played in the retail trade – contemporary depictions of markets and street life are a lively testimony to the active part played by women in this sector and other sources support this impression as well – but most women worked in low-paid jobs or socially marginal occupations. The labour shortages produced by the booming economy were satisfied by immigration rather than by opening up new areas for female employment. Legally women remained second-class citizens in important respects. Daughters were dependent on their fathers, and wives on their husbands and neither were able to act for themselves in the eyes of the law. Widows could enjoy greater legal independence, but few had the means to make much use of this theoretical advantage. In the upper reaches of the bourgeoisie, wives and daughters were already retreating into the domestic sphere, though widows seem often to have taken over as financial heads of their family rather than handing this responsibility over to their eldest sons. At a more modest social level, the widow of a craftsman would usually be allowed to carry on her late husband's business, and was in an advantageous position in the marriage market as she could often offer a new husband the acceptance as a guild master which might otherwise have been difficult or expensive to obtain. Despite the rise in status and numbers of the medical profession, child-bearing remained dangerous, and it is possible that bringing midwives under closer medical supervision made matters worse by substituting unsound theory for traditional practice. The continuing high rates of infant and child mortality must have also added considerably to the emotional attrition of life for mothers at all levels of society.

On the other hand, women in financial difficulties through the death of their husbands, along with orphans, the sick and others unable to make ends meet through no fault of their own were well cared for by the standards of the time, and protected from the worst effects of the abrasive economic climate of the golden century. Of course, help was most readily available for those who fitted into the prevailing prejudices of the social and political elite; in the towns, citizens were better treated than non-citizens, orphans and widows better than the able-bodied unemployed.[7] In a great part these proliferating social problems were the result of the rapid demographic growth which characterised both towns and countryside in the late sixteenth and early seventeenth century. The difficulty of dealing with the side-effects of rapid expansion was most obvious in the towns of Holland where institutions which had grown up to deal with the needs of much smaller communities were faced with demands of an unprecedented scope and complexity. However, the prosperity that accompanied this social and economic change enabled more or less satisfactory solutions to be cobbled together through a mixture of municipal action, the charitable activities of the Reformed Church, and private provision. As the economy faltered, pressure on welfare provision increased and resources failed to keep up with the demand. Even when the Dutch economy was booming dealing with poverty was a major challenge; by the late seventeenth century the existing systems were looking fragile, and new approaches seemed necessary to deal with an ever worsening problem. The poor do indeed seem to have been with us always – a Biblical reference that would certainly have rung true in the Dutch Republic, even at the height of its prosperity.

A new society?

For a brief period the Dutch Republic was the dominant economic power in Europe, and this wealth translated almost directly into the resources to sustain major power status – at least for a while. In these years a form of society developed in the more advanced region of the country – the maritime provinces and especially Holland – which was significantly different from anything that could be found elsewhere in Europe. Visitors' accounts treat the Republic with something approaching the wonder and sheer incomprehension of Europeans encountering the societies of the New World. In the case of the Republic the sense of alienation was possibly all the more acute because, while the various elements of society looked familiar, the way they were put together and the way they worked transformed the commonplace into the exotic, and this helps to explain the sense of outrage and even disorientation that is evident in many reports. Outsiders found the Dutch political system almost impossible to understand, and most were appalled by the degree of religious toleration – which they saw as licence – allowed by the civil authorities throughout the Republic. Equally, while Dutch economic success was generally admired, the single-minded pursuit of wealth which accompanied it was regarded as a moral failing rather than as the inevitable consequence of the unprecedented dominance of capitalism in the country.

The most visible way in which the society of the Republic marked itself off from the rest of Europe by the middle of the seventeenth century was by a level of urbanisation which was not to be equalled anywhere in Europe for another two centuries. Less visible but even more fundamental to the transformation which had taken place was the penetration of the market into all areas and into all levels of economic activity: indeed the countryside of the maritime region was so affected by the power of the market that in terms of social structure as well as economic organisation it was barely distinguishable from the towns. Further, the relative size and wealth of the bourgeoisie in both town and country (if the concept of a rural bourgeoisie is not a contradiction in terms) marked a rather more subtle but nevertheless decisive change in social structure. To put it briefly, the Republic had produced a thoroughly capitalist society before the industrial revolution. More controversially it can be claimed that, although there may be legitimate disagreement among historians about whether early modern Europe in general was a society of classes or of orders, for the Republic there can be little doubt that capitalism had produced a class society – perhaps the first since the Greek city states of the Ancient World – though the classes were rather different to those produced by industrialisation.

This new society, however, did not encompass the whole of the Dutch state but was limited geographically to the maritime region and even here was perhaps only fully developed in Holland. The land provinces retained a great deal of an older form of social structure, though this was modified in response to the power of the Holland market. So while the Republic as a whole was small both in extent and in population, the new society that developed within its borders was even smaller and encompassed perhaps only half the total population and rather less than half its geographical area. The scale is rather that of the city state than of the renaissance monarchies or the modern nation state, and the new society that emerges in the *Gouden Eeuw* is perhaps best seen as that of the late medieval town in the Netherlands writ large. It is hardly surprising that this new society, small as it was in comparison to the rest of Europe, found it distinctly more difficult to break with the past in cultural than in social terms. The social changes which took place in Holland helped to produce a high culture that was strikingly original in painting, but less so in literature. The early end to witchcraft prosecutions in Holland points to a fundamental change in the way people saw the world, but in other ways cultural change appears to have lagged behind the pace of the social transformation of the time. At every level the power of a common European culture was a conservative force, and perhaps nowhere more so than in education where the humanist curriculum of the Renaissance retained its prestige despite appearing in essential ways alien to the spirit of the new society that had emerged by the middle of the seventeenth century. More broadly, conventional religion – both protestant and catholic – played a similar conservative role for the mass of the population, though the difficulty that christianity had in coming to terms with the rapidly changing society within the Republic has not received the attention it possibly deserves.

Just as the towns of the Low Countries in the later Middle Ages were bourgeois islands in a society dominated socially as well as politically and culturally by the nobility, so the maritime region of the Republic was a small capitalist intrusion into a Europe which was still largely traditional in social structure. Nevertheless the impact of this small region was remarkable in range and depth: replicas of Dutch urban society sprang up in Beverwijk (Albany) and elsewhere in New Netherland, the influence of Dutch town planning could be seen in many parts of northern Europe, and the Dutch colonial impact affected for better or worse the history of South Africa, Sri Lanka and Indonesia. More generally Dutch commercial practices and mores became the model the rest of Europe thought it had to emulate in order to achieve economic success. Yet it seems that in a number of important ways the Dutch were just too different for their message to be easily or quickly understood or assimilated. A hundred years after the end of the *Gouden Eeuw* the art of the Dutch School was beginning to be recognised as a major contribution to the history of European culture (though Vermeer had to wait another fifty years or more before he came into his own). Perhaps it took the rest of Europe at least this long to catch up with the profound transformation of society pioneered by the Dutch in the seventeenth century.

Notes

1   C. Busken Huet, *Het land van Rembrandt* (Haarlem, 1882-4); P.L. Muller, *Onze Gouden Eeuw*, 3 vols (Leiden, 1896–8); Johan Huizinga, *Dutch Civilisation in the Seventeenth Century* (London, 1968)), first published in Dutch in 1941.

2   J.I. Israel, *Dutch Primacy in World Trade* (Oxford, 1989), chapter 3.

3   See Pieter Priester, *Geschiedenis van de Zeeuwse landbouw circa 1600–1910* ('t Goy-Houten, 1998), 418.

4   This English term came to refer to the inhabitants of the northern Netherlands only as a result of the emergence of the Dutch Republic, otherwise it would have continued to have a rather different meaning.

5   Though note the dissident view of Israel, *Dutch Primacy*, chapter 9.

6   However, note the argument for greater polarisation in J.L. van Zanden, 'Did Holland's Golden Age breed Inequality?', in Lee Soltow and Jan Luiten van Zanden, *Income and Wealth Inequality in the Netherlands 16th – 20th Century* (Amsterdam, 1998), 23–54.

7   Ophans of citizens received measurably more favourable treatment than orphans whose parents had not been citizens, see for Amsterdam Anne E.C. McCants, *Civic Charity in a Golden Age. Orphan Care in Early Modern Amsterdam* (Urbana/Chicago, 1997).

Bibliography

Aalbers, J., 'Holland's financial problems (1713–1733) and the wars against Louis XIV', *Britain and the Netherlands*, 6 (1977), 79–93.

Albach, Ben, *Langs kermissen en hoven. Ontstaan en kroniek van een Nederlands toneelgezelschap in de 17e eeuw* (Zutphen, 1977).

Appleby, Joyce Oldham, *Economic Thought and Ideology in Seventeenth-Century England* (Princeton, 1978), chap. 4.

Aten, Diederik, *'Als het gewelt comt...'. Politiek en economie in Holland benoorden het IJ 1500–1800* (Hilversum, 1995).

Baetens, R., 'The organization and effects of Flemish privateering in the seventeenth century', *Acta Historiae Neerlandicae*, 9 (1976), 48–75.

Bang, N. E. and Korst, K., *Tabeller over skibsfart og varetransport gennen Oresund, 1497–1660, 1661–1783*, 7 vols (Copenhagen/Leipzig, 1906–53).

Barbour, V., *Capitalism in Amsterdam in the Seventeenth Century* (Baltimore, 1950).

Barnes, D. R. and Brink Goldsmith, J. ten, *Street Scenes: Leonard Bramer's drawings of 17th century Dutch daily life* (Hempstead, 1991).

Baxter, S. B., *William III and the Defence of European Liberty, 1650–1702* (London, 1966).

Beck, David, *Spiegel van mijn leven. Haags dagboek 1624*, ed. S.E. Veldhuijzen (Hilversum, 1993).

Bieleman, J., *Boeren op het Drentse Zand 1600–1910* (Wageningen, 1987).

Black, Jeremy, *A Military Revolution? Military Change and European Society 1550–1800* (Basingstoke, 1991).

Blécourt, Willem de, *Termen van toverij. De veranderende betekenis van toverij in Noord-Oost Nederland tussen de 16de en 20ste eeuw* (Nijmegen, 1990).

Blondé, B., *De sociale structuren en economische dynamiek van 's Hertogenbosch 1500–1550* (Tilburg, 1987) [Bijdragen tot de geschiedenis van het zuiden van Nederland, 74].

Boheemen, P. van *et al.* (ed.), *'Kent, en versint, Eer datje mint.' Vrijen en trouwen 1500–1800* (Zwolle, 1989).

Boon, Piet, *Bouwers van de zee: zeevarende van het Westfriese platteland, c.1680–1720* (The Hague, 1996).

Boon, P., 'Zeelieden te Schellinkhout omstreeks 1700', *Tijdschrift voor zeegeschiedenis*, 6 (1987), 107–23.

Boon, P., 'De sociale en economische positie van schippers in het Westfriese dorp Schellinkhout rond 1700', *Mededelingen van de Nederlandse Vereniging voor Zeegeschiedenis*, 39 (1979), 5–14.

Borg, Adelheid van der, *Vroedvrouwen. Beeld en beroep. Ontwikkelingen in het vroedvrouwschap in Leiden, Arnhem,'s-Hertogenbosch en Leeuwarden, 1650–1865* (Wageningen, 1992).

Bossaers, K. W. J. M., 'Macht, Rijkdom en Aanzien. De regenten in het Noorderkwartier in het midden van de 18e eeuw', *Holland*, 21 (1989), 54–62.

Bossy, John, *The English Catholic Community, 1570–1850* (London, 1975).

Boxer, C. R., *The Dutch Sea-borne Empire* (London, 1965).

Boxer, C. R., 'Sedentary Workers and Seafaring Folk in the Dutch Republic', *Britain and the Netherlands*, II, ed. J.S. Bromley and E.H Kossmann (Groningen, 1964), 148–68.

Braam, A. van, *Westzaandam in de tijd van de Republiek* (Zaandam, 1978).

Briels, J.G.C.A., *De zuidnederlandse immigratie in Amsterdam en Haarlem omstreeks 1572–1630* (Utrecht, 1976).

Briels, J., *Zuid-Nederlanders in de Republiek 1572–1630. Een demografische en cultuurhistorische studie* (Sint Niklaas, 1985).

Bruijn, J. R., *The Dutch Navy in the 17th and 18th centuries* (Columbia, SC, 1993).

Burke, Peter, 'The language of orders in early modern Europe', in *Social Orders and Social Classes in Europe since 1500*, ed. M.L. Bush (London, 1992), 1–12.

Busken Huet, C., *Het land van Rembrandt* (Haarlem, 1882–4).

Christ, M. P., *De Brabantsche Saecke. Het vergeefsche streven naar een gewestelijke status voor Staats-Brabant 1585–1675* (Tilburg, 1984).

Cipolla, Carlo, *Europe before the Industrial Revolution* (London, 1976).

Daelemans, F., 'Leiden 1581. Een socio-demografisch onderzoek', *A.A.G. Bijdragen*, 9 (1975), 137–215.

Davids, C. A., *Wat lijdt den zeeman al verdriet. Het Nederlandse zeemanslied in de zeiltijd (1600–1900)* (The Hague, 1980).

Davids, K., Noordegraaf, L. (eds), *The Dutch Economy in the Golden Age. Nine Studies* (Amsterdam, 1993) [Economic and Social History in the Netherlands, iv].

Davids, K., Lucassen, J., Zanden, J. L. van, *De Nederlandse geschiedenis als afwijking van het algemeen menselijk patroon* (Amsterdam, 1988).

Davids, K., Lucassen, Jan (eds), *A Miracle Mirrored. The Dutch Republic in European Perspective* (Cambridge, 1995).

Degryse, K., 'Fortuin en sociaal prestige. Enkele beschouwingen over het "verraad van de burgerij" tijdens het Ancien Régime', *Tijdschrift voor Sociale Geschiedenis*, 9, 283–93.

Dekker, R., *Holland in Beroering. Oproeren in de 17de en 18de eeuw* (Baarn, 1982).

Dekker, Rudolf, *Uit de schaduw in het grote licht. Kinderen in egodocumenten van de Gouden Eeuw tot de Romantiek* (Amsterdam, 1995).

Dekker, R. M., 'De rol van vrouwen in oproeren in de Republiek in de 17e en 18e eeuw', *Tijdschrift voor Sociale Geschiedenis*, 12 (1978), 305–16.

Dekker, R. M., 'Women in revolt. Popular protest and its social basis in Holland in the seventeenth and eighteenth centuries', *Theory and Society*, 16 (1987), 337–62.

Dekker, R. M., '"Getrouwe broederschap": Organisatie en acties van arbeiders in pre-industrieel Holland', *Bijdragen en Mededelingen betreffende de Geschiedenis der Nederlanden*, 103 (1988), 1–19.

Dekker, R., 'Labour conflicts and working class culture in early modern Holland', *International Review of Social History*, 35 (1990), 377–420.

Deursen, A. Th. van, *Bavianen en slijkgeuzen. Kerk en kerkvolk ten tijde van Maurits en Oldenbarnevelt* (Assen, 1974).

Deursen, A. Th. van, *Plain Lives in a Golden Age. Popular culture, religion and society in seventeenth-century Holland* (Cambridge, 1991).

Deursen, A. Th. van, *Een dorp in de polder. Graft in de zeventiende eeuw* (Amsterdam, 1994).

Deursen, A. Th. van, 'Werkende vrouwen in een Hollandse dorp', *De Zeventiende Eeuw*, iv (1988).

Deursen, A. Th. van, 'Gereformeerd gemeentelijk leven in Nederland in de tweede helft van de zeventiende eeuw', *Bunyan in Nederland*, ed. G.J. Schutte *et. al.* (Houten, 1989).

Deursen, A. Th. van, 'De burgers van Graft. Afhankelijkheid en zelfstandigheid van een Hollandse dorp in de zeventiende euw', *Beleid en bestuur in de oude Nederlanden*. Liber amicorum prof.dr. M. Baelde, ed.Hugo Soly en René Vermeir (Ghent, 1993).

Deursen, A. Th. van, 'De oude dag in een Hollands dorp', in *In gemeenschap met de tijd* (Amsterdam, 1997), 25–36.

Diedericks, H. A., Noordam, D. J., Tjalsma, H. D. (eds), *Armoede en sociale spanning. Sociaal-historische studies over Leiden in de achttiende eeuw* (Hilversum, 1985).

Dijk, H. van, Roorda, D. J., 'Sociale mobiliteit onder regenten van de Republiek', *Tijdschrift voor Geschiedenis*, 84, afl.2 (1971), 306–29.

Dillen, J. G. van, 'Dreigende hongersnood in de Republiek in de laatste jaren der zeventiende eeuw', *Mensen en achtergronden* (Groningen, 1964), 193–226.

Dillen, J. G. van, *Van rijkdom en regenten* (Den Haag, 1970).

Dillen, J. G. van, *Amsterdam in 1585. Het kohier van de capitale impositie van 1585* (Amsterdam, 1941).

Dillen, J. G. van (ed.), 'Summiere staat van de in 1622 in de provincie Holland gehouden volkstelling', *Economisch-Historisch Jaarboek*, 21 (1940), 166–89.

Doorninck, Marieke van, Kuijpers, Erika, *De geschoolde stad. Onderwijs in Amsterdam in de Gouden Eeuw* (Amsterdam, 1993).

Duijvendak, M. G. J., Jong, J. J. de, *Elitenonderzoek: rijkdom, macht en status in het verleden* (Zutphen, 1993).

Duke, A. C., *Reformation and Revolt in the Low Countries* (London, 1990).

Duke, Alastair, 'Nonconformity among the Kleine Luyden in the Low Countries before the Revolt', *Experiences and Explanations*, ed. L. Laeyendecker et al. (Ljouwert, 1990), 9–35.

Egmond, Florike, *Underworlds. Organized crime in the Netherlands 1650–1800* (Cambridge, 1993).

Egmond, Florike, 'Fragmentatie, rechtsverscheidenheid en rechtsongelijkheid in de Noordelijke Nederlanden tijdens de zeventiende en achttiende eeuw', *Nieuw licht op oude justititie*, ed. S. Faber (Muiderberg, 1989), 9–23.

Egmond, Florike, 'Children in Court. Children and Criminal Justice in the Dutch Republic', *Social and Legal Studies*, 2 (1993), 73–90.

Elias, J. E., *De vroedschap van Amsterdam*, 2 vols (Haarlem, 1903–5).

Elliot, J. H., *The Count-Duke of Olivares* (New Haven, 1986).

Enno van Gelder, H. A., *Vrijheid en onvrijheid in de Republiek* (Haarlem, 1947).

Enno van Gelder, H. A., *Getemperde Vrijheid* (Groningen, 1972).

Faber, J. A., *Drie eeuwen Friesland. Economische en sociale ontwikkelingen van 1500 tot 1800*, 2 dln (Wageningen, 1972) [A.A.G. Bijdragen 17].

Faber, J. A., 'De oligarchisering van Friesland in de tweede helft van de zeventiende eeuw', *Afdeling Agrarische Geschiedenis*, Bijdragen 15 (Wageningen, 1970).

Faber, J. A., 'Dearth and famine in pre-industrial Netherlands', *The Low Countries History Yearbook*, 13 (1980), 51–64.

Faber, Johannes A., 'Inhabitants of Amsterdam and their possessions 1701–1710', *AAG Bijdragen*, xxiii (1981).

Faber, Sjoerd (ed.), *Nieuw licht op oude justititie. Misdaad en straf ten tijde van de Republiek* (Muiderberg, 1989).

Faber, S., 'Kindermoord, in het bijzonder in de achttiende eeuw te Amsterdam', *Bijdragen en Mededelingen betreffende de Geschiedenis der Nederlanden*, 93 (1978), 224–40.

Farnell, J. E., 'The Navigation Act of 1651, the First Dutch War, and the London Merchant Community', *Economic History Review*, 2nd series, 16 (1963), 439–54.

Feenstra, H., *De bloeitijd en het verval van de Ommelandse adel, 1600–1800* (Groningen, 1981).

Feld, M. D., 'Middle-Class Society and the Rise of Military Professionalism. The Dutch Army 1589–1609', *Armed Forces and Society*, 1 (1975), 419–42.

Frank-van Westrienen, A., *De Groote Tour. Tekening van de educatiereis der Nederlanders in de zeventiende eeuw* (Amsterdam, 1983).

Frijhoff, Willem, *La société néerlandaise et ses gradués, 1575–1814* (Amsterdam, 1981).

Frijhoff, Willem, *Wegen van Evert Willemsz. Een Hollands weeskind op zoek naar zichzelf 1607–1647* (Nijmegen, 1995).

Frijhoff, Willem, 'Non satis dignitatis. Over de maatschappelijke status van de geneeskundige tijdens de Republiek', *Tijdschrift voor Geschiedenis*, 97 (1983), 376–407.

Frijhoff, Willem, 'Publieke beschavingsoffensieven in de vroegmoderne tijd', *Volkskundig Bulletin*, 11 (1985), 93–101.

Frijhoff, Willem, Gijswijt-Hofstra, Marijke (eds), *Nederland betoverd: toverij en hekserij van de veertiende tot in de twintigste eeuw* (Amsterdam, 1987).

Frijhoff, Willem, Gijswijt-Hofstra, Marijke (eds), *Witchcraft in the Netherlands: from the fourteenth to the twentieth century* (Rotterdam, 1991).

Fruin, Robert, *Tien jaren uit den Tachtigjarigen Oorlog, 1588–98* (Amsterdam, 1861).

Fuks-Mansfeld, R. G., *De Sefardim in Amsterdam tot 1795* (Hilversum, 1989)

Gaastra, F., *Bewind en beleid bij de VOC 1672–1702* (Zutphen, 1989).

Geyl, Pieter, *The Revolt of the Netherlands, 1555–1609* (London, 1958).

Gibbs, C. G., 'The role of the Dutch Republic as the intellectual entrepôt of Europe in the seventeenth and eighteenth centuries', *Bijdragen en Mededelingen betreffende de Geschiedenis der Nederlanden*, 86 (1971), 323–49.

Gijswijt–Hofstra, Marijke (ed.), *Een schijn van verdraagzaamheid: afwijking en tolerantie in Nederland van de zestiende eeuw tot heden* (Hilversum, 1989).

Groenendijk, L. F., *De nadere reformatie van het gezin: de visie van Petrus Wittewrongel op de Christelijke huishouding* (Dordrecht, 1984).

Groenhuis, G., *De predikanten. De sociale positie van de gereformeerde predikanten in de Republiek der Verenigde Nederlanden voor ± 1700* (Groningen, 1977).

Groenveld, Simon, *Was de Nederlandse Republiek verzuild? Over segmentering van de samenleving binnen de Verenigde Nederlanden* (Leiden, 1995).

Groenveld, Simon, *Huisgenoten des geloofs. Was de samenleving in de Republiek der Verenigde Nederlanden verzuild?* (Hilversum, 1995).

Groenveld, Simon, 'The Mecca of Authors? States Assemblies and Censorship in the Seventeenth-Century Dutch Republic', *Too Mighty to be Free: censorship and the press in Britain and the Netherlands*, ed. A.C. Duke and C.A. Tamse (Zutphen, 1987), 63–86.

Groenveld, Simon, 'The Dutch Republic, an island of liberty of the press in 17th century Europe? The authorities and the book trade', *Commercium litterarum. Forms of communication in the Republic of Letters 1600–1750*, ed. H. Bots and F. Waquet (Maarssen, 1994), 281–300.

Guibal, C. J., *Democratie en oligarchie in Friesland tijdens de Republiek* (Groningen, 1934).

Gutmann, M. P., *War and Rural Life in the Early Modern Low Countries* (Princeton, 1980).

Haas, J. A. K., *De verdeling van de landen van Overmaas 1644–1662* (Assen, 1978).

Haks, Donald, *Huwelijk en gezin in Holland in de 17e en 18e eeuw* (Assen, 1982).

Harline, Craig E., *Pamphlets, Printing and Political Culture in the Early Dutch Republic* (Dordrecht, 1987).

't Hart, Marjolein, 'Staatsvorming, sociale relaties en oorlogsfinanciering in de Nederlandse republiek', *Tijdschrift voor Sociale Geschiedenis*, 16 (1990), 61–85.

't Hart, Marjolein, 'Een boerenopstand op Walcheren. De strijd om het waterschap 1655–1657', *Tijdschrift voor Sociale Geschiedenis*, 20e jg., nr 3 (1994), 265–81.

Heijden, Manon van der, *Huwelijk in Holland. Stedelijke rechtspraak en kerkelijke tucht 1550–1700* (Amsterdam, 1998).

Hendrickx, F. M. M., *'In order not to fall into poverty.' Production and Reproduction in the Transition from Proto-industry to Factory Industry in Borne and Wierden (the Netherlands), 1800–1900* (Amsterdam, 1997).

Holthuis, Paul, *Frontierstad bij het scheiden van de markt. Deventer: militair, demografisch, economisch, 1578–1648* (Deventer, 1993).

Houston, Rab, 'Elders and deacons. Membership of the consistory of the scotch (sic) church, Rotterdam (1643–1829) and the kirk session of Tolbooth parish, Edinburgh (1690–1760)', *Tijdschrift voor Sociale Geschiedenis*, 20e jg., nr 3 (1994), 282–308.

Hufton, Olwyn, *The Prospect Before Her. A History of Women in Western Europe*, vol. I *1500–1800* (London, 1995).

Huisman, F. G., *Stadsbelang en standsbesef. Gezondheidszorg en medisch beroep in Groningen 1500–1730* (Rotterdam, 1992).

Huizinga, Johan, *The Waning of the Middle Ages* (London, 1924).

Huizinga, Johan, *Dutch Civilisation in the Seventeenth Century* (London, 1968).

Huygens, Lodewijck, *The English Journal, 1651–1652* (Leiden, 1982).

Israel, Jonathan I., *The Dutch Republic and the Hispanic World 1606–1661* (Oxford, 1982).

Israel, Jonathan I., *Dutch Primacy in World Trade 1585–1740* (Oxford, 1989).

Israel, Jonathan I., *The Dutch Republic. Its Rise, Greatness, and Fall 1477–1806* (Oxford, 1995).

Jansen, P. C., 'Verraad in Holland', *Tijdschrift voor Sociale Geschiedenis*, 9 (1977), 295–8.

Jones, J. R., *The Anglo-Dutch Wars of the Seventeenth Century* (London, 1996).

Jong, J. J. de, *Met goed fatsoen. De elite in een Hollandse stad, Gouda 1700–80* (Dieren, 1985)

Jong, J. J. de, *Een deftig bestaan. Het dagelijks leven van regenten in de 17e en 18e eeuw* (Utrecht and Antwerp, 1987).

Kaplan, B.J., *Calvinists and Libertines. Confession and Community in Utrecht 1578–1620* (Oxford, 1995).

Kappen, O. van, *Geschiedenis der Zigeuners in Nederland: de ontwikkeling van de rechtspositie der Heidens of Egyptenaren in de Noordelijke Nederlanden (1420–c.1750)* (Assen, 1965).

Kaptein, Herman, *Het Schermereiland. Een zeevarend plattelandsgebied 950–1800* (Bergen, 1988).

Keblusek, Marika, *Boeken in de hofstad. Haagse boekcultuur in de Gouden Eeuw* (Hilversum, 1997)

Kistemaker, Renée, 'Amsterdam's Municipal Control of Food Supplies', *Rome–Amsterdam. Two Growing Cities in Seventeenth-Century Europe*, ed. Peter van Kessel and Elisja Schulte (Amsterdam, 1997), 221–34.

Klein, P. W., 'De heffing van de 100e en 200e penning van het vermogen te Gouda, 1599–1722', *Economisch-Historisch Jaarboek*, 31 (1967), 41–62.

Klinkenberg, J. Th., 'Dye quade sieckte. De pest in Maastricht in de zestiende en zeventiende eeuw', *Tijdschrift voor Sociale Geschiedenis*, 16 (1990), 267–86.

Kloek, Els, *Wie hij zij, man of wijf. Vrouwengeschiedenis en de vroegmoderne tijd: drie Leidse studies* (Hilversum, 1990).

Knevel, P., *Wakkere burgers. De Alkmaarse schutterij 1400–1795* (Alkmaar, 1991).

Knevel, P., *Burgers in het geweer. De schutterijen in Holland, 1550–1700* (Hilversum, 1994).

Knotter, A., *Economische transformatie en stedelijke arbeidsmarkt* (Amsterdam, 1991).

Knotter, A., 'De Amsterdamse scheepvaart en het Noordhollandse platteland in de 16e en 17e eeuw. Het probleem van de arbeidsmarkt', *Holland*, 16 (1984), 281–90.

Knotter, A., Zanden, J. L. van, 'Immigratie en arbeidsmarkt in Amsterdam in de 17e eeuw', *Tijdschrift voor sociale geschiedenis*, 13 (1987), 403–31.

Kooijmans, L., *Onder regenten. De elite in een Hollandse stad, Hoorn 1700–1780* (Dieren, 1985)

Kooijmans, Luuc, *Vriendschap en de kunst van het overleven in de zeventiende en achttiende eeuw* (Amsterdam, 1997).

Kooy, T. P. van der, *Hollands stapelmarkt en haar verval* (Amsterdam, 1931).

Kuiper, E. J., *De Hollandse 'schoolordre' van 1625* (Groningen, 1958).

Leeuwen, Marco H. D. van, Oeppen, James E., 'Reconstructing the Demographic Regime of Amsterdam, 1681–1920', *Economic and Social History in the Netherlands*, 5 (1993), 61–102.

Lesger, C. M., *Huur en conjonctuur. De woningmarkt in Amsterdam, 1550–1850* (Amsterdam, 1986).

Lesger, C. M., *Hoorn als stedelijk knooppunt. Stedensystemen tijdens de late middeleeuwen en vroegmoderne tijd* (Hilversum, 1990).

Lieburg, M. J. van, *G.C. Schrader's Memoryboeck van de vrouwen. Het notitieboek van een Friese vroedvrouw, 1693–1745* (Amsterdam, 1984).

Liesker, R., 'Tot zinkens toe bezwaard. De schuldenlast van het

Zuiderkwartier van Holland 1672–1794', in *Bestuurders en geleerden*, ed. S. Groenveld, M.E.H.N. Mout and I. Schöffer (Amsterdam/Dieren, 1985), 151–60.

Lindblad, J. Th., 'Foreign Trade of the Dutch Republic in the seventeenth century', *Economic and Social History in the Netherlands*, 4 (1992), 219–49.

Lis, Catharina, Soly, Hugo, '"Beter een goede buur dan een verre vriend." Buurtschap en buurtleven in Westeuropese steden aan het eind van het Ancien Régime', *De kracht der zwakken*, ed. B. de Vries *et al.* (Amsterdam, 1992), 81–107.

Lucassen, J., *Naar de kusten van de Noordzee. Trekarbeid in Europees perspektief 1600–1900* (Gouda, 1984).

Lunsingh Scheurleer, Th., Fock, C. W., Dissel, A. J. van, *Het Rapenburg, geschiedenis van een Leidse gracht*, 6 vols (Leiden, 1986–92).

McCants, Anne E. C., *Civic Charity in a Golden Age. Orphan Care in Early Modern Amsterdam* (Urbana/Chicago, 1997).

Maanen, R. J. van, 'De vermogensopbouw van de Leidse bevolking in het laatste kwart van de zestiende eeuw', *Bijdragen en Mededelingen betreffende de Geschiedenis der Nederlanden*, 93 (1978), 1–42.

Mann, Golo, *Wallenstein* (Frankfurt am Main, 1971).

Marshall, Gordon, *In Search of the Spirit of Capitalism. An essay on Max Weber's Protestant ethic thesis* (London, 1982).

Meer, Theo van der, *Sodoms zaad in Nederland. Het ontstaan van homoseksualiteit in de vroegmoderne tijd* (Nijmegen, 1995).

Monteiro, Marit, *Geestelijke maagden. Leven tussen klooster en wereld in Noord-Nederland gedurende de zeventiende eeuw* (Hilversum, 1996).

Montias, John Michael, *Vermeer and his Milieu. A Web of Social History* (Princeton, 1989).

Montias, J. M., 'Art dealers in the seventeenth-century Netherlands', *Simiolus*, 18 (1988), 244–56.

Montias, J. M., 'Estimates of the Number of Dutch Master-Painters, their earnings and their output in 1650', *Leidschrift* 6–3 (1990), 59–74.

Montias, J. M., 'Socio-economic Aspects of Netherlandish Art from the Fifteenth to the Seventeenth century: a survey', *Art Bulletin*, 72 (1990), 358–73.

Mooij, Charles de, *Geloof kan bergen verzetten. Reformatie en katholieke herleving te Bergen op Zoom 1577–1795* (Hilversum, 1998).

Mout, M. E. H. N., '"Holendische Propositiones." Een Habsburg plan tot vernietiging van handel, visserij en scheepvaart der Republiek (ca. 1625)', *Tijdschrift voor Geschiedenis*, 95e jg., afl.3, (1982), 345–62.

Muinck, B. E. de, *Een regentenhuishouding omstreeks 1700. Gegevens uit de privé-boekhouding van mr. Cornelis de Jonge van Ellemeet, Ontvanger-Generaal der Verenigde Nederlanden (1646–1721)* (The Hague, 1965).

Muller, P. L., *Onze Gouden Eeuw*, 3 vols (Leiden, 1896–8).

Muller, Sheila D., *Charity in the Dutch Republic: pictures of rich and poor for charitable institutions* (Ann Arbor, 1982).

Nickle, Barry H., *The Military Reforms of Prince Maurice of Orange* (Delaware, 1975).

Nierop, H. F. K. van, *Van ridders tot regenten. De Hollandse adel in de zestiende en de eerste helft van de zeventiende eeuw* (Amsterdam/Dieren, 1984).

Nierop, H. F. K. van, *The Nobility of Holland. From knights to regents* (Cambridge, 1993).

Noordam, D. J., *Leven in Maasland. Een hoogontwikkelde plattelandssamenleving in de achttiende en het begin van de negentiende eeuw* (Hilversum, 1986).

Noordam, D. J., *Riskante relaties. Vijf eeuwen homoseksualiteit in Nederland, 1233–1733* (Hilversum, 1995).

Noordegraaf, L., *Daglonen in Alkmaar* (1980) [Apparaat voor de geschiedenis van Holland, IX].

Noordegraaf, L., *Hollands welvaren? Levensstandaard in Holland 1450–1650* (Bergen, 1985).

Noordegraaf, L., 'Levensstandaard en levensmiddelenpolitiek in Alkmaar vanaf het einde van de 16e tot in het begin van de 19e eeuw', *Van Spaans beleg tot Bataafse tijd* (Zutphen, 1980).

Noordegraaf, L. and Schoenmakers, J. T. *Daglonen in Holland* (Amsterdam, 1984) [Amsterdamse historische reeks vii].

Noordegraaf, Leo and Valk, Gerrit, *De gave gods. De pest in Holland vanaf de late middeleeuwen* (Bergen, NH, 1988).

Nusteling, H. P. H., *Binnen de vesting Nijmegen: confessionele en demografische verhoudingen ten tijde van de Republiek* (Zutphen, 1979).

Nusteling, Hubert, *Welvaart en werkgelegenheid in Amsterdam 1540–1860* (Amsterdam/Dieren, 1985).

Nusteling, Hubert, 'The Population of Amsterdam and the Golden Age', in *Rome–Amsterdam. Two Growing Cities in Seventeenth Century Europe*, ed. Peter van Kessel and Elisja Schulte (Amsterdam, 1997), 71–84.

Nusteling, Hubert, 'De bevolking: van raadsels naar oplossingen', *Geschiedenis van Dordrecht van 1572 tot 1813*, ed. Willem Frijhoff, Hubert Nusteling and Marijke Spies (Hilversum, 1998), 72–108.

Parker, Charles H., *The Reformation of Community. Social Welfare and Calvinist Charity in Holland, 1572–1620* (Cambridge, 1998).

Parker, Geoffrey, *The Army of Flanders and the Spanish Road 1567–1659* (Cambridge, 1972).

Parker, Geoffrey, 'Mutiny and Discontent in the Spanish Army of Flanders, 1572–1607', in *Spain and the Netherlands 1559–1659* (London, 1979), 106–21.

Parker, Geoffrey, 'War and Economic Change: the Economic Costs of the Dutch Revolt', in *Spain and the Netherlands 1559–1659* (London, 1979), 178–203.

Pepys, Samuel, *The Diary of Samuel Pepys*, ed. R.C. Latham and W. Matthews, Vol VIII (London, 1974).

Pincus, Steven C. A., 'Popery, Trade and Universal Monarchy: the ideological context of the outbreak of the Second Anglo-Dutch War', *English Historical Review*, vol. cvii, no. 422 (Jan. 1992), 1–29.

Po-Chia Hsia, R., *Social Discipline in the Reformation. Central Europe 1550–1750* (London, 1989).

Poelhekke, J. J., 'Het geval Zijdewind', in *Geen blijder maar in tachtig jaer. Verspreide studiën over de crisis periode 1648–1651* (Zutphen, 1973).

Pol, Lotte van de, *Het Amsterdams hoerdom. Prostitutie in de zeventiende en achttiende eeuw* (Amsterdam, 1996).

Pol, Lotte van de, 'Vrouwencriminaliteit in Amsterdam in de tweede helft van de 17e eeuw', *Tijdschrift voor Criminologie*, 29 (1987), 148–55.

Polišenský, J. V., *Tragic Triangle. The Netherlands, Spain and Bohemia 1617–1621* (Prague, 1991).

Pot, Peter, 'Door honger gedreven? Voedseloproeren te Leiden in 1709 en 1740', *Tijdschrift voor Sociale Geschiedenis*, 17 (1991), 147–71.

Prak, M., *Gezeten burgers. De elite in een Hollandse stad, Leiden 1700–1780* (Dieren, 1985).

Prak, M., 'Sociale geschiedschrijving van Nederlands ancien regime', *Tijdschrift voor sociale geschiedenis*, 14 (1988), 133–59.

Prak, M., 'Civil Disturbances and Urban Middle Class in the Dutch Republic', *Tijdschrift voor sociale geschiedenis*, 15 (1989), 165–73.

Price, J. L., *Culture and Society in the Dutch Republic during the Seventeenth Century* (London, 1974).

Price, J. L., *Holland and the Dutch Republic* (London, 1994).

Price, J. L., 'The Dutch Nobility in the Seventeenth and Eighteenth Centuries', *The European Nobilities in the Seventeenth and Eighteenth Centuries*, vol.1, ed. H. M. Scott (London, 1995), 82–113.

Price, J. L., 'De regent', *Gestalten van de Gouden Eeuw. Een Hollands groepsportret*, ed. H.M. Beliën, A. Th. van Deursen and G. J. van Setten (Amsterdam, 1995), 25–62.

Price, J. L., 'A State Dedicated to War? The Dutch Republic in the Seventeenth Century', in *The Medieval Military Revolution*, ed. Andrew Ayton and J. L. Price (London, 1995)

Priester, Pieter, *Geschiedenis van de Zeeuwse landbouw circa 1600–1910* ('t Goy-Houten, 1998).

Riley, J. C., 'The Dutch economy after 1650: decline or growth?', *Journal of European Economic History*, 13, 1984, 521–69.

Rink, O., *Holland on the Hudson: an economic and social history of Dutch New York* (Ithaca, 1986).

Rogier, L. J., *Geschiedenis van het katholicisme in Noord-Nederland in de 16e en 17e eeuw* (Amsterdam, 1964³).

Rommes, R., 'Pest in perspectief: aspecten van een gevreesde ziekte in de vroegmoderne tijd', *Tijdschrift voor Sociale Geschiedenis*, 16 (1990), 244–66.

Rooden, Peter van, 'Van geestelijke stand naar beroepsgroep. De professionalisering van de Nederlandse predikant. 1625–1874', *Tijdschrift voor Sociale Geschiedenis*, 17 (1991), 361–93.

Roodenburg, Herman, *Onder censuur. De kerkelijke tucht in de Gereformeerde gemeente van Amsterdam, 1578–1700* (Hilversum, 1990).

Roodenburg, Herman, 'The maternal imagination. The fears of pregnant women in seventeenth-century Holland', *Journal of Social History*, 21 (1987), 701–16.

Roodenburg, Herman, 'Een verfoeilijke misdaad. Incest in het gewest Holland tijdens de 17e en 18e eeuw', *Holland*, 25 (1993), 58–76.

Roodenburg, Herman, 'Naar een etnografie van de vroegmoderne stad: de "gebuyrten" in Leiden en Den Haag', *Cultuur en maatschappij in Nederland 1500–1850: een historisch-antropologisch perspectief*, ed. P. te Boekhorst, P. Burke and W. Frijhoff (Meppel/Heerlen, 1992), 219–43.

Roodenburg, Herman, 'The Autobiography of Isabella de Moerloose: sex, childrearing and popular belief in seventeenth century Holland', *Journal of Social History*, 18 (1985), 517–40.

Roodenburg, Herman, 'Eer en oneer ten tijde van de Republiek. Een tussenbalans', *Volkskundig Bulletin*, 22 (1996), 129–48.

Rooijakkers, G., *Rituele repertoires. Volkscultuur in oostelijk Noord-Brabant 1559–1853* (Nijmegen, 1994).

Roorda, D. J., *Partij en factie* (Groningen, 1961).

Rothenburg, G. E., 'Maurice of Nassau, Gustavus Adolphus, Raimondo of Montecuccoli and the "Military Revolution" of the Seventeenth Century', *Makers of Modern Strategy from Machiavelli to the Nuclear Age*, ed. P. Paret (Oxford, 1986).

Rowen, H. H., 'The Revolution that Wasn't: the Coup d'Etat of 1650 in Holland', *European Studies Review*, 4 (1974), 99–117.

Royen, P. C. van, *Zeevarende op de koopvaardijvloot omstreeks 1700* (Amsterdam, 1987).

Scammell, G. V., *The World Encompassed. The First European maritime empires c.800–1650* (London, 1981).

Schama, Simon, *The Embarrassment of Riches* (New York, 1987).

Schilling, Heinz, 'Confessionalization in the Empire: Religious and Societal Change in Germany between 1555 and 1620', in *Religion, Political Culture and the Emergence of Early Modern Society* (Leiden, 1992).

Schmidt, C., *Om de eer van de familie. Het geslacht Teding van Berkhout 1500–1950* (Amsterdam, 1986).

Schöffer, I., 'La stratification sociale de la République des Provinces Unies au XVIIe siècle', *Problèmes de stratification sociales*, ed. R. Mousnier (Paris, 1968), 121–35.

Schulte van Kessel, E., *Geest en vlees in godsdienst en wetenschap* (The Hague, 1980).

Sellin, Thorsten, *Pioneering in Penology: the Amsterdam Houses of Correction in the Sixteenth and Seventeenth Centuries* (Philadelphia, 1944).

Slicher van Bath, B. H., *Een samenleving onder spanning: geschiedenis van het platteland in Overijssel* (Assen, 1957).

Sogner, S., 'Popular contacts between Norway and the Netherlands in the Early Modern Period', *The North Sea and Culture (1550–1800)*, ed. Juliette Roding and Lex Heerma van Voss (Hilversum, 1996), 185–98.

Soltow, L., 'Income and wealth inequality in Amsterdam, 1585–1805', *Economisch- en Sociaal-Historisch Jaarboek*, 52 (1989), 72–95.

Soly, H., 'Het "verraad der 16e-eeuwse burgerij": een mythe?', *Tijdschrift voor Geschiedenis*, 86 (1973), 262–80.

Spaans, J., *Haarlem na de Reformatie. Stedelijke cultuur en kerkelijk leven, 1577–1620* (The Hague, 1989).

Spaans, Joke, *Armenzorg in Friesland 1500–1800* (Hilversum/Leeuwarden, 1997).

Spahr van der Hoek, J. J., *Samenleven in Friesland. Drie perioden uit de sociale geschiedenis* (Drachten, 1969).

Spierenburg, P., *The Spectacle of Suffering: executions and the evolution of repression. From a pre-industrial metropolis to the European experience* (Cambridge, 1984).

Spierenburg, P., *Elites and Etiquette. Mentality and Social Structure in the Early Modern Netherlands* (Rotterdam, 1981).

Spies, M., 'Charlotte de Huybert en het gelijk; de geleerde en de werkende vrouw in de zeventiende eeuw', *Literatuur: Tijdschrift over Nederlandse Letterkunde*, 3 (1986), 339–50.

Spinoza, *The Chief Works of*, vol. 1, transl. and ed. by R.H.M. Elwes (New York, 1951).

Steendijk-Kuypers, J., *Volksgezondheidszorg in de 16e en 17e eeuw te Hoorn* (Rotterdam, 1994).

Stradling, R. A., *The Armada of Flanders: Spanish maritime policy and European War, 1568–1668* (Cambridge, 1992).

Stradling, R. A., *Philip IV and the Government of Spain 1621–1665* (Cambridge, 1988).

Streng, J. C., *'Stemme in staat.' De bestuurlijke elite in de stadrepubliek Zwolle 1579–1795* (Hilversum, 1997).

Taverne, E., *In 't land van belofte in de nieue stadt. Ideaal en werkelijkheid van de stadsuitleg in de Republiek 1580–1680* (Maarssen, 1978).

Tempel, K. van der, *Schippers van de zee in Graft 1650–1695: aspecten van hun sociale en economische positie* (Leiden, 1981).

Temple, Sir William, *Observations upon the United Provinces of the Netherlands*, ed. G. N. Clark (Cambridge, 1932).

Tex, Jan den, *Oldenbarnevelt*, 2 vols (Cambridge, 1973).

Thissen, P. G. B., *Werk, netwerk en letterwerk van de familie van Hoogstraten in de zeventiende eeuw. Sociaal-economische en sociaal-culturele achtergronden van geletterden in de Republiek* (Amsterdam/Maarssen, 1994).

Thomson, I. A. A., *War and Government in Habsburg Spain, 1560–1620* (Cambridge, 1976).

Tracy, James D., *A Financial Revolution in the Habsburg Netherlands: 'Renten' and 'Renteniers' in the County of Holland, 1515–1566* (Berkeley, 1985).

Tracy, James D., *Holland under Habsburg Rule 1506–1566* (Berkeley, 1990).

Trompetter, C., *Agriculture, Proto-Industry and Mennonite Entrepreneurship. A History of the Textile Industries in Twente 1600–1815* (Amsterdam, 1997).

Trompetter, C., 'Bevolkingsontwikkeling, textielnijverheid en armoede. Een nieuwe visie op de demografische geschiedenis van Twente, 1675–1795', *Economisch- en Sociaal-Historisch Jaarboek*, 55 (1992), 159–89.

Veldhuijzen, G., *Nieuwe Heeren Nieuwe Kussens. Het regentenpatriciaat van Dordrecht 1672–1685* (Dordrecht, 1988).

Venema, Janny, *Kinderen van weelde en armoede. Armoede en liefdadigheid in Beverwijck/Albany* (Hilversum, 1993).

Vermij, Rienk H., *Secularisering en natuurwetenschap in de zeventiende en achttiende eeuw: Bernard Nieuwentijt* (Amsterdam, 1991).

Verpalen, M. P. A. M., *De betoverde stad. Carnaval en feestarchitectuur in Bergen op Zoom* (Tilburg, 1992).

Verstegen, S. W., *Gegoede ingezetenen. Jonkers en geërfden op de Veluwe 1650–1830* (Zutphen, 1990) [Diss. VU Amsterdam 1989].

Vliet, A. P. van, 'The influence of Dunkirk privateering on the North Sea (herring) fishery during the years 1580–1650', *The North Sea and Culture (1550–1800)*, ed. Juliette Roding and Lex Heerma van Voss (Hilversum, 1996), 150–65.

Voorst van Beest, C. W. van, *De Katholieke armenzorg te Rotterdam in de 17e en 18e eeuw* (Den Haag, n.d.).

Vrankrijker, A. C. J. de, *Mensen, leven en werken in de Gouden Eeuw* (The Hague, 1981).

Vredenberg, J. P., *Als off sij onse eigene kinder weren. Het Burgerweeshuis te Arnhem, 1583–1742* (Arnhem, 1983).

Vries, Jan de, *The Dutch Rural Economy in the Golden Age 1500–1700* (New Haven, 1974).

Vries, Jan de, *Barges and Capitalism. Passenger transportation in the Dutch Economy (1632–1839)* (Wageningen, 1978).

Vries, Jan de, *The European Economy in an Age of Crisis* (Cambridge, 1979).

Vries, Jan de, 'The population and economy of the pre-Industrial Netherlands', *Journal of Interdisciplinary History*, 15 (1985), 661–82.

Vries, Jan de, 'Between purchasing power and the world of goods: understanding the household economy in early modern Europe', John Brewer and Roy Porter (eds), *Consumption and the World of Goods* (London, 1993), 85–133.

Vries, Jan de, Woude, Ad van der, *The First Modern Economy. Success, failure, and perseverance of the Dutch economy, 1500–1815* (Cambridge, 1997).

Vries, Johan de, *De economisch achteruitgang van de Republiek in de achttiende eeuw* (Leiden, 1959).

Waardt, Johannes Hendrik Marie de, *Toverij en samenleving. Holland 1500–1800* (Den Haag, 1991).

Weber, Max, *The Protestant Ethic and the Spirit of Capitalism* (London, 1930).

Wee, H. van der, *The Growth of the Antwerp Market and the European Economy (fourteenth-sixteenth centuries)*, 3 vols (The Hague, 1963).

Wee, Herman van der, 'The economy as a factor in the start of the Revolt in the Southern Netherlands', *Acta Historiae Neerlandica*, v (1970).

Wessels, L. H. M., *Bron, waarheid en de verandering der tijden. Jan Wagenaar (1709–1773), een historiografische studie* (The Hague, 1997).

Wijsenbeek-Olthuis, Th., 'Het Hollandse interieur in beeld en geschrift', *Theoretische Geschiedenis*, jg 23, n.2 (1996), 145–61.

Willemsen, R., *Enkhuizen tijdens de Republiek* (Hilversum, 1988).

Wilson, Charles, *Profit and Power: a Study of England and the Dutch Wars* (London, 1957).

Wilson, Charles, 'Taxation and the Decline of Empires, an unfashionable theme', in *Economic History and the Historians* (London, 1969).

Woltjer, J. J., 'Geweld tijdens de godsdienstoorlogen en de Nederlanden: een vergelijking', *Trajecta*, 3 (1992), 72–101.

Woude, A. M. van der, *Het Noorderkwartier. Een regionaal historisch onderzoek in de demografische en economische geschiedenis van westelijke Nederlanden van de late middeleeuwen tot het begin van de negentiende eeuw*. 3 dln (Wageningen, 1972) [A.A.G. Bijdragen, 16] .

Woude, A. M. van der, 'Variations in the size and structure of the household in the United Provinces of the Netherlands in the seventeenth and eighteenth centuries', *Household and Family in Past Times*, ed. P. Laslett and R. Wall (Cambridge, 1978).

Woude, A. M. van der, 'Population developments in the Northern Netherlands (1500–1800) and the validity of the "urban graveyard" effect', *Annales de démographie historique* (1982), 55–75.

Wyntjes, S. Marshall, 'Survivors and Status: Widowhood and Family in the Early Modern Netherlands', *Journal of Family History*, 7 (1982), 396–405.

Zanden, J. L. van, *The Rise and Decline of Holland's Economy. Merchant Capitalism and the Labour Market* (Manchester, 1993).

Zanden, J. L. van, 'De opkomst van een eigenerfde boerenklasse in Overijssel', *AAG Bijdragen 24* (1984).

Zanden, J. L. van, 'Kosten van levensonderhoud en loonvorming in Holland en Oost-Nederland 1600–1850. De voorbeelden van Kampen en Alkmaar', *Tijdschrift voor Sociale Geschiedenis*, 11 (1985), 309–23.

Zanden, J. L. van, 'De prijs van de vooruitgang? Economische modernisering en sociale polarisatie op het Nederlands platteland na 1500', *Economisch- en Sociaal-Historisch Jaarboek*, 51 (1988), 80–92.

Zanden, J. L. van, 'De economie van Holland in de periode 1650–1805: groei of achteruitgang?', *Bijdragen en Mededelingen betreffende de geschiedenis der Nederlanden*, 102 (1987), 562–609.

Zanden, J. L. van, 'Did Holland's Golden Age breed Inequality?', in Lee Soltow and Jan Luiten van Zanden, *Income and Wealth Inequality in the Netherlands 16th – 20th Century* (Amsterdam, 1998), 23–54.

Zumthor, P., *Daily Life in Rembrandt's Holland* (London, 1962).

Zwitzer, H. L., *'De militie van den staat.' Het leger van de Republiek der Verenigde Nederlanden* (Amsterdam, 1991).

Index

Friedrich, elector of the Palatinate, 98
Friedrich Wilhelm, elector of
    Brandenburg, 220
Friesland, 12, 13, 15, 87, 115, 119, 125,
    230, 234
Fruin, Robert, 30

games, 111
Geertruidenberg, 30, 33
Gelderland, 12, 13, 124–5, 172, 230,
    234
Gembloux, 12
Geyl, Pieter, 14
Ghent, 1, 8, 14
Ghent, Pacification of (1576), 4, 7, 8, 10,
    11–12, 58, 272
Gorinchem, 89, 146
Gouda, 89, 97–8, 172, 254, 264
Graft, 22, 116–17, 118, 122, 134, 250
Groenlo, 33, 48
Groningen
    province, 125, 126, 230, 234
    town, 9, 12, 21, 33, 273
    university, 105
Grote Vergadering, 142, 164–5
guilds, 106
Gustavus Adolphus, king of Sweden, 50

Haarlem, 6, 9, 10, 21, 23, 55, 57, 58, 64,
    72, 89, 97, 131, 132, 146, 165, 172,
    188, 193, 247, 261, 264, 272, 275,
    279
Hague, The, 42, 89, 98, 108, 165, 172,
    188, 248, 249, 279
Harderwijk, university of, 105, 127
Hein, Piet, 78
Heinsius, Anthonie, 228
Henri III of France, 9, 29
Henri IV of France, 10, 38
's-Hertogenbosch, 45, 48, 91, 112, 113,
    127
    Meierij, 126

Holland, 1, 2, 3, 4, 5, 6, 15, 30, 44, 57,
    210, 265, 272, 277
    economy, 96–7, 115–20, 165–6, 275,
        278–80
    effects of Revolt, 57–8
    land drainage and reclamation, 16, 69,
        84, 115–16, 252
    migration to, 92–3
    North Holland, 6, 18, 165, 191, 250,
        260–1, 265, 277, 279
    officials, 105
    population, 21, 55, 86–7, 91–2, 249–50
    political power, 31
    provincial finances, 31–2, 236–7, 240
    States of, 5, 179, 218, 226, 230, 231–2
    strength of remonstrants, 42
    towns, 84, 88–90, 165, 248, 258, 275
    urban system, 99
    vroedschappen, 171
Holy Roman Empire, 23, 38, 50, 220
Hondeschoote, 20, 72
Hoorn, 58, 62, 66, 89, 90, 96–7, 165, 191,
    279
Huizinga, Johan, 269

iconoclastic riots, 3
immigration, 63, 91, 93–4, 109, 136, 193
Israel, J.I., 270
Israel, Manasseh ben, 204

Japan, 46
Java, 77, 245, 257
Jews, 95, 138, 203–4
Jonge van Ellemeet, Cornelis de, 180
Juan of Austria, Don, 8
Jülich, succession dispute, 37–8

Kampen, 66, 85, 112–13, 124
Keppel, Arnold Joost van (later earl of
    Albemarle), 169
kermis, 110, 111, 151
Koerbagh, Adriaen, 205